TRACING THE SIGN OF THE CROSS

Gender, Theory, and Religion

GENDER, THEORY, AND RELIGION
Amy Hollywood, *Editor*

The Gender, Theory, and Religion series provides a forum for interdisciplinary scholarship at the intersection of the study of gender, sexuality, and religion.

Tracing the Sign of the Cross

SEXUALITY, MOURNING, AND THE

FUTURE OF AMERICAN CATHOLICISM

Marian Ronan

Columbia University Press *New York*

COLUMBIA UNIVERSITY PRESS
Publishers Since 1893
New York   Chichester, West Sussex
Copyright © 2009 Marian Ronan

Library of Congress Cataloging-in-Publication Data
Ronan, Marian, 1947–
Tracing the sign of the cross : sexuality, mourning, and the future
of American Catholicism / Marian Ronan.
p. cm.
Includes bibliographical references (p.) and index.
ISBN 978-0-231-14702-6 (cloth : alk. paper) — ISBN 978-0-231-52001-0 (e-book)
1. Catholic Church—United States. 2. Liberalism (Religion)—Catholic
Church. 3. Sex—Religious aspects—Catholic Church. 4. Loss—Religious
aspects—Catholic Church. 5. Carroll, James, 1943– 6. Gordon, Mary,
1949– 7. Haraway, Donna Jeanne 8. Rodriquez, Richard. I. Title.

BX1406.3.R66   2009
282'.73090511—dc22   2008044106

Columbia University Press books are printed on permanent
and durable acid-free paper.
This book is printed on paper with recycled content.
Printed in the United States of America

Designed by Audrey Smith

c 10 9 8 7 6 5 4 3 2 1

To my husband, Keith A. Russell,
and to the memory of my grandparents,
Jim Dodds and Elizabeth Turner Dodds

CONTENTS

ACKNOWLEDGMENTS

*T*his book would not have been possible without the help and support of many people. I wish to acknowledge in particular:

My parents, Helen and Joe Ronan, for their unflagging determination that I should receive the college education they didn't. I will never cease to be moved by the memory of walking with my father to the post office, when I was still a small child, to buy stamps to put into a savings book to be converted eventually into one of the bonds that would pay my college tuition. Thank you, Daddy.

The American Catholic sisters who taught me to read, write, and think, especially Sisters of Notre Dame de Namur Maura Prendergast, Claire McCormick, Anne O'Donnell, Mary Hayes, Ann Julia Kinnirey, and Helen James John, as well as Melinda Keane SHCJ.

The members of the Grail Movement, especially Mary Louise Birmingham, Cay Charles, Eva Fleischner, Elise Gorges, Carolyn Gratton, Audrey Sorrento, and the late Eleanor Walker, for showing me the possibilities of a vibrant and committed life.

The distinguished scholars of religion with whom I have had the great good fortune to study over the years, including Robert Schwoebel, Norman Gottwald, and the members of my dissertation committee, Thomas Ferraro, David Watt, and the late Gibson Winter. But most of all, my deepest gratitude to my mentor, my *Doktormutter*, Laura Levitt, whose brilliance and commitment will be an inspiration to me until the day I die. Who could have imagined a dissertation director who not only believes in you more than you believe in yourself but also, on her epic excursions into the world of consignment shops, finds you fabulous clothes that actually fit?

Much gratitude also to former classmates now become respected colleagues and dear friends: Liora Gubkin, Margaret O'Gara, and Tania Oldenhage. Many thanks to my dear, fellow faculty member here at the American Baptist Seminary of the West, Margaret McManus. Without those weekly mutual critiques of our respective works in progress, who knows where we would be today? Also to Tracy Fessenden, whose enormously encouraging comments as the blind reviewer of an earlier version of this manuscript made me value her before we ever met. The years since have proven that I was not mistaken in this. Special thanks to Cecelia Cancellaro, whose editing skills strengthened this book and who then, O happy day, found a publisher for it. And to Janelle Peregoy and David Henson, my graduate students, for their assistance with the manuscript.

Finally, all my love and gratitude to my husband, Keith A. Russell. I suppose some version of this book might have happened without you, my dear, but how much less happy I would have been while I was writing it.

Portions of the introduction to this volume appear in "Blessed Are They Who Mourn: Roman Catholic Sex/Gender Ideology After Vatican II," *Journal for Cultural and Religious Theory* 2, no. 3 (August 2001), available online at www.jcrt.org/archives/02.3/ronan.shtml. Used by permission of the *Journal for Cultural and Religious Theory*. Portions of the introductory chapter also appeared in "The Clergy Sex Abuse Crisis and the Mourning of American Catholic Innocence," *Pastoral Psychology* 56, no. 3 (January 2008): 321–340. Used with kind permission of Springer Science and Business Media. An earlier version of chapter 2 appeared as "A Sliver of Dry Land: Reconfigurations of Catholicism in the Works of Mary Gordon," *U.S. Catholic Historian* 23, no. 3 (Summer 2005): 71–92. Used by permission of the Catholic University of America Press.

TRACING THE SIGN OF THE CROSS

Introduction

Christ suffered for you, leaving you an example, that you should
follow in his steps.   —1 PETER 2:21

For just as the psychoanalytic subject is able to designate itself as
a homogeneous entity over time only by repressing the traces of
its unconscious desires, so the . . . cultural artifact . . . continually
rewrites its own history to expel the traces of its ruptured, heteroge-
neous past. The political task of "liberating" an object, then, takes
the form of opening up its unconscious—detecting within it those
chips of heterogeneity that it has been unable quite to dissolve.
                                    —TERRY EAGLETON, *Walter Benjamin;*
                                    Or, Towards a Revolutionary Criticism

The Easter Vigil, the greatest celebration of the liturgical year,
may seem an odd place for an exchange about American Catholic losses,
but that is where it happened. I was taking part in the 2003 vigil at Newman
Hall, the university parish here in Berkeley, when my companion, a former
Catholic sister, leaned over and said to me, "I remember now why I don't
do this anymore. It makes me so sad. What went wrong?"

My friend's sense of loss resonated with me immediately. But I identified
even more strongly with her question, because it was one that had long preoccupied me. For those of us who came to consciousness during and after
Vatican II, the great renewal council of the church in the early 1960s, the
decline of the American church at the turn of the twenty-first century was
almost incomprehensible. Indeed, what had gone wrong?

Given the date of that particular Easter celebration, a bystander might
have assumed that our sadness was a response to the massive crisis that had
by then been roiling the American church for well over a year.[1] In January
2002, the *Boston Globe* broke the first in a Pulitzer prize–winning series

of stories revealing not only that dozens of Catholic priests had molested hundreds of minors in the Archdiocese of Boston over several decades but also that a number of bishops, though aware of the abuse, had done little or nothing to stop it.[2] Within two years, an official report concluded that 4,392 Catholic priests were accused of abusing 10,667 children and young people nationally since 1950.[3] A distinguished historian of American Catholicism writing at the time called the crisis "the single most important event in American Catholicism since Vatican II and the most devastating scandal in American Catholic history."[4]

Beyond a doubt, the sexual abuse of a significant number of Catholic children and teenagers by an equally significant number of Catholic priests since 1950—and the episcopal mishandling of that abuse—are deeply disturbing phenomena. Yet it is far from clear that the distress experienced by my friend and me, and many other contemporary American Catholics, can be attributed exclusively, or even primarily, to the clergy sex-abuse crisis. Long before the current round of revelations,[5] things had not been going well in the American church. Forty years earlier, the Second Vatican Council filled many of us with hope and expectation, but since then, Mass attendance and financial support have declined steadily, the median age of priests and sisters has skyrocketed, and strife between and within Catholic communities has proliferated.

Yet as all of this unfolded, many of us refused to give up hope, joining reform groups such as Call to Action or the Association for the Rights of Catholics in the Church, earning advanced degrees to prepare ourselves for church leadership, or serving as lay ministers in parishes or hospitals. In my own case, the women's movement in the church, the "*ekklesia* of women," as Elisabeth Schüssler Fiorenza terms it, was for many years the new focus of my hope for Catholicism.[6] Not until the 1990s, as I pursued doctoral studies, did the nature and scope of the crisis begin to come clear to me.

Tracing the Sign of the Cross offers an original and badly needed analysis of the crisis in which the U.S. Catholic community finds itself at the beginning of the twenty-first century. It also explores paths through and beyond that crisis. While acknowledging the genuine grief and anger of some American Catholics over priestly sex abuse, this book argues strongly that the problems currently facing the church are neither the result of clergy sex abuse and episcopal corruption per se, nor of deviation from core Catholic teaching, as many bishops believe. Rather, they are rooted, in part at least, in the dashed hopes and expectations of a significant portion of the American Catholic community after Vatican II and the inability of that community to acknowledge and work through those losses. For many of us, during the third of a century during which this crisis developed, opposition to (or fierce support of) Catholic teaching on sexuality and gender has seemed to be the way forward, but the endless character of these battles suggests their futility. In *Tracing the Sign of the Cross*, I argue that the way forward instead involves grieving for our dashed hopes and expectations, in hope of a chastened but more productive future.

To grasp the nature and extent of these losses, bear in mind that after World War II, white ethnic American Catholics were poised to achieve the enhanced status within state and church for which their immigrant ancestors had labored throughout the previous century. Nothing signified these long-awaited advances more graphically than the election of John Fitzgerald Kennedy to the American presidency and the apparent triumph of liberal American Catholicism at Vatican II. Yet not long after these two events, the ostensibly ideal American way of life for which immigrant Catholics had toiled was torn by multiple social conflicts—over civil rights, women's and gay liberation, and the Vietnam War. Even the economic security of the postwar period was undermined by the inflation, recession, and high unemployment of the 1970s. At the same time, a series of Vatican pronouncements—in particular, those prohibiting artificial birth control in 1968 and women's ordination in 1976—called into question the much-anticipated movement of the "People of God" into some kind of equality with the hierarchy and the clergy after Vatican II. And in the years that followed, things did not improve. Postimmigrant American Catholics, conservatives and liberals alike, have barely begun to come to terms with these devastating disappointments.

Given the history of American Catholicism and of the wider church in the modern period, this resistance to acknowledging post–Vatican II losses is not hard to understand. I delineate salient aspects of that history in this introductory chapter. But the remainder of *Tracing the Sign of the Cross* goes beyond that history to identify and learn from more productive approaches to American Catholic losses. These approaches revolve around four American Catholic writers who, in their fiction, memoirs, and essays, sometimes resist but more often work through disappointments and dashed dreams to offer new, hopeful construals of Catholicism. Through my readings of these works, I challenge American Catholics to draw upon the cross and all that it stands for in order to enable ourselves to engage fruitfully the fractured reality of the postmodern period.

THE CHURCH IN THE "MODERN WORLD"

Ambiguity and Vatican II

My exploration of the current crisis in American Catholicism begins with a reconsideration of the Second Vatican Council. If the 1960 election of John F. Kennedy symbolized the acceptance of Roman Catholics into the American mainstream, Vatican II (1962–1965) seemed to signify something equally long awaited: the ascendancy of the American version of Catholicism within the universal church. After over a century of opposition to the modern values and principles on which the United States of America was founded, the church, at Vatican II, seemed to reverse itself and "enter the modern world."[7]

Yet, as the historical sociologist Gene Burns argues, the changes emerging from Vatican II were more ambiguous than is often recognized.[8] The council was, in part, called to complete the agenda of the First Vatican Council of 1869, at which the doctrine of papal infallibility and its monarchical governance structure was defined. But Vatican II did not suspend that monarchical structure; instead, it shifted the territory over which the pope claimed authority from the entire world in all of its religious and sociotemporal dimensions to the arena of "faith and morals."[9]

In this new economy, states are no longer required to enforce the Catholic faith, which is now obligatory for Catholics only. "Morals," on the other hand, because they are understood to inhere in the natural law rather than in Catholic teaching, continue to be obligatory for all and beyond democratic constraints.[10] Thus, the post–Vatican II church has placed increasing emphasis on "morals," which means, for all intents and purposes, sexuality and gender.

By abdicating some of its earlier positions—the condemnation of the separation of church and state, for example—the church at Vatican II earned for itself a place in the liberal democratic world. But this change did not decouple politics from Catholic doctrine as much as it created a new economy in which Catholic teaching on sexuality and gender took on much greater importance in relation to a number of earlier Catholic norms and prohibitions. In this new structure, "morals"—sexuality and gender—occupies the highest position, faith and religious doctrine occupy the middle ground, and Catholic social teaching is relegated to the lowest rung, intentionally vague and rarely enforced.[11]

Instances of the workings of this new ideological hierarchy abound. Compare, for example, multiple threats of excommunication issued against U.S. Catholic lawmakers who support abortion rights and gay marriage and the actual excommunication of irregularly ordained women priests[12] with the clearly optional nature of the church's teaching on (nonsexual) justice issues. As the pastor of the university parish in Berkeley explained from the pulpit the Sunday after the United States invaded Iraq, although the invasion was contrary to Catholic just-war teaching, those who disagreed with that teaching remained valued members of the parish.

It could seem that this consolidation around issues of sexuality and gender influences American Catholics, or at least liberal American Catholics, less than it does Catholics in other countries. U.S. Catholics, after all, have abortions and support international family-planning programs at virtually the same level as other Americans. Sociologist Michelle Dillon argues that activist groups working to liberalize Catholic sexual teaching generate meaningful Catholic identities for themselves even as they dissent from the official Catholic position.[13] But the very fact that Dillon's book focuses on Catholic sex/gender activists and not on other groups of American Catholics illustrates how central Catholic teaching on sexuality has become, even—perhaps especially—for those working to change it.

The Modern/Antimodern Church

The consolidation of Roman Catholic behavioral norms around sexuality and gender after Vatican II was, in many respects, the culmination of the Vatican campaign to regain the power it had lost in the liberal European revolutions of the eighteenth and nineteenth centuries. This interpretation diverges sharply from the more popular one in which the church "entered the modern world"—came to terms with its values—at Vatican II.

To grasp this alternate construal, it is necessary to recognize that the divorce between the Catholic Church and the modern world emerged quite late in the modern period, if there was a divorce at all. In point of fact, the church was intimately involved in the construction of the modern world. Ferdinand and Isabella, the sovereigns who commissioned Columbus's voyage, for example, were Franciscan tertiaries, and Pope Alexander VI arbitrated the division of Latin America between Spain and Portugal in 1493. Some identify the beginning of the modern era with the expulsion of the Jews from Spain by the Catholic Inquisition in 1492.

Only with its losses in the liberal revolutions of the eighteenth and nineteenth centuries did the church become "antimodern." But this antimodern stance was an effective if not entirely conscious strategy for achieving power. In effect, the church won for itself a distinctive modern identity by portraying itself as apart from the modern world. In the immense Philadelphia parochial school system of the 1950s, for example, we learned that the thirteenth century was the "greatest of centuries," even as we were drilled like military recruits to function successfully in business and industry.[14]

Central to the papal antimodernist campaign was the reappropriation of medieval philosophy and social theory called the Thomist, or neo-Thomist, revival. Initially, this revival of the "perennial philosophy" of the thirteenth-century doctor of the church, St. Thomas Aquinas, seemed life-giving, unifying the church and underpinning the social program of the pope who initiated it, Leo XIII.[15] Under Leo's successor, however, the revival became a weapon against a wide range of supposedly pernicious modern philosophies. It led to a purge of all but the most rigidly Thomistic theologians and scholars from Catholic institutions around the world.[16] In the United States, Sunday sermons and the Baltimore Catechism inculcated most rank-and-file Catholics into this same constricted vision. Even after neo-Thomism evolved into the Transcendental Thomism of Vatican II, with its much more positive understanding of the human, postconciliar Vatican, pronouncements on sexuality echoed the rigid neo-Thomist understanding of natural law and would strongly influence Catholic identity into the next century.[17]

Mourning and the Inability to Mourn

To note all of this is not to deny the success of the neo-Thomist revival and the subsequent consolidation of power around Catholic sexual teaching after Vatican II. Quite the contrary. As massive media coverage of the funeral of Pope John Paul II and the election of Pope Benedict XVI in 2005 made clear, the Roman pontiff is now a universally recognized and widely admired figure.[18] In addition, Roman Catholicism, after losing considerable ground in the eighteenth and nineteenth centuries, is now the world's largest religion.

Yet it is worth asking whether such a triumph is entirely appropriate for a religious tradition whose founder went humbly to his death out of love for all humanity. It is further worth asking whether the consolidation of power around unambiguous teaching is precisely what is needed in an era when dedication to the modern dream of certainty and purity can be seen to have fostered the horrors of colonialism, racial and ethnic genocides, and nuclear atrocities.[19] Indeed, one wonders if, to be faithful to its calling, the Catholic Church wouldn't do better to face up to its many losses in the modern period and use that chastening as a template for ministry to the billions now facing similar and even more devastating losses.

A Conversation About Mourning

In considering these questions, I have been aided by an increasingly prominent conversation in the study of Western religion, that of "mourning and the inability to mourn."[20] Sigmund Freud initiated this conversation in a 1915 article in which he discusses similarities and differences in the reactions of those who undergo the loss of something they love.[21] In each case, the forced withdrawal of attachment to a lost love object results in an extremely painful state. Those whose relationship with the lost love object was relatively conscious and unconflicted can gradually work through the loss and are able to establish new relationships. Others, whose relationship was more unconscious and conflicted, face a more prolonged and difficult process. Freud characterizes this second state as melancholia.

The use of the term "melancholia," or depression, to describe the inability to mourn suggests that the conversation is primarily concerned with individuals, but Freud acknowledges that groups also experience blocked mourning.[22] Theorists since Freud have picked up on that possibility. Two of the earliest were the German scholars Alexander and Margarete Mitscherlich. In *The Inability to Mourn*, the Mitscherlichs argued that many members of the first West German generation after the defeat of the Third Reich suffered from an inability to mourn, in that they failed to engage emotionally with their responsibility for the crimes perpetrated by their government under the Nazis. Instead, they avoided a massive loss of self-esteem by severing all affective links with the immediate past, identifying psychologically with the Allies, throwing themselves manically into rebuilding their country, and understanding themselves as more truly victims than those who perished in the Holocaust.[23] In a more recent study, Anahid Kassabian and David Kazanjian use the framework of mourning and the inability to mourn to examine the Armenian genocide of 1915.[24]

Kassabian and Kazanjian avoid framing the inability to mourn as an illness. Instead, they argue that the two psychic structures, mourning and melancholia, are similar, because each is bound up with the process of working through loss. The difference between them has more to do with degree and context than kind.[25] The form or force of melancholia (and the mania that can accompany it) is closed and rigid, while mourning is more open to a range of identifications.[26] Mourning and the inability to mourn thus have to do with people's ability or inability to tolerate difference and change. In many respects, the post–Vatican II Catholic fixations on abortion, contraception, homosexuality, clergy sex abuse, and women's roles in the church function as a similarly rigid defense against mourning.

THE INCREASING PROMINENCE OF CATHOLIC SEXUAL TEACHING

The Immigrant Trajectory

It might seem that the Roman Catholic Church in the United States would have avoided this inability to mourn if only because its location within a liberal democracy inclined it toward modern ideas in a way that the European historical context did not. Yet by the middle of the twentieth century, certain trajectories within American Catholicism converged to hinder mourning in the church in the United States as well.

In examining this convergence, we observe the massive increase in the number of Catholics in the United States in the century before the post–World War II economic boom. In 1850, Catholics constituted 5 percent of the population of the United States; by 1906, they had grown to 17 percent, or fourteen million out of eighty-two million people.[27] Some of these Catholics were drawn from the upper classes, but the vast majority of them were poor immigrants who had come through Ellis Island or crossed the U.S.-Mexican border. Their lives in the United States were marked by poverty, minimal education, and terrible diseases—though probably to a lesser extent than would have been the case in the overpopulated lands from which they came. Immigrant American Catholics were also looked down upon—indeed, often despised—by a significant percentage of the white Anglo-Saxon Protestant American majority.

Not until after World War II did a significant number of these American Catholics begin to experience equality with their fellow Americans. The popularity of Catholic entertainers such as Bing Crosby and Perry Como and of films and television shows about Catholics such as *Going My Way* and *The Honeymooners* helped to effect, even as it testified to, this long-desired rapprochement.[28]

For many of us, almost coterminous with this cultural acceptance was the sense of promise that accompanied the postwar economic boom. For my own Irish working-class family, owning the tiny stucco "twin" house financed through the GI Bill of Rights was the most thrilling event of our lives, followed only by the prospect of my brother and me someday "going to college."

In 1960, these historic transformations culminated in the election of the first Catholic to the American presidency, John F. Kennedy. When I feel inclined to minimize the significance of that election for many American Catholics, I recall my teenage self, on the night of the election, staying awake well into the small hours of the morning praying the rosary for a Kennedy victory.

The Catholic Gospels of Suffering and Success

But there was nothing automatic about this postwar movement of white ethnic Catholics into the American middle class. Nor did it come about without changes in the immigrant Catholic identity that had developed during the previous century. Central to these changes was the refashioning of the identification with suffering that had characterized immigrant Catholics for decades, an identification I, drawing on the work of the historians James Terence Fisher and Jay Dolan, call "the Catholic gospel of suffering."[29]

A classic portrayal of the Catholic gospel of suffering is *The Madonna of 115th Street*, a study of Italian Catholics in Harlem from the late nineteenth through the mid-twentieth centuries by a scholar of American religion, Robert A. Orsi. As Orsi sees it, Catholic rituals carried out regularly in Italian Harlem—for example, neighborhood processions in which parishioners bear a statue of Jesus on their shoulders—strengthened the bonds between those parishioners by emphasizing their shared suffering. Such rituals were far more than enactments of passive endurance; rather, the voluntary embrace of suffering through ritual gave meaning to that suffering.[30] As a second-generation Irish immigrant, this was also, in part at least, my experience of devotion to the crucified Christ in the Roman Catholic Church of the 1950s.

But if the "gospel of suffering" was a significant component of American Catholic identity before World War II, it was also the case, as Dolan argues, that a fracture in that Catholic identification had appeared as early as the late nineteenth century, especially among immigrant groups who had arrived earlier in the century. This fracture—or tension—came about because of the parallel immigrant encounter with the expectation of success that marked the wider Yankee culture.[31]

Sermons delivered at parish missions provide some of the first evidence of this tension. Although the two emphases—suffering and success—were hardly compatible, visiting priests who preached at parish missions during this period tended to advocate both, because each made sense in its own way; indeed, a degree of immigrant success was essential if the church was to survive.[32]

But in the 1930s, in broadcasts by the famous "radio priest" Father Charles Coughlin, certain changes in the American Catholic formulation of the relation between suffering and success began to emerge, and these changes contributed to a postwar reconfiguration of American Catholic identity. In recent years, Coughlin's name has become virtually synonymous with the shameful anti-Semitism of his late-1930s radio broadcasts. Yet Coughlin's broadcasts strongly influenced Catholic attitudes in other ways as well. In particular, though papal social-justice teaching was a significant part of his message, Coughlin was also intensely aware of the economic aspirations of ordinary Catholics whose longing for success was thwarted by the Great

Depression. His earlier broadcasts thus extended the previously incoherent Catholic construal of the relationship between suffering and success.[33]

Gradually, however, the relationship between the two was reformulated, for Coughlin and eventually for many other American Catholics, into a less ambivalent, more linear schema in which suffering and death are overcome by resurrection. The well-known television priest Bishop Fulton J. Sheen further disseminated this linear "death and resurrection" schema during the 1950s,[34] and this shift was ultimately inscribed in figures of the resurrected Christ that replaced the crucifix in the front of some Catholic churches after Vatican II.

Yet, inevitably, a tension between suffering and success remained. Suffering continued to play a vital role in Catholic ritual—in the Mass, the Stations of the Cross, during Holy Week, and in devotion to the saints.[35] The very loss of the immigrant Catholic community that accompanied the move to the suburbs brought with it a certain insecurity and confrontation with complexity that would only increase as the years passed. And significant segments of the American church—African American Catholics, for example, and the growing Latino Catholic community—continued to suffer from poverty and oppression after World War II, as many of them still do in the early twenty-first century.

The Catholic disposition toward suffering and its spiritual transformations thus continued to inform the children and grandchildren of immigrant Catholics as they became freer and more mobile than their forebears. But it did so in a reconfigured way that allowed room for increasing material success.[36] Within this reconfiguration, prohibitions against divorce, contraception, and abortion played an increasingly prominent role. And while this ideology did in some instances bring about actual suffering—I am reminded here of my high-school classmate Eleanor Bonner, who chose to die of leukemia rather than accept treatment that might endanger her fetus—Catholic sexual prohibitions became signifiers of Catholic identity even for those who, privately, did not conform to Catholic sexual teaching.

The Middle-Class Trajectory

Despite the logic of these developments, Catholic sexual teaching might not have become as prominent as it did after Vatican II except for a second historical trajectory within American Catholicism, that of a small but influential Catholic middle class born in the first decades of the twentieth century.[37] As historian William Halsey argues, the neo-Thomist revival was especially important for members of this group, because it gave them access to the innocence and optimism characteristic of the nineteenth-century Yankee culture from which they had until recently been excluded.

The nineteenth century was a time of poverty and oppression for most immigrant American Catholics, but for many white middle-class American Protestants, it was an era of romance and increasing optimism, especially in the decades after Reconstruction. As the first cohort of immigrant Catholics were moving into the American middle class, however, World War I and, in particular, the failure of the Treaty of Versailles that ended that war heralded a much less optimistic era for the country. By drawing on the sense of reason and certainty that was fundamental to neo-Thomism, however, the emerging Catholic middle class was able defend itself from the implications of these and other developments. In particular, as Halsey contends, neo-Thomism enabled these American Catholics to believe in a rational and predictable cosmos, in moral structures inherent in the universe, and in a didactic or "genteel" rendering of arts and culture.[38]

For the purposes of this book, the most helpful element of Halsey's argument is his emphasis on "American Catholic innocence" and its resistance to intellectual and ethical complexity. Because of the rigid polarities of neo-Thomist logic, middle-class Catholics in the period between the two world wars could condemn modern society without feeling compelled to analyze it in its increasing complexity. They spoke frequently of the "nonsense" of "enemies" or "adversaries" to indicate that it would be a waste of time to engage their arguments.

Neo-Thomist certainty and the optimism it defended did not shape the attitudes of all American Catholics, of course. The onset of the Great Depression postponed the integration of the majority of American Catholics into this vision. With the postwar economic boom, however, American Catholic optimism, rooted in turn-of-the-century Yankee ideology and the neo-Thomism of the catechism, would finally be possible for later generations of Catholic immigrants. As a result, many U.S. Catholics, as well as the Vatican and the hierarchy, were ill prepared to acknowledge and mourn the fragmentation and loss that characterized much of the twentieth century and that would assault them once again at the beginning of the twenty-first.

The Trajectories Converge

The bourgeois American Catholic investment in innocence and certainty and the post–World War II reconfiguration of Catholic identity around prohibitions of divorce, contraception, and abortion converged into a storm over sexuality and gender in the American church after Vatican II. Some of the teachings that generated this storm were, in fact, part of the Catholic campaign against modernity from its inception. The dogma of the Immaculate Conception, for example, which proclaimed that Mary (and, of course, Jesus) were the only human beings free from sin, served as a commentary on the futility of democracy at a time when the pope was in danger of losing the Vatican territories to the new liberal Italian state.[39]

Equally to the point, however, this dogma played a key role in settling the question of exactly when the fetus is ensouled, that is, becomes a human being. Revered theologians such as Augustine and Aquinas had taught that ensoulment occurs between the fifth and sixth months of pregnancy. But, as ethicist Paul Badham observes, "if Mary was, as this dogma argues, untainted by sin from the time of her conception, then she must have been a person from the time of her conception."[40] Thus, in 1869, Pope Pius IX, when issuing excommunication decrees for women who had undergone abortions, dropped the adjective "ensouled" from the phrase used previously to clarify what kind of fetus could not be aborted: an "ensouled fetus." This made early abortions grounds for excommunication for the first time in church history.[41] It is hardly a coincidence that this excision of moral nuance came on the eve of the definition of papal infallibility and the reinscription of polarized Thomist rationalism into Catholic theology.

In the cases just considered, invocations of innocence and certainty strengthened what might be perceived as the conservative end of the Catholic continuum of positions on sexuality. But a conviction of innocence and certainty frequently underpins the liberal end of the continuum as well. Seen in this light, invocations of the innocence of victims of clergy sex abuse, as well as of the purity and innocence of the fetus at all stages of its development, support the American Catholic inability to mourn. As life becomes increasingly threatening and ambiguous, these matters, at least, are clear. Or so it would seem.

By discerning within twentieth- and early twenty-first-century American Catholicism a pattern characterized by the repeated invocation of innocence and certainty, and by suggesting that this pattern betrays a costly resistance to mourning, I do not claim to be describing "objective" historical events. Some American Catholics have surely managed to mourn the losses they and their communities sustained throughout the twentieth century. I also do not mean to suggest that this pattern characterizes all groups of twentieth-century American Catholics to the same extent, or even at all in the cases of most Latino and African American Catholics, whose losses demand their own analyses. My purpose, rather, is to highlight what I believe to be a distinctive rhetorical pattern that has considerable significance for the future of the American church. Much of the language of certainty, optimism, and innocence that plays a foundational role in my analysis in this chapter is drawn from the writings of postimmigrant middle- or professional/managerial-class white American Catholics, not those of Latino or African American Catholics. This is because the former, to a significant and sometimes troubling extent, comprise the very writings that have strongly influenced American Catholicism since Vatican II.

WORKING THROUGH AMERICAN CATHOLIC LOSSES

American Catholics as the Sexual Other

Another dimension of U.S. history also helps to explain the intense preoccupation with sexuality and gender in the American church after Vatican II. Twentieth-century American Catholics were attracted to fantasies of innocence and sexual purity in part because such purity and innocence obscured the sexual vilification, or othering, that had been a significant component of American anti-Catholicism since the 1840s.

Though American Protestant oppression of Catholics was most violent in the period before the Civil War, anti-Catholic prejudice extended well into the twentieth century, up to and including the presidential campaign of John F. Kennedy in 1960.[42] American anti-Catholicism was linked to the Vatican's opposition to the liberal state and the threat that immigrant Catholic loyalty to the pope ostensibly posed for democracy. But another significant component of American anti-Catholicism was the identification of Catholics with illicit sexual behavior. Catholics in popular American literature were frequently highly sexualized.[43] Nuns were perceived as especially threatening to the purity of the Victorian family. They were portrayed as unmarried, unsupervised lesbians and as deadly mothers who killed and buried beneath the monastery the infants they conceived in consort with priests.[44] Even after Kennedy's election, films such as *Agnes of God, Three Mules for Sister Sara*, and *Sister Act* reiterated time-honored connections between Catholicism and sexual lasciviousness, reminding American Catholics of their historic role as one of the sexual others of American culture.[45]

The postwar white ethnic Catholic move out of the ghetto and the accompanying diminishment of Catholic sexual othering were welcome developments. Yet certain hazards attend upward mobility into a group by which one was previously oppressed. These include the danger of assuming the toxic visions that motivated the oppressor group and the need to separate oneself psychically from other "others" who still live beyond the boundaries of acceptable society.

The positioning of innocence and sexual purity at the heart of twentieth-century Catholicism is especially problematic because, as the Jewish studies scholar Eric Santner persuasively argues, it was precisely the fantasy of purity and innocence that fueled the modern project that culminated in the catastrophes of the twentieth century. The expulsion from society of the other, the impure, and the degraded is the corollary of this modern fantasy.[46] Santner identifies the extermination of European Jewry as the preeminent twentieth-century catastrophe marked by the modern drive to eliminate difference.[47] Yet the American Catholic community has not been immune to the compulsion to expel the other, as violent protests by Catholics against racial integration and passivity in response to misogyny and homophobia by others clearly reveal. There is, in fact, an intimate connection between the modern compulsion to expel the other and the experience of being identified as that other.

The French feminist theorist Julia Kristeva provides certain tools with which to analyze this disturbing connection.[48] Primary among these is the notion of the abject. According to Kristeva, the abject is the underside of rationality and control, the loathsome, messy, physical yet also joyous and attractive stuff associated with the mother's body from which the individual must separate in order to become a self. This separation from that which is loathed and loved is achieved, with great difficulty, by transforming the mother into an Other, the abject, and expelling her beyond a psychic boundary that is, necessarily, less than stable. The abject hovers just beyond the borders of the self, yet threateningly close.[49]

Abjection is the structure of the expulsion of the other beyond the boundaries of modern Western society. It also provides the foundation for the religious concepts of sin, purity, and pollution, which the psycho-analytic theorist Diane Jonte-Pace calls the "other side of the sacred."[50] As such, abjection is integral to all religious formations. Unfortunately, as with all mechanisms of repression, when those formations collapse, the abject reappears, but in a new guise.

Recent developments within American Catholicism may be described as precisely such a return of the repressed. On the one hand, sexual pro-hibitions that ostensibly insulate American Catholics from abjection help to legitimize violence against the other, especially the poor, women, and sexual minorities. Unambiguous Catholic condemnation of abortion un-dergirds symbolic and actual violence against women and physicians by pro-life activists. It also increases the suffering of couples who decide, in good conscience, to terminate a pregnancy. Opposition by the Vatican, the hierarchy, and conservative Catholic legislators to the distribution of condoms weakens efforts to reverse the AIDS pandemic. And the liturgi-cal and practical subordination of women within institutional Catholicism reinforces the social subordination of women, at least in Europe and the United States.

On the other hand, the rhetoric used by liberal Catholic activists in their war with the Vatican over sexuality and gender also contributes to a renewed discourse of American Catholic sexual abjection. The election of John F. Kennedy signaled a significant decline in nativist anti-Catholi-cism in the postwar period, but beginning in 1968, time-honored images of the church as the agent of a menacing foreign authority and a bastion of sexual perversion began to circulate again in the media. A number of factors contributed to this resurgence of anti-Catholic images, but, as the religious studies scholar Philip Jenkins has noted, this renewal of media hostility to Catholicism could not have been so open had not American Catholics themselves used such rhetoric.[51] Jenkins highlights, in particu-lar, the inflammatory and inaccurate term "pedophile priests" in a spe-cial clergy sex-abuse issue of the liberal *National Catholic Reporter* as a critical event in the renewal of anti-Catholic rhetoric and images in the secular media. "If Catholics and even Catholic clergy were themselves complaining of . . . an epidemic of clerical sexual perversion," Jenkins asked, how could the reporting of such perversion be considered anti-

Catholic?[52] American Catholics are being identified once again with the sexually tinged abject, a possibility no amount of righteous indignation on our part can entirely offset.

An Alternative to Winning

Throughout the twentieth century and especially since Vatican II, identification with, or opposition to, Roman Catholic teaching on sexuality and gender roles has played an important role in protecting significant numbers of American Catholics from confronting the fragmentation and loss of the contemporary period. The costs of this Catholic inability to mourn the loss of innocence and purity have been enormous—and not only for Catholics.

Change in official Catholic teaching on sexuality and gender is unlikely in the foreseeable future.[53] If anything should have forced a rethinking of Catholic teaching on sexuality and the roles of women, gays, and lesbians in the church, it was the clergy sex-abuse crisis. But at the very height of the crisis, the American bishops renewed their campaign against reproductive freedom, both by condemning abortion at all stages of pregnancy and by once again declaring artificial contraception equivalent to abortion.[54] In an attempt to shift the blame for clergy sexual abuse, the Vatican and the bishops have also redoubled their condemnations of homosexuality. John Paul II's masterful shaping of the institutional church during his pontificate makes it likely that, failing a genuine miracle, all of this will continue.

Yet if the Vatican and the hierarchy are unlikely to abandon in the near future the reconfiguration of the post–Vatican II church around sexual prohibitions and gender roles, neither is it easy to imagine how liberal American Catholics will withdraw from their reinforcement of the pivotal place of sexual teaching within contemporary Catholicism. In many respects, it is only reasonable that highly educated, frequently professional men and women schooled by Vatican II itself to believe they are "the Church" would struggle indefinitely against the authoritarian imposition of sex and gender norms with which they disagree profoundly. And let me be clear here: as I am writing this introduction, I continue to be involved in this opposition. I grow increasingly aware, however, that this seemingly endless struggle defends me and my sister and brother activists from confronting what has become of our Vatican II dreams of a liberal church.

Yet, in our time methods for moving beyond rage and disappointment have been developed. Individuals struggling with the violence engendered by the repression of loss sometimes turn to psychotherapy for assistance. If they are fortunate, these individuals are able to identify, interpret, and come to terms with their losses, a process Freud called "working through."[55] But working through loss in this way can be slow, difficult, and expensive.

For groups struggling to come to terms with unconscious losses, cultural processes can also facilitate "working through." In particular, art, literature, and religion itself are intermediate regions in which the transformation from unconscious violence to healing can occur.[56] In the next four chapters of *Tracing the Sign of the Cross*, I examine fiction, essays, and memoirs by four members of the post–World War II generation of American Catholics as they do and do not engage, interpret, and transform the Roman Catholic preoccupation with sexual prohibition, gender roles, and other aspects of contemporary American Catholic identity. These four writers can be seen as attempting to "work through" the loss that plagues American Catholics. We might say that the works of literature interrogated in this study function as the transferential region by means of which the fragmentation and uncertainty that sexual prohibition holds at bay is or is not integrated into American Catholic identity in the post–Vatican II period. The crucifix, that most Catholic of signifiers, plays a critical role in this interrogation.

Chapter 1 considers the relationship between sexuality and mourning as it is represented in the writings of the novelist, journalist, and former Catholic priest James Carroll. In his widely read journalistic critiques of the institutional church and in frequent public appearances, Carroll's calls for church reform suggest a genuine commitment to acknowledging and coming to terms with Catholic failures and losses. A close reading of Carroll's nine novels and his award-winning memoir *An American Requiem*, however, display a highly gendered pattern of resistance to such mourning.[57]

Symptomatic of these difficulties is the repeated appearance in Carroll's novels of a plot structure in which two male characters compete for a woman's love, with the relationship between the men appearing more charged than the relationship between the woman and either of the men in the triangle. Intermittent accompanying expressions of homophobia distract the reader from these homosocial bonds, which are, in fact, fundamental to the control of women in church and society. Attention to this narrative framework reveals a structuring tension between the liberal stance toward women and people of color in Carroll's journalism and the conquering Christic heroes of his novels. The fantasized conquests of these heroes hold at bay the grief that would otherwise accompany the death of a long-sought, liberal, post–Vatican II American Catholicism. Since Carroll is a virtual icon of U.S. reform Catholicism, this deeper structure points toward an inability to mourn among the post–Vatican II generation of American Catholics more broadly, and not only on the part of church leaders or conservative Catholics.

Chapter 2 addresses the intersection between sexuality and mourning in the works of the Catholic novelist and essayist Mary Gordon. In her first three novels, Gordon portrays the Catholic Church—and the paternal figures who represent it—as bedrock, the sort of unfeeling, impermeable essence favored in neo-Thomist metaphysics. Yet in each book, a struggle ensues between this impermeable essence and its "enemies": ordinary life and love, motherhood, sexuality, but sometimes also intelligence, politics, or having a career. Why, if Catholicism were truly impermeable, would these struggles keep occurring? Gordon's characters cannot leave them behind, because the bedrock church was never really impermeable. The other, the sexual abject, is attached imperceptibly to its underside like a barnacle. Its continued attempted expulsion points toward the encroachment of sexuality and other loathsome substances onto the purity and innocence of mid-twentieth-century American Catholicism, a classic instance of the inability to come to terms with temporality and embodiment.

In the 1990s, when figures of the sexual and racial other appear within representations of Catholicism in Gordon's work, this resistance to mourning begins to give way. In her 1996 memoir, *The Shadow Man*, Gordon confronts abject secrets about her conservative Catholic father, a convert from Judaism—that he was a published anti-Semite and pornographer who had lied about multiple aspects of his life before marrying her mother—and the bedrock church of her earlier fiction is chipped away, rendered porous, and reconfigured.[58] And at the end of her 1993 novella "The Rest of Life," the female Italian American protagonist, after facing painful repressed memories of her youth, celebrates her new vision with a joyous Eucharistic hymn.[59] Gordon's 2005 novel *Pearl* extends this hopeful reconfiguration effected by mourning the loss of an innocent and optimistic American Catholicism at the beginning of the twenty-first century.[60]

Some may find it puzzling that I choose in my third chapter to explore a number of complex essays by a former Catholic, the feminist philosopher of science Donna J. Haraway. Haraway's work can seem far removed from Roman Catholic, post–Vatican II teaching on sexuality and gender. Haraway is most widely known for a 1985 essay in which she uses the "cyborg," a hybrid, part machine, part animal, part human, to represent the postmodern breaching of boundaries. Yet some critics find Haraway's cyborgs lacking in feeling, especially in response to the human and ecological losses of the late industrial era. In effect, they accuse Haraway's cyborgs of a failure to mourn.

I, however, read the appearance of figures of the crucified Christ in Haraway's 1992 essay, "Ecce Homo, Ain't (Ar'n't) I a Woman, and Inappropriate/d Others: The Human in a Posthumanist Landscape," and in her subsequent book, *Modest_Witness@Second_Millennium.Femaleman©_Meets_ Oncomouse™*, as precisely the introduction of the rhetoric of mourning into her cyborg discourse. In Haraway, as in Carroll and Gordon, sexuality and gender circulate around figures of Christ on the cross, culminating, for Haraway, in a pivotal reading of the genetically altered female Oncomouse™ with a crown of thorns on her head.[61]

In chapter 4, mourning and the inability to mourn also illumine Catholic discourses of sexuality and gender in the works of the essayist and television commentator Richard Rodriguez. In his debut collection of autobiographical essays, *Hunger of Memory*, pre–Vatican II Roman Catholicism plays a critical role in defending Rodriguez from painful losses associated with his assimilation into Anglo-American culture.[62] Rodriguez thus expresses scorn and outrage at the loss of the precious ecclesial stability and intimacy he perceives to have accompanied the reforms of Vatican II. However, the title of one chapter in *Hunger of Memory*, "Mr. Secrets," suggests that there may be more hidden under this fantasy of ecclesial stability than meets the eye.

These secrets begin to emerge in Rodriguez's 1992 collection of essays, *Days of Obligation*.[63] This is especially the case in the essay "Late Victorians," in which Rodriguez revises his understanding of Catholicism in light of his own homosexuality and the death from AIDS of his dear friend César. At first, César seems to be a gay version of the privileged, optimistic, American individualism Rodriguez scorns. But gradually, in the face of César's agony and that of so many other gay men in 1980s San Francisco, Rodriguez realizes that a community is gathering over that city much as one gathered after the death of Jesus. The stylized Latin Mass to which Rodriguez once clung is refigured as a band of AIDS volunteers called forth at Holy Redeemer Catholic Church in the Castro district for their service to the dying—a ragtag but utterly committed communion of saints.[64] This loss, mourning, and reenvisioning of Catholicism in turn facilitate the brilliant reconfiguration of American racial and cultural identity in Rodriguez's 2002 autobiographical meditation *Brown: The Last Discovery of America*.[65] In *Days of Obligation* and to an even greater extent in *Brown*, Rodriguez engages his own suffering and loss, which can hardly be separated from his sexuality, in the shadow of the distinctively Catholic crucifix.

Chapter 6, the conclusion, comprises an interrogation of my own losses as a postwar, Vatican II American Catholic and how my readings of Carroll, Gordon, Haraway, and Rodriguez, in light of the scholarly conversation about mourning and the inability to mourn, have transformed this experience. In this chapter, I consider the failure of higher education and professional/managerial-class status in themselves to eradicate the deeply inscribed deprivation and suffering experienced by my parents' immigrant families; the deterioration of American Catholic culture, especially the culture of the American Catholic sisters who profoundly influenced me before and during Vatican II; and the ongoing influence of binarized, idealized, neo-Thomist thought patterns on the reform Catholicism in which I have invested greatly since the early 1970s. Over these thirty-plus years, my inclination has been to battle for power, like the heroes of James Carroll's texts, against the Vatican and the hierarchy for equality and gender inclusion in the church, especially regarding women. And indeed, as I am writing, some of my dearest friends feel called to continue this battle. Yet engagement with texts by Gordon, Haraway, and especially Rodriguez, as they work through their own not insignificant losses, inspires me, increasingly, to identify with a fragmented and porous Catholicism, that sliver of dry earth, as Gordon puts it, which is never beyond the shadow of the crucifix.

In this conclusion, I acknowledge that the process of working through loss is more difficult and protracted than I had once imagined and that I will probably never cease grieving for the death of my youthful dream of an innocent American Catholicism. But I continue, nonetheless, to "trace the sign of the cross," drawing on the Catholic tradition as a source of great encouragement and sustenance in my life.

CHAPTER ONE

Skating Ahead of the Cracks

JAMES CARROLL'S LIBERAL AMERICAN CATHOLICISM

> I told the story of his hurling himself out onto the thin ice at Mount
> Paul Novitiate in 1962, and of my standing with my classmates on
> the shore, crying, "Go, Patrick! Go Patrick!" I intended only to say
> that I'd recognized a man I wanted to be with, but . . . I now recog-
> nized in his story a reminder of that other One.
>
> "Who is that, walking on the water?"
>
> "Isn't that Jesus? The only one we loved?"
>
> And Peter went, right out onto the water, without a thought for
> consequences, or a nod to those who said it couldn't be done. And
> for a moment, he was walking on water too.
>
> — JAMES CARROLL, *An American Requiem*

> Unless the entire discursive field (and each subject's unconscious)
> is changed, these categories will continue to generate particular
> forms of subjectivity beyond the control of individuals . . .
>
> — JANE FLAX, *"The End of Innocence"*

From the beginning, I had certain notions, certain fantasies,
about what my interrogation of the works of four contemporary American
Catholic writers would entail. During the writing process, some of these
notions fell by the wayside. Others have been transplanted, reconfigured,
retooled. One early intuition has remained with me throughout, however.
James Carroll comes first.

The choice of Carroll as my starting point is fueled, in part at least, by
chronology. Born in 1943 and thus older than Mary Gordon, Donna J. Haraway, Richard Rodriguez, and I, Carroll holds a kind of senior rank among
the American Catholics whose work I examine.[1] He is not even technically
a baby boomer, though the imprint of the civil rights and anti–Vietnam War
struggles makes him one, his date of birth notwithstanding.

Geography, too, informs my selection of Carroll as the baseline for this project. The Catholic crescent, that chain of rustbelt cities from Chicago through Detroit and Cleveland to Boston and down the eastern seaboard to the District of Columbia, home to so many of Carroll's Catholics, fictional and real, has long been the territory of my imagination as well. Like Carroll, I studied theology on Catholic Row in Washington, haunted St. Patrick's, the Cloisters, and St. John the Divine in Manhattan, loved and hated Irish Catholicism in parishes on the edges of sometimes vibrant, sometimes dying eastern cities.

Beyond age or geography, however, Carroll stands at the gateway to *Tracing the Sign of the Cross* because his is an archetypal story of American Catholic upward mobility and assimilation and the losses that accompanied them. Already a generation removed from the struggles of immigrant American Catholics, Carroll attended prestigious schools, rode around Europe in the private railway car of his brigadier general father, and socialized with cardinals and popes. Yet even as the young Carroll catches game-winning touchdowns and plans a career as an Air Force pilot, the sign of the cross, ostensibly long left behind in the Chicago Catholic ghetto, resurfaces in his own life. He leaves Georgetown University to enter the celibate Roman Cath-olic priesthood.

However, James Carroll's ordination to the Roman Catholic priesthood was less a resolution of tensions between "the Catholic grammar of suffering" and a liberal American construal of reality than it was a reiteration of them.[2] In his award-winning memoir, *An American Requiem: God, My Father, and the War That Came Between Us*, Carroll narrates a series of attempts to come to terms with these warring trajectories, especially as they are played out in his relationship with his very Catholic and very American father during and after the Vietnam War.[3] In this chapter, I trace Carroll's ability—and inability—to confront the losses that attend this struggle. As I do so, the trajectory of the cross and the late twentieth-century American Catholic struggle with sexuality that is part of it begin to come into view.

GOD, MY FATHER, AND THE WAR

For many American Catholics before World War II, James Carroll's life would have seemed a fairy tale. Carroll's roots were in Bridgeport, an Irish, working-class section of Chicago; his parents, Joe and Mary, were the first members of their large families to trade the old neighborhood for professional possibilities in another part of the country. As his second son would later do, Joe Carroll received most of his education in a Catholic seminary, but, unlike his son, he chose to withdraw just before ordination.[4] He subsequently earned a law degree at night while working in the stockyards, joined the FBI, and married. After masterminding the spectacular capture of a Chicago gangster during World War II, Joe Carroll moved with his wife and growing family to Washington, D.C., where he became a member of J. Edgar Hoover's inner circle. Then, at age thirty-seven, he was commissioned a brigadier general, the youngest general in the United States at the time, to take command of the Office of Special Investigations of the recently established U.S. Air Force.

In *An American Requiem*, Carroll reminds us that his father's meteoric rise from the Chicago stockyards to the military leadership occurred during a period of increasing apparent compatibility between Catholicism and American culture. American Catholics had served in the U.S. armed forces in large numbers during World War II, but it was the convergence of Catholic anticommunism and the outbreak of the cold war that made Catholics feel more at home in America than ever before. In 1949, the year when the first Soviet atomic bomb was detonated, Stalin invaded Czechoslovakia, and Mao captured Peking, Pope Pius XII abandoned the neutrality he had maintained during World War II and, with one stroke of the pen, excommunicated all the communists in the world. He then adapted Catholic just war theory to the cold war—something he had refused to do against the Nazis—and denied Catholics in the West the right to avoid military service by claiming conscientious-objector status. For the first time, American non-Catholics were able to see the pope in Rome as a valuable ally. American Catholics Francis Cardinal Spellman, Bishop Fulton Sheen, Senator Joseph McCarthy, and Dr. Tom Dooley reinforced this impression.

Joe Carroll welcomed the church's anticommunist stance. As a young person, James Carroll "shared [his] father's view entirely," supporting and taking great pride in the pope's actions, while deriving from them and from his father's government career a "vivid and continuous sense of connection to what theorists called 'the state.'"[5] Because of this, the figures of the FBI agent and the military officer began to merge with that of the priest in Carroll's imagination, a convergence that would prove significant later, both in his decision to join the priesthood and in the fiction he would write.

One signifier of the assimilation effected between Catholicism and American culture in this period is the phrase Carroll uses to describe the presidential inaugurations that he, a Washington, D.C., resident, attended regularly for almost thirty years.

> All my life, inaugurations had been like a sacrament of the streets to me, rituals of rebirth, the one true American gala, a quadrennial instance of Jefferson's "peaceful revolution." At inaugurations . . . I had learned the basic lesson of this nation: how to put aside what divides us—*e pluribus*—in favor of a felt experience of what unites us—*unum*. At inaugurations, we could all wear buttons that said "I like everybody."[6]

In some respects, Carroll's "sacrament of the streets" echoes the assertion by the American Catholic studies scholar Robert Orsi that the annual *festa* of Our Lady of Mt. Carmel in Italian Harlem embodied "a theology of the streets."[7] Yet Orsi's "theology of the streets" was concerned with the suffering of the Italian Catholic community and the influence of the *festa* on that suffering. Carroll's "sacrament of the streets," on the other hand, suggests movement beyond such suffering into a sort of transcendent unity. It calls to mind the designation by the feminist science studies scholar Donna J. Haraway, whose own Catholicism I examine in chapter 3, of "the god-trick" or "the unmarked category" as a location ostensibly beyond race, class, or gender and into which competing groups long to disappear.[8]

Carroll's recollections of his family's time in Wiesbaden, West Germany, in the late 1950s give some indication of the kind of experience that might underwrite such a vision. Before then, Carroll believes, his father might as well have been an insurance broker or a meat salesman, but during those "gravy days early in the Cold War," General Carroll had his own private plane, train, and lavish house. Servants waited on the Carroll children, and James, as the son of a general, enjoyed seniority over the other officers' sons. He recalls sitting on the roof of the family's house, "watching the light of the day fade and the windows of houses in the valley turn bright, and then stars overhead would fill the sky. I remember . . . realizing how full of beauty the world was, and that it was put there for me."[9]

This sense of self was enhanced by the genuine happiness Carroll experienced in Germany. Liberated from the all-male environs of the Benedictine Priory School he had attended in the United States, Carroll finds the beginnings of a gratifying sexual relationship with a cheerleader girlfriend and fantasizes a future with her and a career as an Air Force pilot. In a delicious deviation from the deep religiousness his parents expected of him, his idol is Elvis, not yet "The King," but "king to me, my truest Lord, the one in whom I found my first identity, not as my father's kind of Catholic, or my mother's kind of son or my siblings' kind of brother, but simply as myself."[10]

Even the attraction of the priesthood was, in some respects, an extension of this trajectory of selfhood and assimilation. In Germany, Carroll meets the many Air Force chaplains who are his father's friends, and he encounters in them, for the first time, a priestliness that is manly, even glamorous—far removed from the feminization and sorrow he associated with Catholicism back home. So intense is the sense of intimacy he experiences when he caddies for his father and one of his chaplain friends, Monsignor Chess, that he pretends for a while that they are all priests together.

Finally, at the end of his father's tour of duty, the family travels to Rome for a private audience with Pope John XXIII. Instead of allowing James to kneel before him, the pope draws him close and speaks in a way that elates him. "He is seeing through to the core of me, he knows my secret, and he shares it," Carroll writes. In this "counter-Elvis," as he calls him, Carroll glimpses the transcendence of the church and knows, finally, that God has captured him and that he will have to respond. What better way to seal the sense of unity and well-being inscribed in his "sacrament of the streets"?

THE INESCAPABLE CROSS

Yet despite this happy convergence in James Carroll's youth between church and state, between priest and G-man, *An American Requiem* is structured from the outset by a tension between American optimism and a strong undercurrent of suffering and loss. Initially, Carroll attributes this undercurrent to an attack of polio that his older brother, Joe, suffered in 1947, at the age of five. Carroll recalls that during the early phases of Joe Jr.'s polio, he began to see crosses everywhere. "Polio brought the cross back into our family, where it belonged," he writes.[11] Those were also the days when Mary Carroll began to take James and her other sons with her to pray for Joe Jr. at the shrines and monasteries along "Catholic Row" in northeast Washington: "The Shrine (of the Immaculate Conception) especially was the North

Star of my childhood. When Joe was in the hospital, it seemed we went there after every visit. I knelt below the crucifixes, all that writhing, legs as bruised as Joe's. . . . I imitated my mother, lighting candles at the snake-ridden (virus-ridden?) feet of the Blessed Virgin Mary."[12] From his parents' response to his brother's illness, Carroll derives the life-shaping conviction that their Catholicism means only one thing, that "every human has his cross to bear," that "each of us," as he says, "is crucified."[13]

Ultimately, however, Carroll traces the undercurrent of sorrow and loss in his family back to certain events in his parents' lives before he and his brother were even born, specifically to his father's decision to leave the seminary on the eve of ordination. Fundamental to the emphasis Carroll places on this experience is the widespread attitude of many Catholics before Vatican II toward someone who left the seminary, who "lost his vocation" to the priesthood. To have such a person in the family was a source of deep shame, especially in Jansenist Irish Catholic culture.[14] In those days, the role of the "spoiled priest," Carroll reminds us, "was to drink heavily and to fail."[15]

Carroll also believes it highly likely that his parents compounded the shame of his father's failure by having come together while Joe Sr. was still a seminarian. Within this construal, only when their beautiful first son, Joe Jr., was born did Joe and Mary Carroll dare to believe that the stigma of the "spoiled priest" was really behind them. The polio that struck Joe Jr. when he was five years old thus functioned as the final proof that their shame was inescapable; they would never be happy.

James Carroll explicitly links his decision for the priesthood to his brother's illness. From the hour of his birth, in fact, Carroll was identified with his older brother: after a shaky arrival in the world, the future James Carroll received by mistake the name already assigned to his older brother, Joseph, in an emergency baptism at the hospital. But with his brother's affliction, Carroll believes he was officially and irrevocably marked as his father's substitute. One of the significant realizations in *An American Requiem* is that Carroll's "vocation" was, in part at least, an attempt to restore the lost happiness of his young parents, to end their shame by taking his father's place as a priest.

A conversation between Joe Carroll Sr. and his second son during James's years as a priest illustrates the accuracy of this intuition. For the first time in his life, Carroll asks his father why he didn't get ordained. "Because I wasn't worthy," Joe Sr. replies.

"Worthy?" I am mystified, and to my horror, I feel a jolt of anger. "Worthy? What the hell does worthy have to do with it? Who the fuck is worthy? . . . Worthy?" I say again, "You think I'm worthy?"

My father stares at me, thinking. At last he answers, "Yes, I do." . . . I am worthy because I have immolated my will. He is unworthy—here is the very definition of his life—because he would not.[16]

The subtext of this exchange, as any Catholic of the period could have explained, is sexuality. Though priests did immolate their wills in other ways—obedience to the bishop, for example—James Carroll's primary immolation, for which his father respected him, was the renunciation of sexual activity. This was the sacrifice for which he had been designated from childhood and against which he would struggle, in one form or another, for the greater part of his adult life.

BUT WHICH CROSS?

At first blush, James Carroll's priesthood would seem to be situated unambiguously in the trajectory of the cross, the tangible result of his family's conviction that every human being is crucified. Yet the "Catholic grammar of suffering" is more than submission to limitation and pain or bearing the shame and guilt triggered by attempted escape. Rather, as the American Catholic Studies scholar Robert Orsi's interpretation of the *festa* of Our Lady of 115th Street suggests, the Catholic grammar of suffering includes a view of the world in which suffering and limitation can lead to self-respect and freedom if they are embraced as Jesus embraced them.[17] One subtext of *An American Requiem* is precisely the tension between these two different understandings of the cross, that is, between the engagement of mourning and the strategies of shame, guilt, passivity, and triumphant conquest that can, ostensibly, elide the pain of mourning.

Carroll's recollections of his years as seminarian and priest illustrate these tensions very well. Although he endures the typical episodes of "God-wrestling" beforehand, and although it was as much the fulfillment of his parents' deepest wishes as his own, Carroll's priesthood and the years of preparation for it were by no means years marked only by the "immolation of the will."[18] They were also, as Carroll tells us, a time of unexpected joy.

Part of the credit for this joy goes to the group of priests Carroll chose to join, the Congregation of St. Paul, or Paulists. The Paulists are a distinctly American congregation and one of the most liberal in the church. Their founder, Isaac Hecker, was, like Thomas Merton and Dorothy Day, a WASP convert, in this case from Transcendentalism; in the early part of the twentieth century, the Americanist heresy, condemned by the Vatican in 1896, was linked to Hecker's life and teachings.[19] Even Carroll's manner of selecting the Paulists is telling: he signed up with them, in part at least, because the Paulist recruiter he met at a vocation fair at Georgetown was breezy, jocular, and hip. Later, Carroll will see in the distinct sashed cassock of the Paulists both some of the glamour he found in his father's chaplain friends and an indication of the Paulists' elite status.

More significantly, the Paulists' apparently nearly limitless trust in Carroll will significantly strengthen the sense of himself that had begun to emerge in Germany. When he breaks the rules, the Paulists tell him his failures will make him a better priest. When his writing talent becomes apparent, they send him to the University of Minnesota to study with the modernist poet (and Catholic convert) Allen Tate, though it was probably against their institutional interests to do so. The Paulists even support him when, on his first assignment after ordination as campus minister at Boston University, he orders the stained glass and "mournful" Stations of the Cross torn out of the chapel, after which it accidentally burns to the ground.[20]

In the Paulist seminary, the "immolation of the will" that Carroll's father identified with the priesthood changes from a configuration with personal sexual purity and strict obedience at its core to one emphasizing social justice and peace, or so it would seem. Before long, Martin Luther King Jr. is Carroll's newest "lord," and he is praying not to be recognized as he stands outside his father's Pentagon office protesting the Vietnam War.

IF NOT FOR THE WAR?

As its subtitle—*God, My Father, and the War That Came Between Us*—indicates, *An American Requiem* addresses major losses in James Carroll's life under the rubric of the Vietnam War. Carroll's opposition to the war can be interpreted without much difficulty as the continuation of a classic Catholic trajectory, a return, as it were, to the very sign of the cross his parents' entrance into the professional-managerial class prepared him to leave behind. As such, Carroll's antiwar activism is a reiteration of earlier Catholic ritual and theological transformations of suffering, now enacted on behalf of the Vietnamese and other oppressed peoples of the world as it once was for oppressed immigrant American Catholics. Carroll explicitly links the crucifixion to his antiwar efforts. When he and his comrades picket the residence of Cardinal Medeiros of Boston, the sign he carries reads "Another Crucifixion in Indochina." When the self-identified Catholic Worker Roger LaPorte sets himself on fire to protest the war, the crucifixion again comes to mind: "Jesus on the wall above me had never seemed so wretched."

Yet such an interpretation would not have been self-evident to many American Catholics at the time. Indeed, the U.S. Catholic community was bitterly divided over the Vietnam War. By the 1960s, American Catholics had finally achieved the acceptance as "real Americans" that they had coveted for decades, and they did not welcome the erosion of that identity. Large numbers of American Catholics served in the U.S. armed forces during Vietnam. The Vatican and American bishops had been largely successful in their efforts to inculcate opposition to communism in the Catholic community, and the war in Vietnam was frequently represented as a communist attack on a Catholic country.

James Carroll's family is an object lesson in the bitterness of these divisions. General Carroll, a participant in high military decision-making processes, was deeply implicated in the war.[21] He dissented from the call issued by the new Pope, Paul VI, at the United Nations General Assembly in 1965: "Jamais plus la guerre! Jamais plus la guerre!"[22] But he was outraged when other Catholics dissented from *Humanae vitae*, the 1968 papal condemnation of artificial contraception. One of his sons, Dennis, fled the country to escape the draft. Another, Kevin, joined the FBI and pursued Catholic war resisters, including the Jesuit Daniel Berrigan, for their actions against local draft boards.

James Carroll made public his opposition to the war at the celebration of his first Mass, before "the wretched crucifix" in the chapel at Bolling Air Force Base.[23] With his parents and their Air Force associates, including the infamous General Curtis LeMay, in the congregation, the newly ordained Father Carroll proclaimed that Ezekiel's bones were dried and burned not just by desert wind and sun but "most of all, by napalm."[24] The congregation could not have mistaken his meaning.

Carroll makes clear that such traitorous opposition by the son who had been the apple of his parents' eye, the priest who had earned his mother a place in heaven, initiated a grievous breach in their relationship. This war-induced breach is enlarged by his subsequent decision to leave the priesthood, and his wedding, which his parents do not attend because it occurs before he has received official authorization from Rome, makes that breach permanent. When his father dies, years later, they are still unreconciled.

But Carroll has already revealed that the losses he attempts to confront in *An American Requiem* extend well beyond this "beloved priest-son alienated from his father by their differences over Vietnam War" plot line. Conflict and complexity had, in fact, long marked Carroll's relationship with "God and [his] father." Even before their time in Germany, Carroll had dreaded the "vocation" his parents were convinced he had, likening the seminary, in a bad pun, to a "cemetery" and harboring the conviction that by going there he would "entomb himself."[25] In looking back at their time in Weisbaden, Carroll calls himself a coward and a liar for leading his girlfriend on when he knew—or at least feared—that he was destined to be a priest. Because of its indirectness, he even understands as an act of cowardice the reference he makes at his first Mass to the evils of the war. In those days, he admits, the apparent coherence and integrity of his two selves were belied by the fact that he was unable to bring them together.

In addition to being a narrative of "God, [his] father and the war," then, *An American Requiem* is the record of a struggle within James Carroll. It is a struggle Carroll will engage in again and again, a struggle between the entitlement and optimism that his father's professional status and his own formation in a liberal American Catholic religious congregation prepared him for and the immigrant Catholic disposition toward suffering and limitation that neither his parents nor the American church ever entirely left behind. And if, as I will argue, it is a struggle he most frequently resolves in favor of entitlement and optimism, it is also one he engages with bravery, and never more so than in *An American Requiem*.

"The Story Is What Saves Us"

While James Carroll's opposition to the war may be an extension of the trajectory of the cross in American Catholicism, the function of his departure from the priesthood and subsequent marriage is more difficult to determine. From one perspective, Carroll's decision to become a priest, to restore his parents' happiness, can be interpreted as a failure to mourn, an inability to endure the space of difference and possible betrayal that inevitably opens between parents and child. His return to lay status would then be an attempt to confront that void. Or, following Julia Kristeva, the celibate priesthood could be Carroll's effort to push the sexual abject, unleashed by his parents' marriage, back to the margins of the Catholic cultural domain, and the renunciation of it is a willingness to confront that abjection and move beyond it.

Carroll suggests several reasons for his actions. When he goes home to tell his parents of his decision, he adds, almost as an afterthought, that he is leaving the priesthood because he wants to marry and have children. At other times, however, he explains that he resigned in order to be a writer.

While Carroll's first reason is a pragmatic one, his second demands scrutiny, since there is nothing in canon law or even in Catholic practice that forbids priests to be writers. Thomas Merton entered the Abbey of Gethsemani assuming that as a monk he would give up writing, but the Cistercians instructed him to write numerous devotional and historical works—as well as the popular memoirs and volumes of poetry that cannot have done any harm to the abbey's bottom line.[26]

Carroll began his writing career wanting to be a poet, and he showed such early promise that the Paulists sent him, when he was twenty-two, to study with Allen Tate. Carroll stood in a tradition of priest-poets stretching back in this century to the English Jesuit Gerard Manley Hopkins[27] and, in the post–World War II period, to another Jesuit, Daniel Berrigan, who won the Lamont Prize for poetry in 1957. A volume of Carroll's poetry was published by Paulist/Newman Press in 1974,[28] and eight volumes of his spiritual writings appeared between 1967 and 1975, several of them in free verse.[29]

Working with Allen Tate had a significant impact on James Carroll; at one point, he calls Tate his "new father in the Word, but lowercase."[30] Tate was the one who first suggested to Carroll that it would not be possible to be a writer and a priest too. In autographing a volume of his poems for Carroll, Tate wrote on the flyleaf: "Inscribed to James Carroll, with best wishes for his two vocations." He then looked up at Carroll and added, "You know, you're not going to be able to have them both."[31] In *An American Requiem*, Carroll builds on Tate's assertion:

> I am a writer, no priest. I believe that to be made in God's image is to do this: arrange memory and transform experience according to the structure of narrative. The story is what saves us, in this case, with Ezekiel, coming down through valleys and a blue curtain to Jesus, my only God, whose fate was and remains the same as my father's, mine and everyone's. Telling His story, in my tradition, is what makes Him really present.[32]

Later, however, Carroll rejects this polarization. After his marriage, when he preaches at the funeral of a dear friend and fellow Paulist who had also left the priesthood to marry, Carroll concludes that

> storytelling itself can be a priestly act. If there is something peculiarly "Catholic" stamped upon my soul, it is implied by this notion that the imagination is itself sacred. The very act of storytelling, of arranging memory and invention, according to the structures of narrative, is by definition holy. It is a version, however finite, of what the infinite God does. Telling our stories is what saves us; the story is enough.[33]

This reversal was already implied in Carroll's earlier observation that "telling His story, in my tradition, is what makes him really present." It contrasts with the traditional Catholic teaching that what "makes him"—that is to say, Jesus—"really present" is transubstantiation, the "ontological" change of bread and wine into the body and blood of Christ at the Eucharist. This Catholic belief in the Real Presence in the Eucharist has never excluded the presence of Christ in the gospel or God's analogical presence in creation, but it brings it into focus in a way that telling a story does not.

Carroll's move to story calls to mind the position taken by the Protestant Reformers. They agreed that the center of Christian worship and the chief task of a minister of the Gospel is preaching—that is, the telling of "his story"—rather than offering the sacrifice of the Mass, as Catholic theology maintained.[34] It likewise parallels the Protestant removal of the bloody, visual-tactile corpus from the crucifix.

Carroll also justifies his decision to marry and have children with an appeal to the ontological, to the "really-real." Although he once accepted the incompatibility of priesthood and marriage as he did the incompatibility of priesthood and writing, Carroll later becomes convinced that parenthood truly effects the ontological change he once believed to be bestowed by ordination.[35] When he baptizes Jenny, his premature infant daughter, before she dies, he realizes that he has finally become a "real priest."[36]

Others besides Carroll have attempted to shift the ontological, that is, the "really-real," of Catholicism to story. In an article in the *New York Times Magazine*, the priest-sociologist Andrew Greeley argues that images and stories, as opposed to doctrines and rules, are what keep American Catholics Catholic.[37] Drawn loosely from Clifford Geertz's anthropology and David Tracy's theology, Greeley's argument, because it takes "the image" into account, is perhaps less exclusive of the visual-tactile than Carroll's more linguistic notion of story. Yet both versions are marked by a smoothness and coherence that belie their roots in Enlightenment liberalism; to say that the story or the image saves us begs the not insignificant question of which story or image that might be. Even when Greeley asserts the towering dominance of the image of Mary in the Catholic imagination, he fails to make clear which Mary he is speaking about. Is she the Mary of Guadelupe who supports Mexican peasants, the Mary of the Immaculate Conception who undergirded nineteenth-century papal resistance to democracy, or some other Mary altogether?

Carroll's smooth invocation of "story" also calls to mind his earlier description of American presidential inaugurations as "a sacrament of the streets." In response to the increasing priest shortage and other problems, some late twentieth-century American Catholics increasingly identify the sacraments as the essence of Catholicism, much as Carroll emphasizes the centrality of story in Christian salvation.[38] Many of these individuals understand themselves to be working for the reform of Catholicism. Their essentialization of the sacraments per se is, however, unconsciously complicit in centuries-long efforts by the institutional church to concentrate power by controlling the diverse devotional practices favored by the Catholic lower classes in Europe and the United States. In a classic demonstration of the

Nietzschean telescoping of multiple signifiers into one, the scholar of American religion Ann Taves traces this centralization process from the invention of the printing press, the rise of seminary-trained clergy, and the standardization of the Latin Mass through the nineteenth-century consolidation of previously extraparochial devotional confraternities under the control of parish priests.[39] At St. Joseph's, the working-class parish near Philadelphia that my family belonged to in the 1950s, the priests and nuns were still at pains to convince parishioners to relent from saying the rosary and novenas to the saints during Mass.[40] In *An American Requiem*, Carroll's "sacrament of the streets" and his theology of story constitute a similar attempted elision of messy, often painful differences—that is to say, of suffering and limitation.

However, no matter how much one theorizes about "the story" or "the imagination," to be a writer, one must, at some point, write *something*. I have argued that Carroll's move from ontological priesthood to modern but nonetheless ontological storytelling parallels the removal of the tactile-visual corpus from the Catholic crucifix. Another way of framing this argument is to note that even after it is taken down from the cross, the body, the "really-real," is still somewhere. In James Carroll's case, the body continues to appear, even after he turns to story, in his memoir and in the nine volumes of fiction that precede it.

The Christic Hero

The trail of the body liberated from the cross in Carroll's opus begins with a paradigmatic experience recorded early in *An American Requiem*. Before Thanksgiving, during the year Carroll was a Paulist novice, another novice, Patrick Hughes, bet all comers that he could skate across the novitiate's as yet unfrozen lake on December 8. On the long-awaited day, the ice appeared to crack open beneath him as Hughes set off across the lake. His friends were terrified, but

> Then we saw that the ice was breaking and opening not under but behind him. He was ahead of the break, skating so fast and so lightly that even the thin ice was support enough for the instant that he needed it. . . . We began to cry after him, "Go, Patrick! Go Patrick!" As he shot across that ice, leaving behind a great crack, a wedge of black water,

we knew we had never seen such courage before. . . . We had never seen such a capacity for trust—a man's trust in himself. Even before he made it all the way across, and of course he did make it, I thought, This is a man I want to be with.[41]

Carroll's relationship with Patrick Hughes was transformative, opening him to friendship and helping him to believe, eventually, that he "too had what it took, to haul [himself] out onto thin ice and skate ahead of a great crack."[42] This male hero who skates triumphantly "just ahead of the cracks" appears repeatedly throughout Carroll's fiction and most emphatically in the novels where Catholics—often priests or ex-priests—figure significantly. In *Madonna Red*, Carroll's first novel, a priest and Vietnam War veteran, at the last possible moment, prevents a terrorist from committing an assassination.[43] In another thriller, *Fault Lines*, Carroll's preoccupation with fractures is inscribed directly into the title.[44] In *Prince of Peace*, Carroll's most critically acclaimed novel, the priest-hero, Michael Maguire, who had barely avoided death as a POW in Korea and then (literally) skated ahead of cracking ice while he was a seminarian, leads the Vietnam War resistance. "Go, Michael, go," appears like a motif throughout the novel, even in the final scene, Maguire's funeral.[45] And at the conclusion of *The City Below*, Carroll's 1994 novel, Terry Mullen, an ex-seminarian who works for the Kennedys, narrowly fends off the destruction of his marriage and the murder of his wife.[46]

Toward the end of *An American Requiem*, Carroll makes explicit the Christological underpinnings of his triumphant heroes. In a sermon he preaches at the funeral of his original skater, Patrick Hughes, portions of which serve as the epigraph to this chapter, Carroll recalls that he had intended only to say that in Patrick's race across the ice he had recognized a man he had wanted to be with. But then he "recognized in his story a reminder of that other One, Jesus, walking on the water . . . the only one we loved."[47]

Although this passage was written many years later, Carroll's association here of the triumphant (if lovable) male hero with Christ throbs with the optimism of American Catholicism in the post–World War II period, an optimism I shared. I am reminded, for example, that even as I struggled in the 1970s with the implications of feminism for my own Catholic identity, a stanza of my favorite Easter hymn proclaimed "Christ our victor giant / Quells the foe defiant. / Let the ransomed people sing / Glory to the Easter King. / Alleluia."[48]

A study of the "literary imagination" published in 1960 by the Catholic dramatist and literary scholar William Lynch helps to specify the texture and complexity of this era of liberal optimism in American Catholic history. *Christ and Apollo* engages the differences between the univocal imagination, symbolized by Apollo, and the analogical imagination, symbolized by Christ. For Lynch, Apollo represents a kind of Cartesian, gnostic abstractness, but Christ stands for

> the completely definite, the Man who, in taking on our human nature . . . took on every inch of it (save sin) in all its density, and who so obviously did not march too quickly or too glibly to beauty, the infinite, the dream. . . . As the model and source of that energy and courage we again need to enter the finite as the only creative and generative source of beauty.[49]

Lynch, a Jesuit, was an influential figure in the Catholic literary circles of the 1950s and 1960s. In *Christ and Apollo*, he champions what I once called "the incarnational" to designate a concreteness, a definiteness, in contrast to the extreme rationalism of the dominant Catholic philosophy of the first half of the century. Yet as I read *Christ and Apollo* today, I am struck by its own abstractness—by how much more it is Apollonian, one might say, than Lynch had perhaps anticipated.[50]

Carroll's Christic heroes are caught up in a similar dynamic. Carroll's move to the narrative is an attempt to transcend the imaginative rigidity of pre–Vatican II Catholicism, but it carries telescoped within it an orderliness, if not a rigidity, of its own. In *Prince of Peace*, the narrator, Frank Durkin, denounces the dry, restricted, neo-Thomist framework taught in the kind of seminary his priest-friend, Michael Maguire, attended. "The *Summa*," he believes, "fit perfectly with the culture of immigrant Catholicism because, as presented in the seminaries, it embodied that sense Catholics had that there are only so many questions and in the symmetry of God's creation there are just that many answers."[51]

Despite this dislike for the supposed predictability of immigrant Catholicism—which one suspects Carroll shares with his character—there is nonetheless also something unnervingly predictable about a number of his novels. Several hundred pages before the book's conclusion, the reader is able, for example, to predict how Carroll will resolve the culminating crisis in *Prince of Peace*. When Michael Maguire, once "the most famous priest in America," dies, the Archdiocese of New York refuses him a Catholic burial because of his marriage to a divorced woman. His funeral is scheduled, instead, for the Episcopal Cathedral of St. John the Divine in Manhattan, an alternative Carroll portrays as troubling, even unimaginable.

But when the funeral procession winds its way out of the sacristy, the whole cathedral, "the second largest church in the world," as the reader is reminded, is full, not only with every variety of Catholic and Protestant clergy, the famous as well as the obscure, but also ordinary men, women, children, students, nuns, the old and the young, Parthians, Medes, Elamites, and Jews, thousands of them, there to send Michael Maguire "on his way." Maguire's funeral is a Resurrection triumph, as deft an instance of skating ahead of the cracks as any reader could want.

I do not mean to trivialize Carroll's fiction, which is good enough to earn regular and often positive notices in the national press. Critics praise Carroll especially for his ability to weave convincingly into his plots a number of different historical periods and characters. The protagonist in *Mortal Friends*, for example, fights beside Michael Collins, the Irish patriot, while the Kennedys, who had a great impact on Carroll (and on a few of the rest of us as well) move in and out of this plot and one or two others.[52] Carroll's work is also noted for its distinctive "ethical reach"; his characters continually struggle with issues of right and wrong. He has been compared, in this regard, to John Gardner and Graham Greene.[53]

Yet, as with that completely full cathedral, Carroll's fiction is nonetheless marred by its rationality and by the predictability of its plot lines. Too many of the little root hairs have been shaved off, and I am not talking here about mere absence of detail. We have met these guys before, and as much as we enjoy their triumphs, we also wonder, at a certain point, what is lurking down there beneath the ice, and why Carroll and his heroes need so badly to escape it.

The Crone Chorus

A clue to the solution of this mystery appears in a passage in *An American Requiem* in which Carroll, probably not coincidentally, addresses once again the very Catholic grammar of suffering that has had such significant effects on his parents and therefore on himself. In this passage, Carroll explores the prohibitions against success and happiness he believes confronted his parents when they tried to leave the Chicago Catholic ghetto: "Who did you think you were?" he imagines the voices of the immigrant past crying out; "How dare you think you can escape?"[54]

The first time I read this passage, I was riveted. "Who do you think you are?" is the very phrase I had arrived at, after years of introspection, to express my experience of prohibition and shame in the working-class Catholic world of my childhood. But on a second reading, other words leapt up at me. Preceding this chilling interrogation is Carroll's personification of the attitudes that seem to have shaped his family's understanding of various tragic events. These attitudes, Carroll writes, "seized my parents like claws reaching up from the stockyard's bog to haul them back into the fetid world from which they came, a crone chorus—Irish hags, the nuns—screeching, 'Who did you think you were. . . ?' "[55]

Carroll may have had any number of reasons for this misogynist personification. Irish women, even before the postfamine migration, were better educated than Irish men. Because of an inheritance system that left many Irish men unable to support their wives, women emigrated alone to America in greater numbers than men did, often sending their wages back to Ireland to support their families of origin.[56] In the United States, many Irish women were trapped between their own determination and the nineteenth-century Victorian ideology of "the angel in the house." Whether in convents or homes, in fact, many of these women were nobody to mess with. Unmarried Irish aunts, in particular, leapt heroically into the breach on many occasions; I am reminded here of Ann McGowan, sister-in-law of my paternal aunt, Julia Ronan McGowan. Aunt Ann moved in with her brother—Julia's husband—to raise their five children after Julia died in childbirth. When asked why she never had children of her own, Aunt Ann responded that as the eldest daughter, she had delivered the last four of her mother's fourteen children on the kitchen table, and that had been enough for her.

Carroll's reference to Irish nuns as crones and hags might nonetheless be dismissed as an unfortunate, isolated incident were it not for a whole series of problematic female figures linked to this trope throughout his novels. Indeed, my examination of them will suggest that, to extend the metaphor established earlier, the body that disappeared from the cross is that of an

Irish Catholic woman, and the fetid bog that this body lunges out of is a reconfiguration of the dreaded water under the ice at Mt. Paul Novitiate.

Two Irish nuns play pivotal roles in *Madonna Red*, Carroll's first novel. One, a "modern" unhabited nun who has dared to offer Mass, embodies conflict in the post–Vatican II church; the book's protagonist, John Tierney, a Vietnam War hero turned priest, is assigned by the cardinal to prosecute her case. The second is a female IRA terrorist who, disguised as a nun in full habit with a high-powered rifle up her sleeve, attempts to assassinate the British ambassador to Northern Ireland, a Catholic, as he is knighted at a papal ceremony in the cathedral. She fails, and Tierney kills her just as she is about to shoot the ambassador's beautiful upper-class wife, a British Protestant artist for whom the priest-hero obviously has feelings.

Madonna Red is an exciting read. Carroll's positioning of the Irish nun-terrorist opposite the beautiful upper-class Protestant artist is troubling, however, especially since this elegant, upper-class non-Catholic woman appears repeatedly in his subsequent novels. In *Mortal Friends* (1978), for example, nuns are marginal, but Carroll's protagonist, Colman Brady, spends far more time with his WASP artist-lover, Madeline Gardner Thomson, than he ever did with his innocent Irish wife, who is conveniently killed off by Carroll early in the narrative. Later, Brady's son gains entry to the Boston upper class through his marriage to an Episcopalian beauty. It is also perhaps worth noting that Carroll himself is married to a non-Catholic artist, the novelist Alexandra Marshall, who is described in *An American Requiem* as my own "quite American" wife.[57]

In *Prince of Peace* (1984), Carroll reengineers this opposition between "Irish hags, the nuns" and upper class non-Catholic women artists, but the dimensions of the opposition are much the same. As a priest-in-training, the protagonist we encountered earlier, Michael Maguire, is assigned to the same parish as Sister Anne Edward, a young nun who is "the opposite of churchly women enshrined by piety. On the contrary, [she is] caring and vulnerable."[58] Sister Anne struggles with the conflict between being a nun and being a painter. Together, she and Maguire organize a protest over the closing of the parish school by the archdiocese. When Sister Anne is disciplined for her resistance to church authorities, Maguire and his friend Durkin take her to her parents in Dobbs Ferry, the "posh suburbs" Durkin contrasts with "the grim corners of the crowded city."[59] Maguire had already concluded that Sister Anne's assurance has something to do with class, but the Dobbs Ferry mansion and its in-ground swimming pool confirms the transformation of the Irish hag into the upper class, in this instance Catholic, beauty. Maguire goes on to ordination, but Sister Anne leaves the convent and eventually marries Durkin, Maguire's best friend.

The Traffic in Women

The repeated "trading up" from Irish hags to upper-class beauties in Carroll's fiction is distressing in itself. However, a further pattern distinguishes the relationships between these beauties and the Catholic males with whom Carroll pairs them: a pattern that comes into clearer focus when examined under the feminist-theoretical lens of "the traffic in women."

Over the past quarter of a century, feminist scholars have related the oppression of women to maintenance of patriarchy through the exchange of women by men.[60] Heidi Hartmann, a Marxist feminist, defines patriarchy as "relations between men which have a material base and which though hierarchical establish or create solidarity among men to enable them to dominate women."[61] In Carroll's novels, and particularly in the "Catholic" novels, female characters are positioned between male characters who compete for them or collaborate to control them. In *Madonna Red*, Tierney is the protégé and then the antagonist of the cardinal-archbishop of Washington, Justin O'Brien, while in *Mortal Friends*, the central relationship is between the Irish hero, Colman Brady, and his son Collins. Both pairs work to control certain women, with Tierney and O'Brien prosecuting the modern, attractive nun, Sister Dolores Sheehan, and the Bradys *père* and *fils* plotting to keep information out of the hands of Collins's uppity WASP fiancée (later wife). Interestingly enough, in these early works Carroll reveals some ambivalence by making their outcomes uncertain or by at least giving the women some gumption. At the end of *Madonna Red*, Tierney disobeys Cardinal O'Brien and refuses to serve any longer as Sister Sheehan's prosecutor; in *Mortal Friends*, Collins's Protestant fiancée, Janet Lindsay, refuses Brady's demands on several occasions.

The relational pattern in several of Carroll's later novels shifts from fathers and sons to brother and brother, however, and ambivalence about the control of women is much less evident.[62] In *Fault Lines* (1980), for example, David Dolan, the protagonist, defends his brother's widow, with whom he had made love while his brother was still alive, from a violent attack by her second husband, thus securing her for himself. In *Prince of Peace*, Michael Maguire, while still a priest, has an affair with and eventually marries the former Sister Anne, who had until then been married to his best friend. And in *The City Below* (1994), Nick Mullen marries his brother Terry's girlfriend when Terry leaves for the seminary, then subsequently seduces the beautiful, artistic, upper-class woman Terry marries after his return from the seminary, fathering her child in the process.

As Eve Kosofsky Sedgwick argues, much of the feminist theoretical conversation about "the traffic in women" has been synchronic; that is, it hypothesizes the male exchange of women as an unchanging structure throughout recorded history. In *Between Men: English Literature and Male Homosocial Desire*, however, Kosofsky Sedgwick links the erotic triangle—two men erotically involved with the same woman—specifically to the modern period, examining its evolution through English literature from the sixteenth through the nineteenth centuries.[63]

Several aspects of Kosofsky Sedgwick's work are significant for my reading of James Carroll's fiction. First of all, following René Girard, she stresses that in many cases, the bonds between the male rivals in an erotic triangle are more determinative of actions and outcomes than anything in the bond between either of the rivals and the beloved.[64] She calls these bonds between male rivals "homosocial" because they may or may not prove to be genital, or "homosexual." In Kosofsky Sedgwick's analysis, the sexual transactions inscribed in the erotic triangle are richly revelatory of relations of power, including class relations, in the modern period. The status quo cannot tolerate the uncovering of these relations of power, however. In particular, similarities between the male homosocial relation basic to the control of women and genital relations between men must remain obscure. Thus we see the increasing presence of homophobia in the late modern period and in our own.

The intensity of the bonds between the male rivals in *Prince of Peace* and *The City Below* reveals the presence in each of a classic erotic triangle. The cuckolded Durkin was Michael Maguire's best friend from childhood; he admits that he feels wounded over the passion between Maguire and his wife, the former Sister Anne, but that he doesn't know which one he feels jealous of. Maguire's death makes him feel "incomplete, an amputee."[65] In *The City Below*, at a funeral he comes home from the seminary to attend,

Terry Mullen admits to his brother he is not sure what love is, "except for you, you piece of shit." And Nick admits he feels the same way. That night, after Terry leaves, Nick makes love to Didi, Terry's former girlfriend, for the first time, and it is an unusually passionate experience for him. He first wonders if it was "the forbidden thrill of incest" but then characterizes his actions as adultery. Years later, after he seduces Terry's wife, she asks if he feels better, a question he does not understand. "Now that you've fucked your brother?" she replies. "Isn't that the point of fucking me?"[66]

The longing of Carroll's priests and ex-priests for the beautiful, upper-class, female prize is an emblem of both the class insecurity children of the postimmigrant generation may not have experienced directly but certainly learned from their parents and the basic economic insecurity of late industrial capitalism. The misogyny inscribed in their erotic rivalries also exceeds anything implied in Carroll's invocation of "the crone chorus" in *An American Requiem*. In *The City Below*, Terry Mullen refers repeatedly to kicking away the clutching hands that sought to keep him back, a phrase that resonates clearly with Carroll's own description of the voices that haunted his parents. But toward the end of the novel, he realizes whose hands they had always been: not those of his forebears but of his brother, Nick. At least in the ghetto, the hags were credited with some power; the terrorist with a rifle under her habit was surely someone to be reckoned with. The WASP golden girls, on the other hand, seem not to figure in the fraternal struggle at all except as prize, as commodity.

Finally, probably to camouflage the homosocial relations between his male characters, the homophobia theorized by Kosofsky Sedgwick appears intermittently in Carroll's writings. It is not a blatant homophobia, but rather the subtler, more reassuring kind favored by liberals like Carroll (and me). In *An American Requiem*, for example, Carroll speaks, quite movingly, I think, of first learning of real friendship between males from Patrick Hughes, the original hero who "skated ahead of the cracks." Later, in an aside about the high level of comradeship between the Paulists, Carroll recalls that Hughes had been nicknamed "Hugger," a moniker he now suspects to have been a veiled allusion to Hughes's possible homosexuality. Carroll has already made it clear to his reader that the seminarians' allusions were ill founded; Hughes eventually left the priesthood, married, and had children. But this train of thought serves another function. It signals what the relationship between Carroll and Hughes, the man Carroll "wanted to be with," could not have been.[67]

A similar transaction takes place in *The City Below* between Terry Mullen and his lifelong friend Bright McKay. Bright takes Terry to a gay bar to tell him that he is gay. He explains that he had not told Terry before about his homosexuality because he was afraid not that Terry was homophobic but that once Terry learned he was gay, he might never again say to Bright that he loved him. The distinction between this and homophobia may be clear to James Carroll, but it eludes at least one of his readers. In the course of the conversation, Terry also takes the opportunity to state unambiguously that he is straight, but when the topic of straight men's fear comes up, Carroll quickly shifts the conversation to Bright's fear of admitting his love for Terry. By the end of this fairly incomprehensible exchange, two things have been made abundantly, if inartfully, clear: Terry is not gay, and he is not homophobic. The reader is grateful for this clarification, as is, presumably, the gorgeous WASP art curator whose status as Terry's wife has been regularized by the death of the evil brother, Nick, the biological father of the child she and Terry are raising together. As Eve Kosofsky Sedgwick notes, male-on-male homophobia almost always "travels with a retinue of gynophobia and anti-feminism."[68]

The Economy of the Same

On one level, at least, I am surprised by the negative attitudes toward women inscribed in James Carroll's writing. In *An American Requiem*, Carroll writes with gratitude for his mother's love, with admiration and respect for his wife, and with grief over the death of his infant daughter. In his columns and articles, he is also not ambivalent in his support for women's equality in the Catholic Church, including women's ordination.[69]

The telescoping of misogynistic references into broad attitudes or positions is not, for the most part, a personal matter, however. An individual may be highly well intentioned yet, in the absence of enormous attention and effort, still be subject to certain structural realities. In *Working Alliances and the Politics of Differences*, the queer ethicist Janet R. Jakobsen delineates a mechanism whereby extraordinarily well-meaning entities—the women's movement, for example—obliterate within themselves the complexity and diversity that initially characterized them. This mechanism, "the economy of the same," as Jakobsen calls it, reduces multiple issues to a politics of singularity that effects division from and competition with other distinctive, singular entities.[70]

Throughout much of his writing, and with nothing but goodwill, James Carroll engages in the liberal reduction of significant differences to equivalent units. His reduction of women to commodities, albeit splendid commodities, is one example. His formulaic overcoming of difficulties in his saving narratives of the Christic hero is another. In *The City Below*, in the conversation between Terry Mullen and Bright McKay cited above, Bright becomes frustrated with Terry for thinking Bright considers him homophobic. He says, "I'm not talking about homophobia, okay? You don't see me as a nigger, I don't expect you'll see me as a queer. Okay? That's not what I'm talking about. Okay?"[71]

Terry, of course, replies "Okay." But we can't. The logic Bright exercises here is precisely the logic of the economy of the same: if people aren't bigoted toward blacks, they won't be bigoted toward queers. If they oppose the Vietnam War, they won't feel entitled to more than their share of the world's wealth. If only this were true.

Toward Some Future Mourning

James Carroll's use of "Irish hags, the nuns" to personify the Catholic grammar of suffering, especially when that figure appears at the end of a long trajectory of misogynistic signifiers in his fiction, is inevitably disappointing. Yet Carroll comes closer to genuinely mourning his losses in *An American Requiem* than in any of the novels preceding it. It is not inconceivable that in *An American Requiem* Carroll would have renounced the repeated triumphs of his male characters over the women in their lives and instead confronted the loss of his father's love directly, spilling the sacrament of the streets back into the sign of the cross. When in 1974, for example, Carroll journeys to Washington to tell his parents that he is going to leave the priesthood, he is risking more than the exacerbation of divisions between him and them precipitated by his antiwar activism. As the unalloyed hatred in Joe Carroll's response implies, he is also confronting a serious fracture within his father's own makeup, a void that Carroll has refused to grieve by claiming it as his own during much of his life: "I found it possible to stand and say, 'I'm sorry that's the way you feel, Dad.' And I left, admitting for the first time that I could not fill the void in him with anything I did or anything I was. The void was bottomless. He was on his own. So was I. Sad. Free."[72] For this one moment, James Carroll's hero, and the liberal American Catholicism he embodies, has stopped skating, and is looking straight at those dreadful bodies under the ice.

Yet defenses against mourning that have served for a lifetime—depression, projection, denial, guilt—are not easily renounced; Carroll's commitment to American optimism, to the heroic transcendence of cracks and fissures, is deep seated. In the face of such a powerful commitment, even a life-changing separation like the one between Carroll and his father can be rationalized as the result of a personal failing that might not have occurred had one only tried harder or as the unjust theft of something long deserved. In the concluding line of *An American Requiem*, Carroll records an insight that came to him after his father's funeral: "My father was dead. And because I was so much like him, though appearing not to be, I had broken his heart. And the final truth was—oh, how the skill of ending with uplift yet eludes me—he had broken mine."[73] Carroll sidles up to the tragedy of his loss here but then draws back from it once again, suggesting that, had he only tried harder, he might have written a saving story after all.[74]

Between 1996 and 2006, James Carroll has pursued a number of the themes addressed in *An American Requiem* in his regular *Boston Globe* column, in frequent articles in national periodicals, and in a series of books. Most recently, in the aftermath of 9/11 he has strongly opposed the foreign policy of George W. Bush and his administration in his *Boston Globe* columns and in two nonfiction volumes. The first, *Crusade: Chronicles of an Unjust War* (2004), is a collection of those columns; it was followed in 2006 by a longer critique of the war in Iraq, *House of War: The Pentagon and the Disastrous Rise of American Power*.

Increasingly, critics describe Carroll as a voice of ethical or moral authority; historian Garry Wills testifies in a *Crusade* publication blurb that "James Carroll brings to bear—I hope not too late—the moral clarity we so badly need." Given the ethical sinkhole the United States has occupied since 9/11, how can a clear moral critique be anything but welcome?

Nevertheless, it must be noted that in *Crusade*, Carroll assumes once again the stance of the heroic warrior, confronting the evil adversary on behalf of defenseless—in this case, Iraqi—victims. Though Carroll has produced much less fiction lately than he once did, his 2003 spy thriller,

Secret Father, also narrates a series of conflicts between male protagonists, in this case between a father, Paul Montgomery, and his polio-stricken, high-school-age son Michael.

The novel is highly autobiographical, set in the same pre–Berlin Wall Germany where Carroll spent his teenage years. Three overlapping triangles make up the book's framework. In the first, Paul and Michael, who narrate the story in alternating voices, work out the meaning for their relationship of the recent death of their wife and mother, Edie, and of Michael's disability. In the second, Michael and his best friend Rick Healy, accompanied by Michael's sometime girlfriend "Kit" Carson, undertake a dangerous journey to East Berlin, where Kit helps Michael come to terms with his disability. In the third, Paul Montgomery and Rick's German mother, Charlotte, have an affair as they rescue Michael, Rick, and Kit from the Stasi; Rick's cuckolded stepfather, Maj. General David Healy, remains behind in West Berlin.

This is perhaps an unfair simplification of *Secret Father*. Charlotte Healy, in particular, is a more complex and significant character than many of Carroll's previous heroines. As Ed Block writes in the Jesuit periodical *America*, Charlotte's love for Rick shapes the dramatic climax of the thriller, just as the love of the deceased Edie provides Michael with a moral compass.[75] It is nonetheless the case that the beloved Edie is dead and voiceless, even as her husband and son pursue their adventures and narrate Carroll's novel. Kit Carson, the army brat with the comic name, fares little better; she is primarily a foil for the development of Michael's character. The male homosocial structure of Carroll's books is perhaps somewhat mitigated in *Secret Father*, but it is hardly effaced.

From a Catholic perspective, however, Carroll's most significant achievement in the decade after *An American Requiem* was the publication in 2001 of *Constantine's Sword*, his 750-page history of the relationship between the Catholic Church and the Jews. While adding little to the historical record on Catholic anti-Judaism, *Constantine's Sword* is distinctive for making that history accessible to a popular audience. Awards and symposia followed its publication.

An analysis of *Constantine's Sword* would require a chapter of its own, but "The Silence," an article on Vatican complicity in the Holocaust that Carroll published in *The New Yorker* well before *Constantine's Sword*, suggests the contours of Carroll's approach to Catholic anti-Judaism.[76] In "The Silence," Carroll questions the ethics of Pius XII's neutrality toward the Nazis when condemnation of their actions might have shortened the war; he is equally disturbed by the Vatican's subsequent refusal to acknowledge this failing. He finds especially troubling John Paul II's request for forgiveness for "the sins of Christians" during the Holocaust but not for the church's own sins in this regard. Ultimately, Carroll characterizes the Vatican's refusal to take responsibility for its failures in relation to the Holocaust as a defense, however unofficial, of papal infallibility.

Since I am inclined to agree with parts of Carroll's assessment of Vatican behavior during the Holocaust, it is tempting to interpret this article and the massive volume that follows it as the work of a Catholic writer coming to terms with the "chips of heterogeneity" rejected by previous generations of his own ecclesial community. In the middle of the article, however, Carroll describes an interview with Hans Küng, the German Catholic theologian whose license to teach Roman Catholic theology was revoked by the Vatican in 1979 for his dissent from papal infallibility. Küng was another of the heroes of Carroll's youth; at one point in *An American Requiem* Carroll calls him "our Elvis, our John Lennon, our Dylan," and at another, the embodiment of the vision of the beloved Pope John XXIII.[77]

Carroll had heard Küng lecture in 1963, but a face-to face meeting with this hero—who was "more handsome in person than [Carroll] had remembered"—must have been truly exciting.[78] Küng serves Carroll champagne, and they begin to talk. Before long, they agree that the Vatican's behavior toward the Jews is like its refusal to allow women to be ordained; in each case, a proud and arrogant institution is defending its interests, its infallibility, at the expense of the less powerful. The Vatican, Carroll notes, is "playing for keeps."[79] Suddenly, Carroll and Küng are struggling with the Vatican for control over a feminized figure, much as the priest-hero competes with father, brother, or male friend for prized females in Carroll's fiction. Maybe James Carroll will give up skating ahead of the cracks one of these days, but then again, maybe he won't.

CHAPTER TWO

Flowers, and Dirt, and a Few Stones

MARY GORDON'S PERMEABLE CATHOLICISM

> As Gary and I are still going through issues [of *America*] from 1938 and 1939, Pat Samway comes downstairs looking amazed. He's writing a book about Walker Percy, and is listening to tapes of conversations he and Percy had. . . . And just now, as I am sitting two floors below him, Pat hears Percy mention my name on the tapes. He says he thinks I'm a pretty good writer. Percy's wife gets furious; she says I'm not a Catholic at all. Percy tells her gently to calm down.
>
> — MARY GORDON, *The Shadow Man*

> What are the possibilities for politicizing disidentification, this experience of misrecognition, this uneasy sense of standing under a sign to which one does and does not belong?
>
> — JUDITH BUTLER, *Bodies That Matter*

$\mathcal{A}$s we have seen, James Carroll is in many respects an archetype of American Catholic success and upward mobility. Despite his immigrant origins, Carroll's novels are reviewed widely, his memoir won the prestigious National Book Award, he is much in demand as a speaker, and his denunciations of Vatican dishonesty stud the pages of leading newspapers and magazines. However, a closer reading of Carroll's books and articles reveals a different archetype — one in which two white males struggle mightily to keep at bay their immigrant, feminized past and the mourning that accompanies it. Underpinning this seemingly endless struggle is an unanswered question: what would happen if those Irish hags and the cross they are nailed to should reappear?

In this chapter, I seek an answer to this question in the work of the American Catholic writer Mary Gordon. For if Carroll's heroes struggle to keep ahead of those "Irish hags," some of the most memorable characters in the seven novels Gordon has crafted over her distinguished career are precisely Irish American Catholic women. And many of the rest are the worthy successors of these characters, or their mirror images. But unlike Carroll's heroes, a significant number of Gordon's characters come to terms with the social fractures signified by those cracks in the ice, delineating as they do so an alternative Catholic future.

For many years, Mary Gordon's books, especially her novels, have meant a great deal to me as an American Catholic and a feminist. Although I encountered a volume of James Carroll's poetry in the 1970s, when Carroll was still a Paulist priest,[1] I did not read another of his books until *An American Requiem*, two decades later. But I read each of Gordon's novels as they appeared, beginning with *Final Payments* in 1978. I have never been much for ice skating, but I know a few things about the difficulties of having one foot in an immigrant church and the other in a world that is coming apart. And I know a sister when I see one.

A WRITER'S BACKGROUND

The engagement of conflict and complexity in Mary Gordon's writing can in part be traced back to her own early experience. Gordon's father, David, was a Catholic intellectual of the most conservative sort who, before his death when his daughter was seven years old, went to great lengths to pass on to her his intense loyalty to the church. Gordon took this ideologically emphatic Catholic background into the antiwar and student movements of the 1960s and 1970s, participating, as an undergraduate at Barnard, in the student uprising at Columbia.[2] She then fulfilled all the requirements for a Ph.D. in English from Syracuse University except the dissertation. Since 1976, she has published thirteen books, nine of them fiction, as well as a large number of short stories, articles, reviews, and interviews.

The tensions between Gordon's Catholic upbringing and the social upheavals of her college and graduate-school years might well have been sufficient to render the representations of Catholicism in her work complex and dynamic. Yet well before Gordon's young adulthood, her experience of Catholicism had been considerably complicated by the fact that her father was a Jewish convert to Catholicism. After his early death, members of Gordon's mother's Irish-Italian Catholic family invoked her father's Jewishness to explain her sexual failings and supposed intellectual elitism. These experiences may have contributed to Gordon's feminism. In any case, from early on, race, ethnicity, and sexuality struggled uneasily within Mary Gordon's sense of herself as a Roman Catholic, and an engagement with this struggle is at the heart of her literary *oeuvre*.

Catholicism provides the context for a number of Gordon's novels and short stories, and she frequently addresses her own experience of the church in essays and interviews. Some critics, not without encouragement from Gordon herself, draw a division between these works and Gordon's "non-Catholic" or "secular" works, as if a writer's religious identity were a suit of clothes to be put on or taken off at will.[3] A series of tensions and conflicts relating to Catholic identity appear repeatedly throughout Gordon's work, however. These reach a climax and are substantially reconfigured in two books published in the 1990s: *The Rest of Life*, a collection of novellas, and *The Shadow Man*, a memoir of Gordon's confrontation with shameful truths about her idealized father and the impermeable Catholicism he had come to represent. But it can be difficult to maintain such a reconfiguration of identity in the face of shifting circumstances, as we shall see.

ECCLESIAL BEDROCK: PRE–VATICAN II CATHOLICISM

The quality of impermeability associated with the father figures in Mary Gordon's early novels call to mind the metaphysical structure of the neo-Thomist revival. Although Leo XIII's revival of the "perennial philosophy" of St. Thomas Aquinas invigorated late nineteenth-century Catholicism,[4] the rigid Thomism that emerged triumphant from the modernist crisis brought severe consequences for the U.S. Catholic Church.[5] Hyperclear distinctions between substance and accidents, the essential and the nonessential, exerted significant effects on the American Catholic imagination. This influence reached its culmination in the 1950s, when Gordon and I, and many other members of the postwar generation of American Catholics, absorbed its unambiguous framework through the Baltimore Catechism and the structures of parish life.[6]

In a 1987 interview, Gordon describes this church in distinctly neo-Thomist cadences, characterizing it as "bedrock": "It was all about standing up to the enemy. . . . It could be Communists, Jews, Protestants, or atheists, but it was also pornographers, intellectuals, and sociologists, almost without distinction. What you were made to understand was that all those things were nonsense, and that you were holding on to pure bedrock."[7] This formulation of the stark Catholic boundary between truth and error can be traced back through the century. In a memoir of his training as an American Jesuit in the 1940s, for example, F. E. Peters writes, "and the *adversarii* of each thesis, those pagans, heretics, apostates and Dominicans . . . were refuted so succinctly and yet so devastatingly that I imagined them very wrongheaded indeed. What, after all, did Descartes and Kant know about the *philosophia perennis*?"[8] Along these same lines, at the turn of the century the Belgian Thomist Canon Becker asked, "What good is it to read the writings of adversaries, since they don't have the truth?"[9]

The seduction of clear distinctions shapes Gordon's recurrent questioning of the sufficiency of her own belief and that of a number of her female characters. In her first novel, *Final Payments*, Gordon's protagonist, Isabel Moore, begins instinctively to pray after her father's death but then recognizes that "having given up the rigors and duties of belief, [she] had no right to its comforts."[10] For Gordon, counterpoised against this bedrock Catholicism is the abject, in the form of the racial and sexual other.[11] In many of Gordon's texts, this polarization is displaced onto the relationship between her female characters and the fathers, biological and clerical, who represent the church for her. When Gordon confronts in her work this attempted exclusion of the racial and sexual abject from these linked figures, both the father and the church begin to change.

GORDON'S NOVELS: THE IMPERMEABLE CHURCH

Linkages between father figures and a rigid, impermeable Catholicism are evident throughout Mary Gordon's novels. The relationship between a daughter and a father is central in Gordon's first two novels, and in each of these, the father is a rigid, conservative Catholic. In *Final Payments*, Isabel Moore, the protagonist, struggles with the implications of having remained at home throughout her twenties to care for her incapacitated father, a conservative Catholic college professor. Dr. Moore supported "the Royalists in the French Revolution . . . the Fascists in the Spanish Civil War," and truly believed that those who did not find their way into the one true church would be held accountable by God for all eternity.[12] And in her second novel, *The Company of Women*, another daughter, Felicitas Taylor, struggles with a father-surrogate, the conservative Catholic priest Father Cyprian, and the "company of women" around him, including her mother.[13]

In both of these novels, an initial binary is established between young women on the brink of life and their suffocating, if beloved, Catholic fathers. Isabel Moore stays at home like a recluse for eleven years to care for her father, who had a stroke soon after finding her in bed with his best student. After her father's death, Isabel's love affairs and her attempt to have a career end in further humiliation; she atones by moving in with her family's repellent old former housekeeper, Margaret. Isabel breaks out of this second suffocating relationship and goes on to a new life, but at the book's conclusion, suspicion lingers that the conflict is not fully resolved. And, *voilà*, in Gordon's next novel, the young Felicitas Taylor begins the process again. She escapes from the narrow life she has known with Father Cyprian and her mother's friends to the Columbia University of the 1960s, where she becomes pregnant. Her return with her daughter to the upstate retreat where Cyprian and the women now live is more convincing than Isabel's transformation, but Felicitas, like Isabel, counts herself out of the belief system figured by her Catholic Father.

In her next novel, *Men and Angels*, Gordon turns her attention to ostensibly non-Catholic themes.[14] In particular, motherhood and the failure of a mother's love are figured by an emotionally disturbed fundamentalist Christian, Laura Post, nanny to the children of the book's secular protagonist, Anne Foster. Because Laura's parents failed to love her, and because Anne fails to do so, Laura commits suicide. In *Men and Angels*, Gordon appears to set off a rigid religiousness against an apparently separate secularity. It may be that by writing a book not set within her own religious tradition Gordon was able to confront even more directly than in her previous novels the inadequacy of rigid impermeable religion; clearly, Laura Post benefits even less from it than do the Catholic figures in *Final Payments* and *The Company of Women*.

In *The Other Side*, published after *Men and Angels*, Gordon returns to Catholicism as a context, chronicling the lives of an Irish immigrant family, Vincent and Ellen McNamara, their children, grandchildren, and great-grandchildren.[15] Once again, the father—in this case, the patriarch

Vincent McNamara—figures Roman Catholicism, though a more patient and benign form of it than we have seen in Gordon's work thus far. His outraged if heroic wife, Ellen, on the other hand, will have nothing to do with what she takes to be the church's mediocrity and hypocrisy. The polarization between Vincent's Catholicism and Ellen's ferocious, prosocialist secularity is one of the structuring principles of the novel.

Gordon's use of this ostensibly polarized structure in novel after novel raises questions about whether the church is as impermeable for her as it would seem and whether her female characters have truly left it behind. If they had, wouldn't one book on the subject be enough? Why would Gordon invoke repeatedly the polarization between secularity and "bedrock" if that "bedrock" were completely other, if it truly were completely and utterly impermeable? Rather, this site of ambiguity, this site of disidentification with a Catholic signifier, is precisely where figures of bedrock Catholicism in Gordon's work are open to transformation.[16]

Disidentifications appear throughout Gordon's fiction. Intermittently the reader will catch a glimpse of something on the margins of the text, frequently a minor character who calls into question the binary the story seems to assert. As *The Company of Women* concludes, Linda, the beloved young daughter of the unbelieving Felicitas, announces to the conservative Father Cyprian that she is going to be a priest when she grows up; Cyprian admits that she would make a better priest than most men and from that time on, prays daily for women's ordination. In *Men and Angels*, the only character to bring much insight to Laura Post's suicide is a Christian, Jane Watson, who mediates between traditional religious wisdom and secular freedom. And in *The Other Side*, the division is undercut by Gordon's selection, however ironic, of the eve of the Feast of the Assumption for the gathering of the McNamaras around the deathbed of their apparently secular matriarch, Ellen.[17] Even in *Final Payments*, the most linear of Gordon's novels, the protagonist, Isabel, is freed to reclaim her ostensibly secular life by her reinterpretation of a New Testament verse, "the poor you have always with you."[18]

One of the more striking examples of the binary between bedrock Catholicism and its opposite in Gordon's early fiction is her emphasis on the Irishness of the American church. Gordon has in fact stated that all American Catholics are Irish Catholics, whatever their ethnicity.[19] She is not entirely wrong, of course—Irish Catholicism dominated the American church for generations. Gordon replicates this hegemony by portraying the vast majority of Catholic characters in her earlier novels as Irish, or at least as rarely members of other Catholic ethnic groups. When Italian and Jewish protagonists begin to converge with Gordon's figuration of Catholicism in her fiction, therefore, the movement underway is likely to be significant.

THE NOVELLAS: TOWARD A MORE PERMEABLE COMMUNION

In *The Rest of Life*, Gordon's 1993 collection of novellas, such movement is evident on multiple levels.[20] Most obvious is the change of genre. After four novels, Gordon turns now to a form that, though shorter, still allows for considerable complexity and a more lyric and less linear construction than *The Other Side*.[21] The three novellas in *The Rest of Life* are marked, in fact, by a nonchronological flow of episodes and a receptivity to ambiguity that are, for the most part, unprecedented in Gordon's writing. She refers to this "meticulously controlled ambiguity" as "permeability."[22] Given the figures of an impermeable, bedrock Catholicism in Gordon's earlier work, her use of the word "permeability" here is striking.

The Rest of Life seems to concern itself more with the secular than the religious. The critic Alma Bennett, in her 1996 study of Gordon's *oeuvre*, acknowledges the presence of Catholicism in the collection but treats it as something external and inaccessible to Gordon's three female protagonists. For Bennett, each novella concerns a woman in the middle or later stages of life telling the story of her most intimate relationships, with husbands, former husbands, lovers, and with children, mentors, and parents. Religion is secondary at best.[23]

Yet the collection begins with the narrative of a love affair between an unnamed protagonist, X, and a Roman Catholic priest, Clement Buckley. Nor is Clement Buckley some generic priest; he is specifically a Paracletist, a member of the same religious order to which Father Cyprian belonged.[24] And the word "immaculate" in the title of the first novella, "Immaculate Man," calls to mind the Virgin Mary with an ambivalence similar to that expressed in *The Other Side* by the gathering of the McNamara clan around the deathbed of their resolutely secular matriarch on the eve of the Feast of the Assumption. It is always possible, of course, that in this book Gordon's preoccupation with Catholicism will come to an end. Some of the characters in "Immaculate Man" even seem to be saying this, such as when the unnamed female protagonist admits that she doesn't really understand "all that . . . the Catholic Church. That way of thinking. That whole world, gone now, and what was implicated in it."[25] And when she tells Clement that he would be better off with someone who knows more about "all that," he disagrees with her because he, too, places the church in the past: "It's all gone away. What was is gone."[26]

Even old Father Boniface, Clement's mentor, talks about the church as something that has ended. "It was complete. It stood. It helped us for a very long time. And then it went away. It only took twenty years from the first slip. There's no place I could take you now that wouldn't be dead. I must make you believe; it used to be alive. You can only understand [Clement] if you know that."[27]

Yet although X, Clement, and Boniface pronounce "it" gone, it continues, though in a changed, or perhaps changing, form, and all three of them struggle with what that might mean. When the Paracletists stopped attracting new members, the Archdiocese of New York turned their motherhouse into a battered women's shelter where Clement now works; Clement and X also become lovers there. But Clement doesn't stop being a priest when he falls in love with X. Rather, he talks it over with Boniface, and together they decide that his sexual relationship is not a sin. Clement even takes X to meet Boniface, and they develop a friendship based on their shared love for Clement. One thing they agree upon completely is that Clement must remain a priest; he cannot be what he is without being a priest.

Furthermore, Clement's relationship with X is nothing new or shocking to Boniface, because he himself has had male lovers—other priests—throughout his life and has struggled over the years to keep his attraction to Clement hidden. Thus, for all that Boniface claims from time to time that "it" is gone, he is also not sorry "it" broke up. "It wasn't really the truth about life. So many lies to keep it up. . . . It's better now. More truthful. I'm very hopeful about the way things are."[28]

Similarly, Clement has managed to integrate important aspects of his Catholicism into the new life he has taken on—continuing, for example, to tell a certain luminous kind of truth to the women and children at the shelter, a truth telling that both Boniface and X identify with the priestly Clement they love. Even the name he goes by, Clement, is the name he was given by the Paracletists. And although the identity that this name symbolizes is vulnerable—one of the women at the shelter whom X perceives to be a threat calls him by his name before ordination, Frank, though jokingly—Clement, for the most part, continues his priestly identity in his new life.

The otherness, the impermeability of the church seems primarily to be a problem for the apparently non-Catholic X, then, and she reflects on this problem more than once throughout her narrative. She notes, for example, that when the old people in the nursing home where Boniface lives ask him to bless them, they believe he does so to protect them from evil, but Boniface understands that he is blessing them to let them know that they are not alone. Later, X tells Boniface that Clement thinks his mother was a saint. Boniface replies, "I don't know, but I know that she did the best she could. Maybe that means she was a saint."[29]

Yet for all that she sees Clement and Boniface struggling with this ambiguity, struggling with the passage from "all that" to something else, X for the most part maintains "it" as something separate. At one point she tells of taking Boniface, in his wheelchair, to a Brazilian concert where everyone is dancing, Clement and X, children, women in their sixties, the rich and the poor. And for a few minutes, X believes that life could be like this, "that everyone . . . would come together. I wanted a world that was more like this more of the time." This is the closest she could come to faith, she adds.[30]

But X will not share this understanding of faith with Clement or Boniface. She fears they might say that they understood her; they might even believe that they understood. But X knows that to themselves they would be saying, "That's not 'it'"—not the kind of faith they had when "it" stood—"That isn't what we had at all." After which Gordon adds, with a final blow of the hammer, "And they'd be right."[31] Similarly, on a trip with Clement to Paris, X compares her lack of belief in eternity—"since what I can't see or even hope for is the face at the end of motion, the embracing arms"—with Clement's and Boniface's conviction that "they will remain forever in a paradise of lodgment and eternal rest. *Eternal rest grant unto them O Lord and let perpetual light shine upon them.* This is their prayer for the dead. But it was never mine."[32]

It is hard not to wonder who is really speaking here. How would the unchurched X know the Roman Catholic prayer for the dead? Who feels the need to assert that a mere vision of universal inclusion is nothing like the faith in "all that" that Boniface and Clement once had? Or when Boniface assures Clement that his relationship with X isn't a sin, why is X unwilling to believe him? Why does she care? Is Gordon not once again struggling with her own vision of Catholicism in these echoes of earlier characters who so often figured the polarization between a bedrock, impermeable faith and its many opposites?[33]

But Gordon undermines this polarization even as she invokes it. To begin with, she inserts a New Testament story toward the end of "Immaculate Man," as she did toward the end of *Final Payments*. This time, the protagonist is not reinterpreting the story; rather, Clement is telling it to her. It's the story of the Ascension of Jesus into heaven. In the middle, Clement stops because he believes he's not telling it right. X reassures him, but later admits that

> he told the story very badly, he was no good at telling stories. You couldn't listen for the story, just the occasional remarkable sentence, something about emptiness, something about looking up at the soles of Jesus' feet. It always seemed to happen with Clement: the badness of the storytelling left spaces you could fill in so in the end you saw more, understood more, than you would have from somebody who'd told it well.[34]

This acknowledgment of seeing and understanding more in a porous, fragmentary religious situation is a new vision of Catholicism moving in from the margins, where it often figures in Gordon's earlier work, toward the center of her fictional universe. The insight expressed in the passage is, of course, X's, not Clement's. In her reading of *The Rest of Life*, the critic Alma Bennett argues that throughout "Immaculate Man," Clement's Catholicism remains impermeable for X—"a fundamentally unknowable, unsharable world."[35] But for the writer, who enjoys the privilege of trying on all these points of view at once, the limitations of a single character don't really matter. Even if X is convinced, for her own reasons, that "all that" is gone forever, Gordon has discovered that more can be understood in the current, fragmentary situation than when "it" was complete, when "it" stood. And she has done this by creating two characters, who figure "it"—Roman Catholicism—while leading sexual lives beyond the official boundaries of the church, boundaries carefully honored by her previous Catholic father figures.[36]

The transaction in "Immaculate Man" between a pure, essentialized Catholicism and its worldly opposites takes on added significance because *The Rest of Life's* three novellas are clearly connected, each circling around Gordon's core concerns—ambiguity, porousness, permeability—but each in its own distinctive fashion. Thus while X wonders about the continuity between different aspects of Clement's personality, the unnamed protagonist in Gordon's second novella, "Living at Home," a psychiatrist, is also having trouble grasping, as do the autistic children she works with, "the idea of what makes up a person, a person consistently recognizable, consistently the same."[37] And Paola, the much older protagonist in the third novella, "The Rest of Life," struggles with her own possible continuity, trying "to understand that all the things that happened in her life happened to *her.* . . . That there is some line running through her body like a wick."[38] An examination by each protagonist of the elasticity and the inadequacy of language coheres with this other exploration of the ambiguity of personhood.[39]

Given the clear linkages between these three novellas and the careful attention Gordon pays to Catholicism in the first of them, *The Rest of Life* is a riff on the permeability of Catholicism as well as on that of her more obvious concerns—erotic love, motherhood, language, personhood. The tendency to overlook this may be attributed, in part at least, to the apparent secularity of Gordon's second protagonist, Y, a nonreligious Jew who has divorced three husbands and undergoes an abortion over the course of the novella. Yet "Living at Home" is positioned between "Immaculate Man" and Gordon's third novella, which is also, though more subtly, informed by Catholicism. In this context, "Living at Home" is as much a reversal, a photographic negative of Gordon's religious preoccupations, as it is a "secular" novella. This is especially the case since the second female protagonist, Y, relates, toward the end of her narrative, as do the other two protagonists, a vision of a kind of universal harmony, but one from which she herself is excluded. Finally, it seems possible that this setting, like that of *Men and Angels*, far removed from the Catholic Church, frees Gordon to do something she had never done before—to insert into the body of her work a Jewish protagonist, one of the others who were expelled from the bedrock Catholicism of her childhood.[40]

Gordon's third protagonist, an elderly Italian widow, Paola Smaldone, reinforces this move beyond the confines of the Irish church. For the first time in Gordon's opus, the westward direction of immigrant Catholicism is reversed, and we find Paola traveling, in the company of her son and his fiancée, back to the Italy of her youth.[41] And instead of attempting, as Isabel and Felicitas do, to break out of the suffocation of her rigid past, Paola returns to reexamine and ultimately to be healed of the deadening damage incurred in this earlier life. She is, in particular, burdened by the suicide of her teenage boyfriend, Leo, and the shame called down on her family by her refusal, at the last moment, to join him in that suicide. This shame resulted in the worst punishment Paola could imagine, banishment to the United States and permanent separation from her beloved father, killed soon after by the Italian fascists.

At the heart of Paola's suffering is her aloneness; she has never told anyone this story. Her son had hoped that by taking her back to Italy for the first time in sixty years she would do exactly that: tell him of her past. But Paola cannot even imagine telling anyone these dreadful memories. As the story proceeds, it seems more and more likely that her narrative will end in an ambivalence parallel to those at the conclusions of the previous two novellas, in which X is uncertain how long Clement will stay with her and Y does not know what will happen to her, either.

But unexpectedly, as her narrative is drawing to a close, Paola sets out alone from the hotel where she is staying to visit the site of her young lover's suicide. Once there, she weeps passionately. On the way back, her train is stalled in a dark tunnel, and instead of resisting it as she has "all this time," Paola gives in to the darkness, an action that enables her to see not just her dead boyfriend's face but those of innumerable young men, soldiers, actors, sons, prisoners. Wanting to tell them that they are not alone, she prays, rhythmically, to the "brave boys" who "died for nothing" in a multitude of ways, begging their forgiveness, "for you have died and we have lived."[42] And when she returns to the city, Torino, she is filled with joy because she has received something:

Just a hint, a possibility: a suggestion of a face to whom to tell her story. All the different stories. All the different ways it could have happened, each of them true. . . . From within darkness, something was knowable. It was not a replica of what one was. It was distinct, but multiple, and liable to change. Leo's face was swallowed up in darkness. Yet there were things that she could see. The most important thing was this: The dead, being one and many, knew there was nothing to forgive.[43]

Contrasting strikingly as it does with the face at the end of motion, the static eternity that X, in "Immaculate Man," couldn't see or even hope for, this vision is the culmination not simply of Paola's story but of all three novellas. In a splendid lyric passage that parallels but surpasses X's and Y's much more ambivalent visions of universality, Gordon describes Paola, after she has received this vision, as "full of gratitude":

> It doesn't matter that she doesn't know to whom. She lifts her heart in thanks. She thanks the red glow of her father's cigarette, the almond cake they ate, the feel of stones through the thin soles of her espadrilles, the fly resting on her hand, intricate as a jeweled watch. . . . She thanks her sons for allowing her to teach them to read, the men whose limbs she helped to straighten, the globes of red tomatoes ripening thousands of miles away without her, her cousin's satin coverlet, the harsh sheets and thin towels of the Turinese hotel, the water in the fountain in the square, the birds at daybreak, wheeling high above the roofs, all that has gone before us, everything, all things, the living and the dead.[44]

The story ends with Paola thanking the doorman who opens the door to the hotel where her son and his fiancée are waiting. "*Si, grazie*," she tells him.[45]

There can be little doubt that Paola's vision and her subsequent paean of gratitude are religiously coded. They constitute the culmination not only of Gordon's protagonists' struggles with the meaning of ambiguous memory, personhood, language, loss, and pleasure but with ambiguous religion as well. Throughout "The Rest of Life," Paola expresses a range of thoughts and feelings about Catholicism. Some of them are quite skeptical, as when she resists visiting her father's grave: "To imagine that there was a kind of presence in those bones was to think the way that priests forced you to, pretending that Christ was in the bread."[46] Or when she begins her prayer for forgiveness: "She doesn't know who would hear the words. She doesn't care. The God that people pray to is an empty word, a husk, lighter than air. Only the rhythm of old prayers are called for now. She clasps her hand."[47]

But to know that Paola resists imagining the way that priests "forced you to, pretending," is hardly to know how she herself imagines or prays. We do know that the church goes on being part of Paola's life, despite her ambivalences. In America, she, like many immigrant women, goes to the church, which, in contrast to her cousin's comfortable life, "had no softness to it. The Irish priests who made the Latin sound like German, the vestments that looked brand new, the stained glass in the windows that sliced the air like knives."[48]

Paola's reference here to the hardness—the impermeability, shall we say—of the church and the Germanic sound of the Latin in the mouth of the Irish priests is significant. The turn from an Irish to an Italian protagonist is a critical element in the transformation of Gordon's representation of religion. As Robert Orsi indicates, previous generations of Italian Americans enjoyed a more relaxed, culturally based Catholicism than did the "American" (read: Irish) Catholics who controlled the parishes. Whether they went to church or not, Italian Americans continued, tenaciously, to understand themselves as Catholics; they did not, for the most part, allow themselves to be alienated from their own long-established sense of the sacred by a certain lack of correspondence between it and official church positions. Theirs was a Catholicism removed from the formal, triumphalist faith of Joseph Moore, Father Cyprian, and, further, from the kind of Catholicism rejected by Gordon's ex-Catholic characters.[49] Gordon's portrayal of it, in the person of the Italian American Paola, facilitates the new religious vision X was drawn to but wary of in "Immaculate Man."

We get an insight into this new configuration at the point in *The Rest of Life* when Paola attempts to write down for her son and future daughter-in-law the story she has kept hidden for so long. "It happened when I was fifteen years old," she begins. "But what was *it*? She sees the small word—*it*—the enemy, hard as a bullet. Was it the death, their history, the history of Italy, the history of poetry, the history of men and women? Whose name should be included: Goethe, Leopardi, his parents, her aunt, Mussolini, a host of female martyrs, the Virgin Mary, her dead mother, her father whom she loved above all things? *It*."[50]

Two things are striking about this formulation. The first is the easy, almost natural coexistence of the Virgin Mary and a host of female martyrs with multiple other figures and dimensions of life. This is not the list of an institutional ideologue but that of an actual Catholic—a theology of the streets, to use Orsi's designation. But in this case, it is a theology of the bourgeois Italian streets between the two world wars. The second striking aspect of this formulation is Gordon's use of "it" here. X, Clement, and Boniface repeatedly designate as "it" the Catholicism that is no more.[51] But now, under the template of Paola's rich, porous, religious as well as very human past, "it" begins to look quite different.

Gordon provides a clue to this reconfiguration of American Catholicism in a 1991 essay, noting what an excellent training ground regular attendance at Mass was for an aspiring novelist, with the consecration occurring "way past the middle." She acknowledges that as a child she couldn't have consciously understood this connection between the Mass and the structure of fiction. "But I absorbed it unconsciously, this elaborate and varied and supple use of language. From a very early age I had it woven into my bones."[52]

This is precisely the structure that informs "The Rest of Life." The opening stories of Paola's life are like the confession of sins or the Scripture readings with which the Mass begins. Her narrative then moves into a priestly prayer that transubstantiates those memories and culminates in a great hymn of thanksgiving. Gordon has been repeating this action all along, not simply building a transforming event into her story line "way past the middle" but actually using a story from the Gospel to bring that transformation about.

In "The Rest of Life," however, Gordon's "elaborate, varied and supple" Eucharistic structuration moves steadily closer to consciousness. For Paola's hymn of gratitude after her prayer for forgiveness is patterned directly on the Eucharistic canon. "Lift up your hearts," it begins, and Paola "lifts her heart in thanks." "It is right and just, always and everywhere to give thanks," the canon continues, and Paola does it. "All creation rightly gives you praise," the canon trumpets, and Paola responds, yes, "all that has gone before us, everything, the living and the dead."[53] Linda, Felicitas's young daughter who wanted to be a priest, has finally become one, but she is Paola Smaldone.

Fundamentalist and sacramental traditions have their reasons for resisting women's ordination, however.[54] Paola has celebrated her liturgy; she has learned that something is knowable, not a replica of what once was, but something new—something, someone to whom she can tell her story and be freed. But she doesn't know exactly who this is, and she doesn't care. She is full of gratitude, but "it doesn't matter that she doesn't know to whom."[55]

Paola's lack of concern for knowing exactly differs markedly from the neo-Thomist preoccupation with the absolute truth of revelation.

The story of Paola's transformation is a culminating variation on themes running throughout *The Rest of Life*. Gordon indicates this by using the novella's title as the title of the entire collection. Paola's vision of something, someone, bestows a certain resolution on the uncertainty that marks the conclusions of "Immaculate Man" and "Living at Home." Yet this something is, paradoxically, inexact, multiple, subject to change.

This resolution, though temporary, is for Gordon a religious and, in fact, a Catholic one. The title of the collection signifies "all that rest of life" which is not tragic or high but can incorporate even the greatest tragedy. Gordon describes the outcome of that process as something "more incarnational," invoking a signifier used by Catholics to imbricate the transcendent with the ambiguous, nonsensical things of this earth.[56]

CATHOLICISM RECONFIGURED: *THE SHADOW MAN*

Published three years after *The Rest of Life*, *The Shadow Man* is a memoir of Mary Gordon's search for, and coming to terms with, hidden truths about her beloved father, David, a Jewish convert to Catholicism who died when she was seven years old.[57] In it, we learn that Gordon's long-idealized Catholic father turns out to have been not only a published pornographer who lied about the most significant details of his past but also an anti-Semite who, during and after the Holocaust, repudiated that past in the name of Catholic anticommunism.

Gordon had not been totally unaware, before *The Shadow Man*, of discrepancies in the idealized image of her father. As a girl, she had discovered an issue of the pornographic magazine he published before his conversion to Catholicism; she later found his unpublished diatribe against "the infection of the Jews."[58] Yet the degree of deception in her father's presentation of himself exceeded anything she had anticipated. Far from the sophisticated intellectual he had made himself out to be, David Gordon had actually been a high-school dropout who worked as a bookkeeper before his unsuccessful career as a magazine publisher. His only overseas experience had been in Lithuania, where he lived before emigrating to the United States with his Jewish parents and sisters.

Anti-Semitic, anticommunist Roman Catholicism was an ideal barrier between David Gordon and the past he tried to repudiate. By the time of his 1937 conversion, he was a protégé of Leonard Feeney, the right-wing Jesuit aesthete later excommunicated for a triumphalist separatism that even midcentury separatist Catholicism could not tolerate. Letters from David Gordon to the well-known Jesuit weekly *America*, while Feeney was its literary editor, provided some of the documentation of anti-Semitism that would most distress his daughter. By 1942, he was a member of the League of Social Justice, which was led by the anti-Semitic radio priest Charles Coughlin.

Even before Gordon confronted the repudiated racial and sexual other in her father's dream of a pure Catholicism, however, that purity had been undermined for her because her mother's Irish-Sicilian family, to whom she and her mother had returned after her father's death, consistently used Gordon's Jewishness to explain her sins and failings. "It's the Jew in you," they would say, referring not only to her sexual transgressions but also to more arcane faults such as reading too much.[59] This taunting was an opening wedge in Gordon's courageous pursuit of truths about the father she had idealized for years: if he were perfect, she wondered, how could he have left her in this situation?

The effect of these disidentifications is evident in the style of *The Shadow Man*. Gordon portrays herself, her father, and the Catholicism that bound them together in chains of minutely reiterated images. From the first chapter, in which Gordon explores her memories of her father, a number of literary figures are established and then woven throughout the memoir. Specifically, Gordon describes her job—remembering her father—as "enclosing my understanding of his life and death in one of the shining vessels that the Church provided . . . chalice, ciborium, monstrance, pyx."[60]

At first, the same old binary seems to apply to these figures—the body and blood of Christ and the memory of Gordon's beloved father polarized from the profane things of this world. But the space between the ideal father and the profane is far narrower than it was in earlier books; there is such a danger of ordinariness creeping in that the memory of Gordon's father must be "transubstantiated."[61] Yet here the process of transubstantiation is futile, because Jewishness, as Gordon knows, is ineradicable. Gordon thus reconceives her task as one of running and rerunning a series of silent films. Some of the memories Gordon runs through the projector are happy ones, but more often, a bad father, a disidentification with the ideal father, is introduced. In one of the films, Gordon cannot forgive her father for a perceived failing; when he gives her a large white peppermint heart bearing the words "I love you" to make it up to her, Gordon takes a bite out of it. Gordon compares the peppermint heart to the Communion host, with the words "I Love You" in red "like the trace of blood on the chest of the crucified Christ."[62] The act of biting the host—something pre–Vatican II Catholics were strictly forbidden to do—figures the changes taking place in Gordon's bedrock Catholicism as she explores the identity of her idealized father.

Gordon draws these images of a permeated Catholicism through the remainder of *The Shadow Man*. Teeth and biting, in particular, figure the division between Jewishness and Catholicism, as when Gordon and her cradle-Catholic mother are repulsed by her father's practice of leaving his dentures out—a figuration of Jewish excess—or when, after having been begged by Gordon to keep those same dentures in during a family party, he squats down to her level and snaps them at her.

In the face of these disintegrating memories, Gordon turns to her father's published writings. But she is humiliated by much of it. Gradually, Gordon grasps that the real ambiguity in her attempted identification with the perfect father is that the reading and writing part of his legacy to her, the smartness that her mother's family despised her for, conflicts with the repudiation of Jewishness that he also tried to leave her. All of these painful discoveries are assimilated to Gordon's reconfiguration of Catholicism: she feeds into the movie projector her father's crumbling magazines, "those pages that turn to flakes that I could put on my tongue and melt like the Communion Host."[63]

Subsequent archival discoveries—her father had lied about his birthplace, his siblings, his education, his previous marriage—force Gordon to admit that her goal in undertaking the investigation cannot be achieved. She simply could not continue to identify with him or to believe that there was never a time when she was not a part of him. She thus turns to doing what she best knows how to do: she tells her father a series of stories. In a theme-and-variations structure reminiscent of *The Rest of Life*, many of the figures established earlier in the memoir are reassembled in these stories. In the first, an archaeologist excavating her destroyed native city discovers that there is not enough evidence to allow her ever to learn what she wants to know. In the second, a woman discovers that a bank vault whose contents she believes she owns is actually empty. And in the last, a daughter tries to fashion many objects received after her father's death into a whole to be named "THIS IS MY FATHER."[64] But when she tries to do this, "nothing will hold," so she puts all the objects in a row on a bench a few inches off the floor, where they are "constantly interchangeable, constantly ready to be in different relations to one another."[65]

Some of these endlessly recombinant objects call to mind passages in Gordon's earlier work. Two fragmentary messages—"If only once more I could see your face" and "Among the dead there are so many thousands of the beautiful"—echo Paola's vision of the dead and her subsequent hymn of joy at the conclusion of "The Rest of Life." Like Paola, Gordon has come to realize that "something" about her father "is knowable," but that something is "distinct . . . multiple . . . and liable to change."[66]

Other items recapitulate earlier segments of *The Shadow Man*, making apparent that it is not only Gordon's vision of her father that is being reconfigured but also the Catholicism that he shared with her. They include a skull with many missing teeth (the biting father), a chipped valentine (the Communion host), and a "devotional weapon," a crossover implement somewhere between the purity of religion and the violence of war. In these items converge the by now far better understood self-repudiation of Gordon's father, the transformation of Gordon's own identity that this new understanding has helped to bring about, and a Catholicism they still share, though it is far less pure than it once seemed.

Gordon extends this reconfiguration of Catholicism to the present in the final chapter of *The Shadow Man*, "Transactions Made Among the Living." The second section of the chapter is Gordon's journal of the removal of her father's body from her mother's family's cemetery plot and its reburial in a plot she herself has purchased. Why should he lie "among people who at best tolerated or patronized him, at worst despised him?" Gordon wonders.[67]

Traces of the old, pure, separate Catholicism continue through this final section. As she plans her father's reburial service, Gordon decides to have the psalms said in Latin, not simply because her father would have liked them that way but also because they are "formal words, emptied of particularity. It is from this emptiness that their solace comes," reiterating the Thomist form-accident distinction.[68]

Elsewhere, however, earlier polarizations are visibly overcome. Gordon describes the distinctly Catholic reburial service as "a confusion of the symbolic and the actual."[69] She draws texts for the service both from the Latin and from the modern English order of worship, noting that "some of the new passages are superior to the old . . . much better than the sin-ridden prayers of the old lectionary."[70]

During the reburial process, Gordon again questions the sufficiency of her own faith; she doesn't know "what she believes about the fate of the life these bones represent" and wonders if her decision is "a hateful, cowardly hedging of the bets?" Yet she refuses to give up the Catholic "form of belief" that seems to her "deeply precious, irreplaceable." She refuses to do so, she says, because this form can contain "more than most other forms, and is therefore conducive to more beauty, more truthfulness."[71]

In this final chapter, the clear division between Gordon's mother's unambiguous Catholicism and her father's unsuccessfully repudiated Jewishness also no longer obtains: Gordon's mother's beautiful teeth, once so distinct from her father's excessive, Jewish toothlessness, have become black holes in her head as well. And Gordon explicitly links the swim she takes after her father's reburial to the melting of distinctions between the physical and the spiritual. While swimming, she thanks both her parents for their extreme, excessive, passionate, exclusive love, absorbing into her relationship with them the excess—Catholic *and* Jewish—that she had previously resisted.

Finally, on the last page, Gordon realizes that the reburial of her father has not made her sad at all; she's really very happy. She has traversed a considerable distance, from the once impermeable memory of her idealized father to the simple items and actions associated with this new happiness: "There was something to touch, to be lowered . . . to which it was possible to bid a farewell." Similarly, Gordon's earlier bedrock Catholicism, with its precious golden vessels, is transformed as it converges with the humble components of this service: "flowers . . . and dirt, and a few stones."

MOURNING CATHOLICISM

As we have seen, a trajectory of signifiers appears in novels published by Mary Gordon between 1978 and 1993 and in her memoir that affords a privileged perspective on American Catholicism in the post–Vatican II period. One factor contributing to this achievement is the sheer multiplicity of signifiers that intersect in Gordon's representations of Catholicism.

Initially, this does not appear to be the case. Gordon's portrayal in her early novels of young women struggling against rigid, conservative Catholic fathers tends to confirm the image of sexual self-sacrifice as the "sign of the cross" at the heart of postimmigrant American Catholic identity.[72] With the publication in the 1990s of *The Rest of Life* and *The Shadow Man*, however, Gordon's take on Catholicism grows wider and more complex, as questions of race and ethnicity become irrevocably intertwined with those of gender and sexuality. Gordon had reinscribed Irish hegemony in the American church by portraying the vast majority of the Catholic characters in her earlier novels as Irish or, at least, as not members of other Catholic ethnic groups. But in *The Rest of Life*, Gordon brings this Irish dominance to a close, making her female protagonists WASP, Jewish, and Italian. And in *The Shadow Man*, she displays, in her adored father's flight from his own Jewishness, the anti-Semitism telescoped within the fantasy of a pure Catholicism in the 1930s, 1940s, and 1950s.

In *The Shadow Man*, Gordon likewise portrays the inextricable linkage between Catholic anti-Semitism and the repudiation of sexuality and femaleness. Gordon's mother's Irish-Sicilian family used the Jewishness she inherited from her father to explain the "sins of impurity" Gordon was continually confessing.[73] They also used her Jewishness to explain another gender-linked failing: her "excessive" intelligence, which they might have perceived as less problematic in a son. The oppression that was produced in Mary Gordon's childhood along with misogyny and the repression of sexuality needs to be recognized here for what it was: racism, not "anti-Judaism" or some other putatively less reprehensible practice. Gordon was a baptized Catholic and a pious, practicing one at that. Her "Jewishness" was not a matter of religion.

The attempted repudiation of gender and sexuality as well as race from the Catholic cultural domain is part of what made the pre–Vatican II church appear to be impermeable, to be utter "bedrock." That it was constructed in this way helps to explain the repeated and unambiguous presence of the work of mourning in Gordon's writing. In point of fact, experiences of suffering and loss intersect with figures of Jesus and the church in all of the writing by post–World War II American Catholics that I examine in this study. But in Gordon, sexual and racial "chips of heterogeneity" are explicitly reincorporated into the Catholic cultural domain as Gordon's characters—and Gordon herself—grieve the losses and betrayals they have sustained. For example, in her first novel, *Final Payments*, Gordon begins the story of her protagonist, Isabel Moore, not merely with her father's death but specifically with his funeral. In *The Rest of Life*, struggles by two sexually active priests to let go of what the church once was parallel Paola Smaldone's passionate grief for the dead lover of her youth, a grief that unleashes in her a very Catholic and very permeable hymn of thanksgiving. Similarly, Gordon's confrontation in *The Shadow Man* with her father's "otherness," with those Althusserian "chips of heterogeneity" he longed to expel from his identity, is, at its very foundation, a work of mourning. Gordon's decision to conclude the memoir with the reburial of her father in the new cemetery plot where she and her husband will eventually be buried underscores the central significance of mourning throughout the work. Gordon's coming to terms with the differences between herself and the father with whom she was closely identified is tied, at a profound level, to her mourning for and eventual reconfiguration of the Catholicism they shared.

There can be little doubt that the reincorporation of sex, gender, and racial differences into the Catholic cultural domain demands great courage and determination. To leave unexamined the dissonance between one's private life and official representations of a pure, impermeable Catholicism is a good deal less demanding. I am thus deeply grateful to Mary Gordon for her refusal to be forced to choose, as neo-Thomist epistemology inclined us to, between Catholicism and the rest of life, which is also "deeply precious, irreplaceable."[74] For if the fragmented, porous, human faith Gordon depicts in *The Shadow Man* has room in it for her, it has room in it for me as well. On such loyal disidentifications, as Judith Butler has written, the future depends.

CODA: INTO THE TWENTY-FIRST CENTURY

At a time when institutional representations of the church can seem pinched and meanspirited, Gordon's Catholicism is capacious and welcoming. This is so much the case that in a previous version of *Tracing the Sign of the Cross*, I positioned my reading of Gordon's Catholicism last, making it the culminating chapter of my interpretation of the post–Vatican II American church.

But the writing of books is a lengthy process. By the time I undertook the current revision of this book, Gordon (as well as Carroll and Rodriguez) had published other books and articles. In Gordon's case, this included two novels, *Spending* (1998) and *Pearl* (2005).[75] Initially, I believed I discerned in both of these an extension, or at least a continuation, of the reconfiguration of Catholicism that meant so much to me in Gordon's memoir and her 1993 novellas. I argued as much in an article that appeared in 2005.[76]

I was especially enthusiastic about what I perceived to be the reiteration of a porous, supple, and highly ethical Catholicism in *Pearl*. *Pearl* is the story of childhood companions, Maria and Joseph, who rush to Dublin to save the life of Maria's biracial child, Pearl. Pearl has undertaken a hunger strike in recompense for the death of a young Irish revolutionary, Stevie, and is approaching death herself.

The novel reprises many of the themes of Gordon's previous treatments of Catholicism. Maria, a tough feminist activist, left the Catholic Church during the social turmoil of the 1960s and was still unreconciled with her father, a devout Catholic convert from Judaism, when he died. But in *Pearl*, Gordon conveys the ambiguity of her protagonist's ex-Catholic identity: "she has left [the church]—unequivocally, she believes—in protest."[77] And in the face of the imminent death of the daughter she adores, Maria prays, whether she believes in such a thing or not. In point of fact, Gordon's omniscient narrator sounds frequently like the God Maria thinks she has left behind, and the last hundred pages of the book are one great riff on the deeply Catholic themes of forgiveness and gratitude previously engaged by Paola Smaldone in "The Rest of Life." Maria's belief that "the center of the world is not impenetrable, but porous, and susceptible to change"[78] may sound, at first, doctrinally vacuous, but *Pearl* is a book about characters named Maria and Joseph and the desire of a child they love to sacrifice her life in recompense for violence.

While Gordon used specific Gospel texts to change the direction of her earlier stories, the conclusion of *Pearl* incorporates multiple New Testament allusions in a lyric, antiphonal fashion. When Breeda, Stevie's mother, retracts her condemnation of Pearl for the death of her son and asks Pearl's forgiveness for her accusations, Maria in turn is able to ask her dead father's forgiveness and to forgive him for failing her. She begins by believing such a thing is impossible: there is no resurrection of the dead, she asserts, and so the dead cannot forgive. But then she considers that it might be possible to change the ending of the story: that there might be "some ground now, not a place of stone, but a sliver of dry land on which, for a moment, she might get her footing."[79] Given that here Maria is offering a new ending not only to the story of her relationship with her father but also to the story of death, this image of a sliver of dry land instead of a place of stone calls to mind other visions of a shifting, contingent, but nonetheless precious Catholicism in Gordon's work. As she stands in this new place, Maria speaks her own variations on the words that Jesus spoke from the cross:

> Father, forgive me.
> Father, I forgive you.
> Father, forgive me, but I knew exactly what I did.
> I wanted to harm you. And I did.
> And there was no repairing it. You died. You did not rise.
> Repair us now, Father; forgive me, keep her safe.
> Roll back the stone.[80]

In a similar fashion, Joseph is able to forgive himself for his near-psychotic proposal of marriage to Pearl, which set back her recuperation significantly. He identifies with the story of Judas, who betrayed Jesus much as Joseph betrayed Pearl. At first, he wonders what might have happened to Judas if, instead of hanging himself, he had just gone back to his job, keeping the community purse. But after Pearl forgives him, Joseph remembers a Brother at Portsmouth Priory who told him that he was sure that Judas was in paradise, along with the Good Thief, even if he hadn't asked for forgiveness.

The bond between Maria and her daughter is restored in this web of reconciliation, and Pearl develops a new desire to live. In the end, there is no miraculous transformation of Maria's vexed relationship to Catholicism: she would like to say "Go with God" to Joseph as he departs for Rome, "but she won't allow herself to."[81] Nonetheless, we leave Maria and Pearl reunited, even laughing. "We will hope for the best," the narrator tells us.[82]

FURTHER QUESTIONS

When I wrote about them in 2005, then, the connections between *Pearl* and the reconfigurations of Catholicism in Gordon's earlier work seemed undeniable. More recently, however, I have begun to wonder whether the porous, transfigured Catholicism of *The Rest of Life* and *The Shadow Man* is, in fact, as evident in Gordon's recent work as I first believed. There are echoes of it, certainly. Maria Myers's "sliver of dry land" recalls the "flowers, and dirt, and a few stones" of *The Shadow Man*. And the foregrounding of Maria, the daughter of a Jewish convert, and Pearl, Maria's interracial child, reiterates the integration of race and ethnicity into the Catholic cultural domain embodied by the protagonists in *The Rest of Life* and by Gordon's own Jewish-Catholic father.

But if Gordon has indeed gone beyond the hegemonic Irishness of the American church, why, I find myself asking, does she choose to send these characters back to Ireland? And does painter Monica Szabo's portrayal in *Spending* of the "post-coital" Christ taken down from the cross signify the integration of sexuality into the Catholic cultural domain, an integration inextricably linked to the loss and mourning Gordon addresses previously? Or is this portrayal of Christ a kind of displacement activity, a faintly shocking flaunting of sexuality in the face of a decline liberal American Catholics seem incapable of engaging?

At times, I also respond with disappointment to Gordon's nonfiction articles about Catholicism. "Women of God," published in the *Atlantic Monthly* in 2002, weaves Gordon's own childhood attraction to the life of a contemplative nun into a consideration of the precipitous decline in the number of American Catholic sisters over the last third of a century and what that decline implies. It incorporates Gordon's interviews with a wide range of nuns in different parts of the United States and abroad. The nuns and their lives are appealing; the article goes down easily.[83]

But it is hard for American Catholics of a certain generation—my generation as well as Gordon's—to avoid nostalgia when writing about nuns. I am embarrassed to find this fine writer, with whose earlier work I identify so closely, weeping romantically over her youthful decision against a way of life I know to be as fragmented and difficult as my own (and Gordon's as well, I'll warrant). Another article, this one about the rosary as a feminist spiritual practice, also embarrasses me, invoking as it does a piety virtually unmarked by the fractures and historical specificity with which Gordon engages deftly in her own previous work.[84]

Yet even as I experience this sense of disappointment over Gordon's apparent retreat from a high-water mark, the portrayal of Catholicism in her books of the early and mid-1990s, I recognize that this is as much a statement about me as about Gordon. *Tracing the Sign of the Cross* is a record of my search for figures of Catholicism that make me feel welcome, at home. I found these, paradoxically, in a series of representations by Gordon of a porous, sometimes even fragmented church, representations that seem to me to be genuinely brilliant. But my search is not Gordon's search. And brilliance is, by its very nature, difficult to sustain.

Coming to terms with this disidentification helps me to see Gordon's recent work differently. In point of fact, some of it does call to mind the author of *The Shadow Man*. Gordon's writing on the Catholic clergy sex-abuse crisis, for example, exhibits subtlety and nuance.[85] This is not to suggest that Gordon pulls any punches about the gravity of the situation or the hierarchy's failure to examine its responsibility for it forthrightly.[86] Yet she also chooses to write sparingly, publishing one article and one review in the midst of a virtual feeding frenzy on the subject by other liberal Catholic commentators.[87] She also acknowledges the hazards of entering such a conversation, wondering aloud if there is anything to be added to "the amount of ink, the number of television hours devoted to the issue."[88]

This self-interrogation is no ploy. In both articles, Gordon implements strategies that extend the ambivalence she experiences in writing on this fraught topic. These include the use of questions rather than statements and outright disclaimers to avoid being misunderstood. In "The Priestly Phallus," for example, she writes:

> I fear that I am approaching dangerously near a territory I do not wish to enter: the territory that suggests that the only reasons for entering the priesthood and staying in it are pathological. I know many priests whom I respect deeply, and while I am not privy to the details of their sexual lives in all cases, I know that some make the kinds of compromises that many of us who have taken vows have made at one point or another in our lives.[89]

"Unholy Orders," Gordon's review of David France's *Our Fathers: The Secret Life of the Catholic Church in an Age of Scandal*, is similarly nuanced, a model of how to discuss clergy sex abuse in much of its complexity without giving an inch on ethical matters.[90] Her refusal, following France, to exclude from consideration priests "from whom we can only withhold sympathy," others who are "less simple villains," and even one who, "in an ancient Catholic mode . . . repented, asked forgiveness of his victims and turned himself into a hermit, living alone in filth and squalor in the woods," is a model, in its careful understatement, for others who would wade into these perilous waters.

Facing up to the gap between Gordon's purposes and my own has also enabled me to see differently some of her articles that I had previously disliked. Although I was embarrassed by "Holy Women," a second reading brings to the surface Gordon's own second thoughts about some of her responses. At the conclusion of the article, in fact, she renounces her schoolgirl "idea of the higher calling. The one right way . . . the old dead images, the grip of a past that will no longer serve" in favor of " 'the freedom of what is unsettled' . . . The risk of partial understanding."[91]

Some of Gordon's oscillation is the occupational hazard of the professional writer who publishes a great deal. But it is also, I think, something more. For the work of mourning is arduous and unending. Those whose circumstances allow it—and I include myself in this category—find almost irresistible the intermittent escape into comfort and coherence. But then the deadness of "a past that will no longer serve" assails us. We oscillate. We struggle. We search for allies whose visions can bolster and transform our own.

CHAPTER THREE

The Passion of Oncomouse™

DONNA HARAWAY'S DIFFRACTED CATHOLICISM

> He was despised and rejected by men; a man of sorrows, and acquainted with grief, and as one from whom men hide their faces he was despised, and we esteemed him not. Surely he has borne our griefs and carried our sorrows; yet we esteemed him stricken, smitten by God, and afflicted. But he was wounded for our transgressions, he was bruised for our iniquities; upon him was the chastisement that made us whole, and with his stripes we are healed.
>
> —ISAIAH 53:3–5

> And the Oncomouse™ doesn't have a crown of thorns on her head for no reason.
>
> —DONNA J. HARAWAY, *Modest_Witness@Second_*
> *Millennium.FemaleMan©_Meets_Oncomouse*™

*O*ne of the premises of *Tracing the Sign of the Cross* is that it is difficult for human beings, individually and collectively, to come to terms with loss. It is so difficult that they go to great lengths to protect themselves from it. And when human beings do manage to acknowledge and work through loss, they frequently do so only with the help of others who support them in the work of mourning. Partners, friends, children, pastors, psychotherapists, musicians, writers, visual artists, and others all serve as such allies at times.

Seen in this light, the two previous chapters of *Tracing the Sign of the Cross* may be read as narratives of the search for allies in the work of mourning the losses of post–Vatican II American Catholicism. James Carroll and Mary Gordon reach out with more or less success to fictional and nonfictional characters for help in confronting the failures of the Catholic Church and the fragmentation of the society their immigrant forebears struggled to enter.

Tracing the Sign of the Cross can also be read as the narrative of my own search for such support. Much as Carroll turns to Hans Küng and Gordon to Paolo Smaldone, I have looked to Carroll and Gordon for "visions to transform and bolster my own." And like theirs, my search has met with more success at some moments than others. Certainly, there are times when the scope of liberal American Catholicism, even at its best, strikes me as hardly adequate.

SEEKING FEMINIST ALLIES

During one such time, the early 1990s, I expanded my search for allies to the burgeoning discourse of feminist theory. Feminist theory (or theories) comprises a body of overlapping concepts and conversations about women and gender stretching back to Sojourner Truth and Virginia Woolf and forward to scholars such as the queer theorist Judith Butler, the film theorist Trinh T. Min-Ha, and the black feminist sociologist Patricia Hill Collins. It is influenced by philosophy, literary and cultural studies, postcolonialism, psychoanalysis, and poststructuralism.[1]

In some respects, my exploration of feminist theory is like Gordon's turn to non-Catholic and non-Irish characters in her fiction.[2] I hoped that by immersing myself in a network of concepts and conversations little concerned with American Catholicism I would acquire some of the tools needed to approach that same Catholicism in the context of the fractured reality of late twentieth-century society. Imagine my surprise when a distinguished practitioner of such ostensibly secular feminist theory turned out to be not only a potential ally in the work of mourning the losses of the twentieth century but a participant, albeit an ambivalent one at times, in the very American Catholic discourse that forms the center of my investigation.

This feminist theorist is the philosopher of science Donna J. Haraway. Haraway's sophisticated melding of science and technology with feminist studies, Marxism, and literature, especially science fiction, struck me as a stunning instance of the possibilities offered by feminist theory. Like many others, I was especially taken by the figure of the "cyborg," which Haraway introduced into feminist theory in 1985 in her famous essay, "A Manifesto for Cyborgs: Science, Technology, and Socialist Feminism in the 1980s."[3] "A cyborg," Haraway writes, "is a cybernetic hybrid of machine and organism, a creature of social reality as well as science fiction . . . a kind of disassembled and reassembled postmodern collective and personal self."[4]

At first, the cyborg seemed to me far removed from the losses of postim-migrant American Catholicism and the mourning those losses require. And I was by no means alone in misreading this creature. Because it is drawn partially from feminist science fiction, for example, some readers understand Haraway's cyborg to be purely a figure of the imagination. And because of the technological devices that form part of it, others believe the cyborg to be pure machine, the binary of the body.

However, a closer reading of Haraway's quirky, multidisciplinary discourse suggests that these oversimplified interpretations of the cyborg miss the mark. The very purpose of the cyborg is to signal the breaching of ostensibly impassable boundaries that organize the modern world—between humans and animals, between organisms and machines, and between the physical and the nonphysical world overall. In "A Cyborg Manifesto," Haraway specifically proposes the cyborg as a "partial, ironic, intimate, and perverse figure" of the "transgressed boundaries, potent fusions, and dangerous possibilities" needed in our time.[5]

CHRISTENING A CYBORG

As a figure of ruptured boundaries and powerful intersections, the cyborg facilitates certain insights into the fragmentation of Western society throughout the twentieth century, including the fragmentation of post–Vatican II American Catholicism. Seen from the perspective of Haraway's later scholarship, however, the cyborg is more directly implicated in American Catholic mourning and melancholia than an initial reading of "A Cyborg Manifesto" suggests. Haraway explores one element of this implication in her 1997 book *Modest_Witness@Second_Millennium.FemaleMan©_Meets_Onco-mouse™: Feminism and Technoscience.*[6] "U.S. scientific culture," Haraway writes, "is replete with figures and stories that can only be called Christian. Figural realism infuses Christian discourse in all of that religious tradition's contested and polyvocal variety, and this kind of figuration shapes much of the technoscientific sense of history and progress."[7]

In her discussion of Christian figural realism, Haraway is influenced by the work of the mid-twentieth-century literary scholar Eric Auerbach. Within Christian figural-realist discourse, two people or events are connected in such a way that the first signifies the second and the second fulfills the first;

at its heart, according to Auerbach, is the practice of reading Christ back into the Hebrew scriptures.[8] The narrative frame of this relationship is the Christian promise of fulfillment at the end of history, whether salvation or damnation. Haraway argues that this narrative frame and the representations it organizes infuse secular as well as religious histories of progress and apocalypse, including technoscientific ones.

From this examination, Haraway's readers derive insight into the discursive structure of Western science and technology. But we also gain insight into the multiple Christian figures and frameworks that stud Haraway's own articles and books.[9] In a 1989 study, *Primate Visions*, for example, Haraway asserts that primatology is chiefly concerned with stories of origins and endings, that is, with "salvation history."[10] The title of the section in which this observation appears is "Primatology is (Judeo-)Christian Science."[11] "Implicitly and explicitly," Haraway writes, "the stories of the Garden of Eden emerge in the sciences of monkeys and apes, along with versions of the origin of society, marriage, and language."[12]

This preoccupation with science as "salvation history" continues in *Simians, Cyborgs, and Women* (1991), as evidenced by the title of one of its articles, "In the Beginning Was the Word: The Genesis of Biological Theory."[13] Yet in this book, something has changed: the religious discourse here overflows Haraway's previous carefully contained critique of Western science as "(Judeo-)Christian stories of origins and endings" to function as part of Haraway's analysis of Western culture more broadly. In the introduction, for example, Haraway refers to "the one Subject of monotheism and its secular heresies."[14] In this volume, too, she first uses the term "the god-trick" to highlight similarities between God's ostensible transcendence of material location and the practices by which members of privileged social groups occupy a class unmarked by social specificity ("the unmarked class"), thus obscuring the material interests that inform their opinions and actions.[15]

Gradually, however, Haraway's engagement with religious figures in *Simians, Cyborgs, and Women* moves beyond even this broader critique; bit by bit, Haraway incorporates religious and Christian figures and terms into her constructive argument as well. The most striking such engagement of religious rhetoric occurs in "A Cyborg Manifesto," the very piece in which the ostensibly technological—thus irreligious—cyborg appears. The religious components of this article are apparent from the opening paragraphs, in which Haraway describes it as a manifesto of a new "ironic political myth."

Haraway signals here the appearance of something akin to religion when she tells us that this myth will be "faithful to feminism, socialism and materialism," but in the way that "blasphemy is faithful" rather than in the way that reverent worship and identification are.

The binary Haraway seems to construct here between her list of secular "-isms" and traditionally religious worship and identification calls to mind the binaries enacted in Mary Gordon's earlier novels between vibrant young women and their rigid Catholic fathers, for example, or between secularity and bedrock Catholicism. And like Gordon, Haraway destabilizes these binaries. Much as Isabel Moore frees herself from Catholic rigidity by quoting a verse from the New Testament, Haraway uses religious language to criticize religion. She has gone beyond analysis or critique: she's proposing a new myth. And it isn't sufficient to dismiss or even eviscerate traditional, nonliberatory religion; Haraway feels the need to blaspheme it, and blaspheme it "faithful[ly]." However much her intention, here and elsewhere, may seem to be antireligious, the frequency of the appearance of Christian figures and frameworks suggests as much ambivalence as opposition.

The intersection between Haraway's critique and engagement of religion becomes even more evident in the language she uses to describe the cyborg itself. The cyborg is "outside salvation history," we are told, yet Haraway uses Christian-inflected terminology to describe this unsaved figure: it is an "incarnation."[16] She also constructs her ironic political myth within an explicitly Jewish and Christian millennialist literary form. As a "response to crisis," she tells us, her "manifesto" turns out to be a close relation of the very "Judeo-Christian" stories of the end-times Haraway finds troubling elsewhere. This dynamic plays out through the entire article: "cyborgs are not reverent, and they cannot re-member the universe," yet exchange in the world "transcends" the universal translation effected by capitalism; cyborg society is "committed to building a form that actually manages to hold together" not only "witches, engineers, elders, perverts . . . mothers and Leninists" but Christians as well.[17]

AMBIVALENT ORIGINS

The kind of ambivalence Haraway exhibits in this oscillation between critique and engagement of Christian figures and frameworks could, I suppose, be totally outside a writer's awareness. But Haraway knows she is ambivalent. In "A Cyborg Manifesto," she explicitly acknowledges the contradictions that attend her location: "I am conscious of the odd perspective provided by my historical position—a Ph.D. in biology for an Irish Catholic girl was made possible by Sputnik's impact on U.S. national science-education policy. I have a body and mind as much constructed by the post–Second World War arms race and cold war as by the women's movement."[18]

Haraway's primary interest here is to suggest that political contradictions—being constructed as much by the cold war as by progressive activism—are actually grounds for hope. But I doubt it is entirely a coincidence that Haraway acknowledges her Catholic origins, for what I believe is the first time, in the context of this discussion of contradictions. Haraway is not merely offering a scholarly analysis of "salvation history," of secular narratives of origins and endings here; she is engaging her own fragmented experience as at once a scientist, a feminist, and an "Irish Catholic girl." Indeed, the very phrase "salvation history" played a prominent role in Catholic religious education in the 1950s when Haraway and I—another "Irish Catholic girl"—were being catechized.

This acknowledgment of a fractured Irish Catholic identity, in some ways like my own, by a "secular" feminist theorist I had hoped to recruit as an ally in the work of mourning came as something of a shock to me. But it was nothing compared to the shock I sustained when I came upon "*Ecce Homo*, Ain't (Ar'n't) I a Woman, and Inappropriate/d Others: The Human in a Posthumanist Landscape," an essay Haraway published a year later in a popular feminist studies anthology.[19]

Like Haraway's earlier essays, "*Ecce Homo*" addresses the fractures and fusions that are the scourge and hope of our time. When crises such as those at the end of the twentieth century emerge, Haraway tells us, the more normal rhetorics of systematic analysis are replaced by another practice, that of figuration. But, we are reminded, the crisis of postmodernity is already a crisis of figuration, specifically, a crisis of the universal figures and narratives of modernity, which have proven delusory in light of world wars, genocide, and nuclear incineration. To resolve the current crisis, we must have figures of the human, but not of the universal, generic, Enlightenment human that has enabled such evil and destruction. Instead, we must have figures of a broken and suffering humanity, which, in ambiguity, contradiction, and noninnocent translation, signify a certain hope.

To play this role, Haraway offers a "Judeo-Christian"/humanist Trickster embodied in the figures of the Suffering Servant of the book of the prophet Isaiah, Jesus, and Sojourner Truth.[20] The way in which Haraway presents this series of figures will prove problematic. Yet she offers it because she finds it to be, as the postcolonial feminist theorist Gayatri Spivak phrases it, that which we "cannot not want." Despite its "stolen symbolism," Haraway tells us, this posthumanist human signifies a "possible hope."[21] If the cyborg, an "incarnation" of the crises and fragmentation of postmodern society, might help to illumine the losses of post–Vatican II American Catholicism, how much more so the Suffering Servant, the broken body of Jesus, and the abused, enslaved body of Sojourner Truth in "*Ecce Homo.*" The crucifix, after all, stands at the center of the devotional system that has for generations helped immigrant American Catholics to recognize and work through suffering and loss.[22]

A PRECIPITOUS ALLIANCE?

Yet even as I grew increasingly encouraged and excited by "*Ecce Homo,*" other feminists were questioning the usefulness of Haraway's figures for working through the losses of late modernity. For example, in response to Haraway's statement that the cyborg's embodiment "is prosthesis," the feminist religious-studies scholar and single amputee Sharon Betcher reads the cyborg as the very binary of the natural, technologically unimploded human/female body.[23] For Jill Marsden, another feminist critic, the cyborg is the apotheosis of militarism, phallocentrism, and commodification, the perfect representation of the subjugation of the flesh by invasive technologies.[24]

Betcher's analysis is, in some respects, a curious one. Haraway's work is frequently located within a subset of feminist theory called feminist-standpoint epistemology. Some members of this school propose, as an alternative to disembodied, "objective," and therefore unaccountable knowledge, supposedly inherent female qualities known as "women's ways of knowing."[25]

Haraway is less concerned with objectivity per se than with threats to accountability that accompany the social constructivism to which some postmodernists subscribe. Indeed, Haraway's strategy of figuration is intended to offset the supposed relativism of the postmodern position. In "Situated Knowledges," another of the articles in *Simians, Cyborgs, and Women*, Haraway uses visual metaphors to bring attention to what she calls the privilege of partial perspective, or embodied vision, as the feminist epistemological alternative to the supposedly all-seeing eye of patriarchy. Using the color-weak eyes of her dogs, the compound eye of an insect, and the diverse eyes of contemporary technological devices to illustrate her point, Haraway underscores the unique and active nature of this kind of knowing:

> The "eyes" made available in modern technological sciences shatter any idea of passive vision; these prosthetic devices show us that all eyes, including our own organic ones, are active perceptual systems, building in specific translations and specific *ways* of seeing, that is, ways of life. . . . All these pictures of the world should not be allegories of infinite mobility and interchangeability, but of elaborate specificity and difference and the loving care people might take to see faithfully from another's point of view, even when the other is our own machine.[26]

To illustrate what this active, faithful, and partial perspective is like, Haraway then introduces into her essay an "actor," another in the series of literary figures including the cyborg and Jesus that appear throughout her writing. Haraway has been legitimately criticized because the particular "actor" she appropriates in this instance, the Coyote, or Trickster, is a mythological figure drawn from a culture not her own, but rather that of the Indians of the American Southwest. Nonetheless, her move here reconfigures knowing as a power-charged and personal conversation rather than as a hegemonic and impersonal act of "discovery."

The feminist philosopher Jill Marsden deems interpretations that hypothesize a binary between the body and technology in Haraway's work "highly misconceived," but she finds Haraway's work disappointing in other ways.[27] For Marsden, Haraway's project is a "reinvention of nature," one that reconceives as "immanent thresholds" the kinds of boundaries that presumably divide bodies from machines.[28] Far from being a reinstantiation of Western binaries, then, Haraway's cyberfeminism implies the "uninhibited explosion" of external controls in favor of an internal system that moves by rerouting and reconfiguration. But Marsden understands Haraway's use of the language of responsibility—as expressed in her call in the "Cyborg Manifesto" for "pleasure in the confusion of boundaries and responsibility in their construction" and reiterated throughout her writing—to comprise the reinscription of an extrinsic moral vantage point that undercuts Haraway's "philosophy of immanence" and short-circuits the very reinvention of nature that Marsden finds most significant.[29]

The most disturbing aspect of these criticisms, for my purposes, is that although Betcher and Marsden would seem to present opposing arguments—Haraway's cyborg feminism does/does not reinscribe the binary between technology and nature—they arrive at much the same conclusion. Each discerns in Haraway's work resistance to mourning the losses that attend the mortal body. Betcher notes that in evoking the cyborg Haraway specifically "rejects this figure's mortality and its need to mourn. . . . Cyborgs," she reminds us, "do not remember the cosmos and . . . cannot dream of returning to dust."[30] Marsden, while attaching a different meaning to it, also discerns in Haraway's "cyberfeminism" a failure to mourn, suggesting that in her return to an external ethical language, Haraway "refuses to face the full trauma of dismantling the biological order" that she otherwise advocates.[31] In these construals, the fragility, the mortality of the whole biological realm becomes that which is rejected or expelled to or beyond the margins of the cultural domain.

It would be comforting to hypothesize at this juncture that the inability to mourn may be inscribed in Haraway's earlier cyborg discourse but that with "Ecce Homo" Haraway leaves all that behind. Unfortunately, a series of troubling omissions and interventions in "Ecce Homo" raises questions about what even "Ecce Homo" can offer to the work of mourning. For example, although Haraway announces at the beginning of "Ecce Homo" her intention to write about a series of figures signifying suffering and dismemberment, including Isaiah's Suffering Servant, Jesus, and Sojourner Truth, she soon begins to refer to two figures only, and specifically, two Christian ones. This elision of the Jewish body as well as use of the expression "Judeo-Christian" at several points in the article (as well as in earlier work) opens Haraway to accusations of supersessionism, the practice of writing and speaking as if Christianity has replaced Judaism.

Similarly troubling is Haraway's practice in "Ecce Homo" of invading and emending texts from the Hebrew Bible while leaving intact multiple citations from historic and contemporary Christian sources. Particularly egregious is the insertion after Isaiah 54:1 ("'For the children of the desolate one will be more than the children of her that is married,' says the Lord") of a parenthetical comment: "'Is this a threat or a promise?' ask both women, looking tentatively at each other after a long separation."[32] Given the massacre of six million European Jews less than a century ago, it is hard to believe that any contemporary person of Christian background would inquire in supposed jest whether God's promise to multiply the (unarguably Jewish) children of the desolate is in fact a threat.[33]

YET MOURNING NONETHELESS

Initially, I found these feminist critiques, including my own, discouraging, but at least they seemed to concur on one point. Traces of the late modern inability to mourn are inscribed in Haraway's figures and narrative structures. But as I reread "Ecce Homo," the essay that inspired so much hope in me, I became genuinely puzzled. For however much the "inability to mourn" may characterize Haraway's writing, in "Ecce Homo" something else, something very nearly the opposite, is happening as well. Even as Haraway's work fails to register the grief that surely must attend the incinerated bodies of millions of European Jews, she also begins there to move gradually toward such mourning. This movement is manifested from the very first paragraphs, in which Haraway reaches toward the consciousness she will also resist. "I want to focus on discourses of suffering and dismemberment," she begins. "I want to stay with the disarticulated bodies of history as figures of possible connection."[34]

Several changes in Haraway's writing practice signal this movement toward mourning in "Ecce Homo." The first is a more explicit openness there toward the recognizably human. Previously, Haraway tended toward less identifiably "human" figures—cyborgs, coyotes, lenses—even if she also argued for their agency. In "Ecce Homo," even as she admits that the new face of feminist humanity that she seeks cannot be the Enlightenment human, she nonetheless asserts that "we must have feminist figures for *humanity*."[35] And indeed, the figures she deploys there are human ones.

Second, Haraway signals the presence of stronger affect in "Ecce Homo" by linking her desire for new, feminist figures of the human with Gayatri Chakravorty Spivak's frequently quoted claim that postmodern deconstruction of hegemonic structures is directed precisely at "that which we cannot not want."[36] In this acknowledgment of longing for the human, Haraway moves to a language of feeling that is more direct and more unabashed than her earlier "cyborg" discourse.

Finally, Haraway registers this increasing affect by a change in her manner of relating to the Christian/Catholic tradition to which her selected figures of the posthumanist human are inextricably bound. While in the past the tone and style of Haraway's treatment of the figures of Christian realism were primarily distant, ironic, or critical, in *"Ecce Homo"* she makes direct and positive use of these figures. For this brief period, at least, Haraway's defenses are down.

THE SUPPLEMENT

To better understand this discursive shift, this breach of boundaries between mourning and denial that emerges in the work of Donna Haraway, it can be helpful to consider once again the relationship between the cyborg and the series of Jewish and Christian figures that appear in *"Ecce Homo."* While some readers understand that relationship as one of polar opposition, I propose that we interpret it as one of supplementarity. The supplement is a term used by Virginia Woolf to add women to existing history and to occasion its rewriting beyond what mere addition can effect. It is also one of the markers Jacques Derrida uses to resist and organize binary opposition without constituting a "third term" or "dialectical resolution."[37]

The significance of this swerve in the direction of Haraway's work becomes clearer if our attention shifts from her figures per se to the integuments of those figures, the articles themselves, and the wider contextual realities they engage. Although the Suffering Servant of Isaiah, Jesus, and Sojourner Truth may not be "recognizably imploded with (material) technology" as the cyborg is, the two texts in which we find them are nonetheless intimately connected.[38] They supplement one another. Each offers, in response to the global crises of the late twentieth century, figures that signify the risks and possibilities of a new reality. In the first case, the new, multiple, nonoriginal, noninnocent global women's experience figured by the cyborg is both fiction and fact of the most "crucial" kind.[39] It engages in a struggle over life and death; the task facing it, the hope it promises, is one of survival. The Jewish and Christian figures that emerge in *"Ecce Homo"* do so at a time of crisis as well, a time when historical narratives are in crisis around the globe. In this instance, however, instead of focusing on the cyborg, Haraway focuses on the figure of a broken and suffering humanity despite its "ambiguity, contradiction, stolen symbolism," and implication in the genocides of this century.[40]

A further clear connection between these texts is the presence in each, despite the great dangers of such a move by a white female academic of U.S. nationality, of the internally fragmented figure "women of color." In point of fact, "women of color" in one or another manifestation is an alternate articulation of what Haraway's central figures stand for. In "The Cyborg Manifesto," "women of color" is an alternative to the "offshore women" positioned in the "integrated homework circuit" and laboring for transnational corporations around the globe.[41] In "Ecce Homo," "women of color" are figured as Sojourner Truth, the heroic ex-slave and feminist abolitionist who cannot be pinned down. The promise of all of these figures is that they may enable connection among diverse groups without at the same time reinforcing the domination inscribed within the claims of universality, rationality, and mastery that plague the figure of Man, the Enlightenment human. As with her use of the Coyote, or Trickster, much is problematic about the white, professional Haraway's "use" of this figure, and much is illuminating, even inspiring, about it.

Finally, Haraway draws our attention to the relation of supplementarity between cyborg and posthumanist human figures. Near the beginning of "Ecce Homo," Haraway states that her reading of a series of trickster figures in a "rich, dangerous, old, and constantly renewed tradition" of Jewish and Christian "humanism"[42] initiates a larger project, a conversation between three groups of powerfully universalizing texts. These texts include two versions of the United Nations discourse on human rights; recent physical-anthropological reconstructions of science, species man, and its science-fiction variant, female man; and the Human Genome Project, the transnational, multibillion-dollar project to map the genetic structure of "man."[43] If enacted, such a conversation would be a continuation of Haraway's complex, multilayered project in critical feminist technoscience of which *Primate Visions* and *Simians, Cyborgs, and Women* comprise earlier stages. Yet Haraway explicitly links this undertaking with—indeed, she launches it with—her nongeneric figures of suffering and dismemberment, the Suffering Servant, Jesus, and Sojourner Truth.

In 1997, Haraway's "staging" of this conversation did in fact occur. I remember clearly coming upon it—her newly published book, *Modest_Witness@Second_Millennium.FemaleMan©_Meets_Oncomouse™: Femi-*

nism and Technoscience—at the book exhibit of a scholarly meeting. Although I had by that time been thinking about Catholicism in Haraway's writing for several years, I laughed out loud when I saw the illustration on the book's front cover. It was a classic Renaissance annunciation, and while the angel in it looked fairly normal, if a bit excited, the Virgin next to the angel was, as they say, something else—a female cyborg, with her hair cut in a pageboy.

But when I got the volume home, the illustration on the back cover, which I had overlooked, spoke even more powerfully to me. In it, a large rodent with distinctly human breasts, arms, and hands stands in a kind of cell while seven menacing pairs of eyes watch it through observation slits. The rodent, I later learned, is Oncomouse™, a real animal genetically altered to develop breast cancer for purposes of research and then patented. On her head is a crown of thorns.

TEACHING A CYBORG TO MOURN

There cannot be much doubt that *Modest_Witness*, with its multiple and ornate glosses, puns, citations, and illustrations, is yet another of Donna Haraway's complex and demanding texts. Nonetheless, with this book Haraway's discourse moves to a higher level of complexity. Already in her earlier prose Haraway both elicited, and to some extent textually transcended, the oversimplified, noninnocent certainties of post-Enlightenment, late industrial capitalism. But in *Modest_Witness*, by virtue of the complex relationships between its parts and levels, the text itself, not merely the figures and illustrations in it, conveys the intricacy and danger of life at the end of the second millennium. Take, for example, the title. Because *Modest_Witness@ Second_Millennium.FemaleMan©_Meets_Oncomouse*™ looks very similar to an Internet address, if I type it into this word-processing document without turning off the hypertext function, the computer will cause the rest of the file to turn blue and "hot." Sometimes doing this even activates my e-mail program.

Part 1 of *Modest_Witness* identifies a new series of languages that are necessary if the conversation Haraway projects in "*Ecce Homo*" is to take place. These languages or "differential literacies" resist the misleading oversimplifications and hegemonic effects undergirded by languages rooted in old Christian-realist narratives of origins and endings. They make it possible to read the world differently. Along with the e-mail address of the book's title, Haraway cites the speculum, statistics, and ethnography as instances of these differential literacies that provide the dizzying possibility of altering the current "World Order." Yet the interconnectivity they embody also brings with it the risk of real change—mutating, skewing, and swerving once predictable outcomes.

Part 2 assembles the actors for the conversation, actors whose names appear in the book's title. To some extent, this assembly embodies a move on Haraway's part from isolation to community and conversation.

The first of these actors is Modest Witness him/herself. "Modest witness" is the term once used to designate eighteenth-century gentlemen scientists who served as witnesses to the objectivity of laboratory experiments. Such "modest witnesses," for example, testified that small laboratory animals actually suffocated when Robert Boyle used his famous air pump to remove the oxygen from an enclosed portion of his laboratory. They witnessed much as the seven sets of eyes observe Oncomouse™ in Lynn Randolph's painting on the back cover of *Modest_Witness*. At the end of the second millennium, however, these modest witnesses have become participants as well as observers; they themselves occupy the technoscientific spaces—"wormholes," Haraway calls them—through which contemporary actors are swept up into genetically, immunologically, mechanically, or market-altered embodiments and dimensions.[44]

As such, Modest Witness is intimately related to the two other partners in Haraway's conversation, FemaleMan© and Oncomouse™. FemaleMan© is a figure adapted from Joanna Russ's 1975 science-fiction novel *The Female Man*. In it, four genetically engineered clones, Janet, Jael, Joanna, and Jeannine, disrupt stories not only of the universal Man but also of the universal Female. Haraway's version of these four characters both brings out the potential that exists in our time for transgressing gender categories and illustrates FemaleMan©'s kinship with "other sociotechnically—genetically, historically—manipulated creatures."[45] Haraway's visible assignment of copyright to FemaleMan© rather than to the author—to whom it is traditionally assigned—shows that, for Haraway, it is not the supposedly unique creator who is essential to every act of knowledge production but rather the web of workers who surround that "creator."[46]

We have already met the third conversation partner. Oncomouse™ is a rodent into which a gene that produces breast cancer, an oncogene, has been transplanted; this trait makes her highly marketable for research purposes. After their successful feat of genetic engineering, Oncomouse™'s academic "inventors" patented her, and the patent was assigned to E. I. DuPont de Nemours & Co. The Oncomouse™, who is identified as the sibling not only of Modest Witness and FemaleMan© but also of Haraway herself, stands at the dense intersection of research, commerce, gender, the military, the academy, technology, Christianity, and animal life. The rhetorics of purity, of the natural, or of rights have never been able to address adequately such a dense and conflicted intersection.

Lynn Randolph's painting "The Laboratory, or the Passion of Oncomouse™" is more successful at achieving this. In it, the Oncomouse™ is clearly human, with human arms and legs, but also clearly rodent—and not an entirely attractive rodent at that; we are quite sure that she isn't Mickey or Minnie.[47] Through seven small windows, non-gender-specific faces of varied skin colors, eerily reminiscent of the modest witnesses of Robert Boyle's suffocation by air-pump experiments or of the panopticon, observe the Oncomouse™ and her crown of thorns.[48] Although Haraway believes that her "promise is decidedly secular," she describes the Oncomouse™ as

> a figure in the sense developed within Christian realism: S/he is our scapegoat; s/he bears our suffering; s/he signifies and enacts our mortality in a powerful, historically specific way that promises a culturally privileged kind of salvation—a "cure for cancer." Whether I agree to her existence and use or not, she suffers, physically, repeatedly, and profoundly, that I and my sisters may live. In the experimental way of life, she is the experiment. S/he also suffers that we, that is, those interpellated into this ubiquitous story, might inhabit the multibillion-dollar quest narrative of the search for the "cure for cancer."[49]

The second sentence of this passage establishes the relationship between Oncomouse™ and that figure of "suffering and dismemberment" in "*Ecce Homo*," Isaiah's Suffering Servant, while the crown of thorns links him/her to the Jesus of that text as well—but in each case, now, with male/female slash marks.

Then, in Part 3, "Pragmatics," Haraway examines the kinds of connections that must be fostered if feminist freedom projects are to advance. As a metaphor for this practical connectivity she chooses hypertext, "computer software for organizing networks of conceptual links that both represents and forges webs of relationships."[50] Haraway is attracted to hypertext because of the connections it makes possible but also because of the risks that accompany it. Hypertext cannot determine "which connections make sense for which purposes"; it is, to use one of Haraway's favorite descriptors, "non-innocent."[51]

Throughout this third section, Haraway displays connections between the layers upon layers of meaning that hypertext embodies. First she identifies a category of objects that contemporary society generally takes for that which is "really-real," the thing in itself, including chip, gene, fetus, fetish, seed, brain, and ecosystem. Then she displays the extremely diverse languages and rationalities by which these things are inextricably tied up with and dependent upon other sticky, fragmented, and contingent phenomena. Individual chapters zero in on the three of these entities most frequently accorded the status of unchangeable essence—gene, fetus, and race.

Finally, in her conclusion Haraway offers the scientific concept of diffraction to illustrate the function of the network of figures she has created for queering, skewing, and mutating the New World Order. In this final move, Haraway returns to the emphasis on visual and optical metaphors that characterized her earlier essay on feminist-standpoint epistemology, "Situated Knowledges." Haraway settles on the metaphor of diffraction because it offers "more interesting interference patterns," the chance to "make the end swerve."[52] Accompanying her narrative is another of Lynn Randolph's paintings, in which a (white) woman moves forward in space, her face and hands eerily doubled, that is, diffracted, and surrounded by a collection of floating objects.

NONINNOCENT DIFFRACTIONS

Donna Haraway's previous representations of complex, nonidentificatory connection and partial perspective converge powerfully in *Modest_Witness*. On multiple levels, this book embodies her network of "immanent thresholds," the internal system that changes by rerouting and reconfiguration.

Some of the most powerful instances of this rerouting and reconfiguration are those in which Haraway revisits positions she herself has previously taken. In *Simians, Cyborgs, and Women*, Haraway uses the term "noninnocent" to characterize practices and positions that, though highly motivated, are nonetheless "contaminated," because their occupants cannot transcend their material locations and be shielded from accountability. This attention to her own noninnocence as well as that of others is an aspect of Haraway's work that I have found especially helpful as I analyze the loss in the last third of the twentieth century of the sense of innocence and optimism that had previously characterized much of American Catholicism.[53]

In *Modest_Witness*, Haraway addresses her own noninnocence by reconsidering earlier stances and finding them wanting or by retaining a position at one level while reconfiguring it at another. She examines, for example, her attraction, and that of her fellow "radical scientist activists," to millenarian discourse. Initially, Haraway had criticized traditional science's belief in millenarian solutions to catastrophe, but now she acknowledges similarities between these scientific stories of "origins and endings" and the frameworks within which she and her "radical kin" operate. They, too, she realizes, pursue deliverance from catastrophe, but from "capitalist commodification" and "technoscience domination" rather than from epidemics or famine. "Disaster," she writes, "feeds radiant hope and bottomless despair, and I, for one, am satiated."[54]

Haraway likewise scrutinizes her practice of appropriation, acknowledging, for example, the problematic nature of her use of the phrase "keep your eyes on the prize" to suggest that solidarity can only emerge from conducting science studies from the point of view of marked groups.[55] But feminist inquiry, she concludes, is "no more innocent, no more free of the inevitable wounding that all questioning brings, than any other knowledge product."[56]

Haraway similarly revisits her use of the term "Judeo-Christian." She attempts to avoid the terms "Judeo-Christian" or "monotheist" and to use "Christian," she tells us, because the visual and narrative materials throughout *Modest_Witness* are specifically secular Christian renditions of shared origin stories. They are "overwhelmingly inflected by both Catholic and Protestant Christian accounts in which Jewish materials are brought into 'salvation history' with its figurations and appropriations."[57]

Haraway also considers criticisms of her externally ethical, modernist vocabulary of accountability, truth, justice, and freedom that, for some, signals her inability to face the full trauma of the dismantling of the biological order. Haraway by no means renounces this vocabulary but instead explicitly links it to the longing already introduced in "*Ecce Homo*," this time reconfigured as "yearning."

> It does not matter much to the figure of the still gestating, feminist, antiracist, mutated modest witness whether freedom, justice, and knowledge are branded as modernist or not; that is not our issue. We have never been modern. . . . Rather, freedom, justice, and knowledge are—in bell hooks's terms—about "yearning," not about putative Enlightenment foundations. Keep your eyes on the prize; keep our eyes on the prize. For hooks, yearning is an affective and political sensibility allowing cross-category ties that "would promote the recognition of common commitments and serve as a base for solidarity and coalition." Yearning must also be seen as a cognitive sensibility. Without doubt, such yearning is rooted in a reconfigured unconscious, in mutated desire, in the practice of love, in the ecstatic hope for the corporeal and imaginary materialization of the antiracist female subject of feminism and all other possible subjects of feminism.[58]

This reference to a "reconfigured unconscious" alerts us to another act of "rerouting," in this case a rerouting of the cyborg itself and of its inability to mourn. In an interview published in 1991, Haraway admits that she resisted giving the cyborg an unconscious because the psychoanalytic unconscious is irreparably contaminated with conservative, heterosexist, and putatively universal oedipal narratives. Yet in the course of protecting the cyborg from the oedipal narrative, she also deprived her of "that which in the unconscious resists," the imposition of those narratives.[59] But the ability to tolerate difference—to resist universalizing discourses such as the oedipal narrative—is precisely the ability to mourn, to work through rather than harden oneself against loss. Modest Witness's reconfigured unconscious is the place of convergence between Haraway's repressed "younger" cyborgs and the Suffering Servant, Jesus, and Sojourner Truth of "*Ecce Homo*" who do indeed suffer and mourn.

Nowhere is this convergence, this attribution to technologically imploded entities of the ability to feel, suffer, and mourn, more compelling, however, than in the chapter on the fetus in *Modest Witness*. For Haraway, the fetus, along with the microchip and the gene, is the archetypal example of what in late twentieth-century Western culture is portrayed as "the really-real," as "life itself." Haraway undercuts this reification of the fetus by making pellucid its connection with scientific devices without which the fetus is highly inaccessible: the sonogram, the computer, the speculum, public-health statistics, and ethnography. More than anything in her previous work, Haraway's encounter with the fetus in this chapter disproves "pious certainties" about the body being elided from her discourse.[60] It also constitutes, in an understated sort of way, an extension of the Catholic trajectory in Haraway's work. After all, if the fetus is an instance of the "really-real" in late twentieth-century American culture, it is the hyper-really-real of late twentieth-century Roman Catholicism. This convergence between Catholicism and Haraway's thought culminates in an extended close reading of an ethnography about infant mortality in Brazil written by a feminist scholar whose work is strongly influenced by Catholic liberation theology.

LIFE SEEN AND UNSEEN

The second part of the final section of *Modest_Witness* is titled "FETUS: Virtual Speculum in the New World Order." In it, Donna Haraway turns once again to the visual metaphors introduced in "Situated Knowledges" to call into question disembodied and unaccountable truth. At the end of the Second Christian Millennium, she tells us, the glowing, free-floating, human fetus, like the cloud-swathed Earth as a whole, has become the symbol of "life itself," signifying for many the immediately natural and embodied, the tactile "real," over against violating technoscientific culture. A series of illustrations in which visual technologies and the supposedly autonomous fetus are clearly interdependent enable Haraway to challenge this bifurcation and the Western Christian realism that supports it.

The first of these heuristic devices is a Bell Telephone commercial in which a pregnant woman reaches out to touch a picture of her fetus on the screen of a sonogram's monitor while describing it over the telephone to the father of the fetus. It is followed by Lennart Nillson's celebrated "The Drama of Life Before Birth," a collection of photographs of fetuses that appeared in the April 1965 issue of *Life*. Finally, Haraway examines a cartoon in which a woman who resembles both Michelangelo's Adam and a classic reclining nude uses a computer keyboard to connect with a fetus on a monitor; electrical wires emerge like an umbilical cord from behind the computer.

All three illustrations display the inextricability of visual technologies from late twentieth-century constructions of "life itself." For the woman receiving the sonogram, "life" no longer manifests itself in the quickening of the fetus, as it did for her female ancestors, but comes into focus for her as she views the electronic screen. For antiabortion activists, photographs like Nillson's that make the fetus visible constitute hard evidence of "life itself." Yet according to Haraway, the subjects of most of Nillson's photos were actually fetuses that had been recently aborted, not live fetuses.

The reclining nude cartoon likewise conveys the noninnocent complexity of visually produced "life." The actions of what Haraway calls FirstWoman are not a matter of self-identical reflection as in the Odalisque, nor is she the object of Adam's gaze as Eve is in Michelangelo's painting of her. Rather, she looks straight into late twentieth-century virtual reality to call up an extrauterine fetus of indeterminate origin. Since FirstWoman is clearly not organically pregnant, is this fetus the product of her own writing and thinking, the record of a pregnancy now over, or someone else's fetus altogether? In any case, it is clearly a mixed, and in some sense artificial, life form. Yet, Haraway argues emphatically, it is not disembodied. "These ontologically confusing *bodies* and the practices that produce specific embodiment are what we have to address, not the false problem of *dis*embodiment. Whose and which bodies—human and non-human, silicon based and carbon based—are at stake, and how, in our technoscientific drama of origins."[61]

Haraway then reconfigures the "fetus in cyberspace" as an entity that is constituted by many variously related communities of practice. She cites feminist studies that locate women and their fetuses in diverse, complex, interrelated worlds: during a genetic-counseling session in New York City, in legal conflicts over surrogacy contracts, responding in diverse ways to a performance video about abortion, and participating in the women's-health movement of the 1960s and 1970s as symbolized by the speculum.

One instance in which Haraway connects the free-floating image of "life itself" with the multiple and conflicted communities of practice that constitute it is her description of a project led by Charlotte Rutherford of the Black Women's Empowerment Program of the NAACP Legal Defense and Educational Fund (LDF). In the 1980s, after intensive meetings with African

American women's groups and extensive internal debate as well, the LDF redefined reproductive freedom as a civil-rights issue for African Americans. As such, it includes not only the right to contraception and abortion but also to a much wider network of reproduction-related services. These include access to diagnosis and early treatment for AIDS, STDs, and cancers; access to prenatal care, including drug treatment for pregnant and parenting drug abusers; access to infertility services; freedom from coerced or ill-informed consent to sterilization; economic security, which could prevent possible exploitation of the poor through surrogacy contracts; freedom from toxins in the workplace; healthy nutrition; and living space.[62] The matter is thus shown to be far more complex than a decision for or against "life."

Finally, in a stunning inversion, Haraway turns her attention to an aspect of "life itself" that generally receives far less consideration than the preborn fetus. For those who cannot afford visualizing apparatuses such as cameras, computers, or even public-health clinics, what does not get seen can be as deadly as abortion, Haraway argues, and the assumed naturalness of certain ways of living and dying can be as devastating as the "technicization" of over-developed nations.[63] By way of illustration, she ends her essay on the fetus with a reading of an ethnographic study of infant mortality in one of the sugar-producing regions of Brazil. In *Death Without Weeping*, Nancy Scheper-Hughes documents the infant mortality rate in the Brazilian Nordeste for infants younger than a year old between the early 1960s and the late 1980s, a rate that increased despite widespread evidence of the "modernization" of Brazil during that period. So invisible were the deaths of these infants that the only "record" Scheper-Hughes could find to determine the number of otherwise unrecorded infant burials were estimates of the quantity of materials ordered by village coffin makers. In an approach similar to that advocated by Haraway throughout the chapter, Scheper-Hughes explores the "communities of practice" linked to these dead infants, emphasizing the "oral, social, and emotional relations of mothers and whole communities to the extreme levels of infant death among them."[64]

Haraway's retelling of Scheper-Hughes's discoveries is a profoundly moving one. The "angels" of the *favela* die from diarrhea brought on by malnutrition, she tells us: "their bodies turn to water."[65] But no matter how extensive the suffering of these infants, Haraway never resorts to the discourse of "natural" bodies to convey it. Rather, she consistently shows that these deaths from starvation and dehydration are linked to the same national and transnational forces that make advanced visual and reproductive technologies available to the wealthy. In particular, according to Haraway, economic structural-adjustment policies and new agricultural technologies have forced the transition in the Nordeste from rural subsistence to urban day labor and the falling real wages that accompany it. At the same time, powdered milk provided to poor Brazilian women by the U.S. Food for Peace Program and the subsequent aggressive marketing of infant formula by transnational corporations caused a massive decline in the culture and practice of breastfeeding.

Haraway notes that four phenomena are linked to the decline of breastfeeding in the Nordeste. First, older women lost the ability to teach younger women to breastfeed, just as "modernization" and commodification convinced those younger women that their own milk was far inferior to manufactured products. Second, although some women of the professional and managerial class may enjoy the privilege of breastfeeding at work, this privilege is not accorded to female day laborers in Brazil. Third, even though Nestlé and other corporations were forced to reduce their aggressive marketing campaigns and began printing consumer warnings on their breastfeeding substitutes, grocery shelves in Brazilian shantytowns were crammed with cans of formula throughout the period in question. Finally, it had become the practice in the informal, consensual family structures of the urban Nordeste, where men circulated intermittently from one family unit of woman and children to another, that paternity was established by a man bringing the first weeks' supply of infant formula to a mother. A woman who breastfed, who thus did not receive such formula, was considered an abandoned woman. What kind of unconscious might emerge, Haraway wonders, from a process of family formation in which the father gives not semen but formula; where papa, not mama, equals baby's milk?

By positioning these "dead angels" of the Brazilian Nordeste at the conclusion of her chapter on the fetus, Haraway overcomes the inability to mourn that feminist critics have discerned in her work. No more than a fetus on a sonographic monitor are these dead angels the natural, technologically untouched "bodies" of cultural feminism; they are, rather, as Haraway writes, "cyborg kinship entities" shaped by the technological and market realities of late industrial capitalism. Yet along with their technological implosion, these bodies signify suffering not only in their deaths by dehydration but also in the mourning that their mothers, their ethnographer, Haraway, and now her readers must undergo. This mourning is linked to political action by the very nature of Haraway's analysis. The longing to understand and change the "fluid dynamics" of these overlapping realities is what Haraway means when she speaks of "yearning in feminist technoscience studies."[66]

CONCLUSION: DIFFRACTED CATHOLICISM

Two distinct movements within Donna Haraway's feminist technoscience suggest that she is not as far removed from the discourse of late twentieth-century American Catholicism as I first imagined. At the most apparent level, Haraway's work evidences a distant, critical, and frequently ironic relationship to Catholic/Christian tradition. This relationship becomes more direct and intimate as figures from that tradition surface in her writing. Then, as this Catholic/Christian figuration is emerging, a more direct engagement with suffering and death also becomes apparent, an engagement that reverses the "failure to mourn" for which Haraway has been criticized. Haraway's figures are thus revealed to be part of the trajectory of the cross that I am tracing in this study.[67]

Much more than was the case with my readings of James Carroll and Mary Gordon, I find myself concerned about what Donna Haraway would think of this interpretation of her work. I suppose this is so because whatever else we might say about Carroll and Gordon, they are each unambiguous and public Catholics. But Haraway's Catholicism is, to use a term she favors, highly diffracted.

Even in *Modest_Witness*, Haraway is ambivalent about the Christianity with which her work is also increasingly involved. She undercuts repeatedly the secular drama of technoscience with ironic theological language; figures are "incarnated" fictions that collect people up into an ending that story redeems and restores; advertising is a chief teacher of theology in postmodernity; the fetus, like the gene, is a technoscientific sacrament.[68] Although Haraway acknowledges her "non-innocent" and "disreputable" use of Christian figural-realism,[69] she also implies that a primary goal of her writing is to move from her address @ the end of the second (Christian) millennium to another address altogether, to "press enter" and move to another screen. And sometimes her rejection of the Christian tradition isn't even ironic. In her gloss on "The Annunciation of the Second Coming," the Renaissance annunciation on the front cover of *Modest_Witness*, Haraway insists that the shocked angel who gestures toward a cyborg madonna an-nounces "*not the birth of Christ*, but the warning that life on earth is chang-ing irrevocably."[70]

If anything, these multiple disavowals serve only to strengthen my sense of Haraway's ongoing if ambivalent identification with Catholicism. Is it not peculiar that as skilled a deconstructionist as Donna Haraway—who, within the covers of the same volume, offers nine or ten possible interpretations of a woman looking at a fetus on a computer screen—should be this rigid, this black and white, regarding the significance of an annunciation? And what of her equally strong assertion, also in *Modest_Witness*, that she will "critically analyze, or 'deconstruct,' only that which [she loves] and only that in which [she is] deeply implicated?" "Those who recognize themselves in these webs of love, implication, and excavation," she adds, "are the 'we' who surf the Net in the sacred/secular quest rhetoric of this chapter."[71]

Haraway offers a few insights into the significance of her nonetheless disavowed Catholicism. Regarding the plasticity of oedipal narratives, Har-away observes, in a 1991 interview, "And I know in my heart that by analogy, I could have remained a Roman Catholic and thought anything I·wanted to think if I was willing to put enough work into it, because these universal stories have that capacity, they really can accommodate anything at all."[72]

This remark can perhaps be brushed aside since it so clearly relegates Haraway's Catholicism to the past, though it does suggest what she con-tinues to think about. More telling is a comment in *Modest_Witness* that Haraway is "genetically Catholic," an especially interesting allusion in light of her effort to deconstruct the gene as an embodiment of the "really-real."[73] I am drawn to Haraway's *obiter dictum* that the Oncomouse™ "doesn't have a crown of thorns on her head for no reason."[74] Presumably, the crown of thorns is a reminder of the secular Christian realism that highlights similari-ties between the sacrificial Oncomouse™ and Christ. But Haraway doesn't actually tell us the reason for that crown of thorns. I wonder if her desire to deconstruct secular technoscience totally exhausts that reason.

Finally, I am preoccupied by Haraway's reading of Nancy Scheper Hughes's *Death Without Weeping*. *Modest_Witness* is an extraordinary mélange of history, cartoons, puns, narratives, song lyrics, paintings, adver-tisements, and interpreted texts; Haraway's utilization of Scheper-Hughes's ethnography may be nothing more than one of these. But there is also some-thing noteworthy, something almost excessive, about Haraway's treatment of *Death Without Weeping*. For one thing, it is the longest single reading in the book (though Haraway's intermittent readings of Lynn Randolph's paintings are, in the aggregate, longer).

The tone of Haraway's treatment of Scheper-Hughes is even more worthy of note than its length. Haraway, as I have already mentioned, regularly uses, borrows, steals, appropriates, and treats with familiarity the works of a wide range of individuals and groups—Native Americans, African Americans, Jews, the prosthetically enabled. In *Modest_Witness*, she greatly increases her acknowledgment of these noninnocent practices—but that is what she does, acknowledges them. In her reading of *Death Without Weeping*, however, Haraway apologizes to Scheper-Hughes. "Besides drastically reducing the complexity of accounts in her book, my sketch adds analogies, renarrativizes, and uses parts of her story in ways she did not," Haraway writes. "But we are enmeshed together in webs spun by yearning and analysis."[75]

I do not believe it entirely a coincidence that Haraway should be thus uncharacteristically—undefensively, unironically—responsive to a text written by a(nother) Roman Catholic woman, using it as the culmination of a chapter on, for better and for worse, that most Roman Catholic of subjects, the fetus. Nor do I believe it a coincidence that Scheper-Hughes's book explicitly elicits the very thing which had been, before the publication of "*Ecce Homo*," deemed lacking in Haraway's work—the suffering and mourning of her subjects and all that that implies. Before reading *Modest_Witness*, I had misremembered the title of Scheper-Hughes's fairly famous enthnography as *Death Without Mourning* rather than *Death Without Weeping*. But Haraway does not escape in *Modest_Witness* from mourning those cyborg angels washed away in their own diarrhea.

It does not actually matter, of course, whether Haraway agrees with what I make of her writings or not. Discourse by its very nature has a life of its own, with consequences that overflow the intentions of its creator; the materiality of discourse applies as much to religious discourse as to any other kind. In early twenty-first-century America, figures that seem almost entirely secularized in one generation may be resacralized in another, as many a parent has learned to his or her astonishment.[76]

My intuition that Haraway was drawn to *Death Without Weeping* in part because of Scheper-Hughes's Catholic sensibility is, of course, nothing more than that, an intuition. But by including in *Modest_Witness* a reading of an ethnography as deeply influenced by Roman Catholic liberation theology as *Death Without Weeping* is, Haraway implicates herself in that tradition whether she intends it or not.[77] Similarly, the incorporation of her reading of Jesus and Sojourner Truth into the feminist Christology of my colleague Karen Trimble Alliaume enmeshes Haraway in Catholic feminist theology as well.[78]

To push this line of reasoning a little farther, my inclusion of a close reading of Haraway's texts in a study of American Catholicism in the second half of the twentieth century folds Haraway back into that collectivity whether she chooses it or not. But when I think about my efforts to reclaim Donna Haraway as part of the American Catholic web of yearning and analysis that I call the trajectory of the cross, I am struck by Haraway's affinity with one particular thread of that trajectory. As I acknowledge in my introduction, I want particularly to attend in this study to the visual-tactile Catholic devotional figures that parallel biblical texts in their significance for American Protestantism. *Modest_Witness* contains twelve reproductions of Lynn Randolph's paintings, the majority of them bearing no Christian markings whatsoever. But on the front cover of *Modest_Witness* is Randolph's cyborg annunciation, which, interestingly enough, Haraway believes is "not about the birth of Christ." And on the back cover is Randolph's "The Laboratory, or The Passion of Oncomouse™," complete with the Oncomouse's crown of thorns. The original of that painting hung over Donna Haraway's desk as she revised *Modest_Witness*, even as a bronze crucifix, complete with crown of thorns, hangs before me as I write this chapter now.[79]

CHAPTER FOUR

The Company of the Blessed

RICHARD RODRIGUEZ'S BROWN CATHOLICISM

> How shall we sing the song of the Lord on alien soil?
>
> —PSALM 137

> He is not the sort of man any gay man would have chosen to be-
> come in the 1970s. Something of the old dear about him, wizened
> butterfly, powdered old pouf. Certainly he is what I fear becom-
> ing. And then he rises, this old monkey, with the most beatific
> dignity . . . and strides into the sanctuary to take his place in the
> company of the Blessed.
>
> —RICHARD RODRIGUEZ, *"Late Victorians"*

$\mathcal{T}$o speak of a particular generation seems, on the face of it, a straightforward matter. My dictionary supports this notion, offering this as a first definition: "the entire body of individuals born and living at about the same time: *the postwar generation*."[1] Approached from this perspective, Richard Rodriguez and the other writers whose works we have interrogated thus far can all be described as members of the same postwar "generation" of American Catholicss. All were born into devout Catholic families and were educated in Catholic schools. All benefited from high-quality postsecond-ary educations and went on to become celebrated writers, something almost unimaginable to the vast majority of U.S. Catholics a few decades earlier. All were deeply influenced by the liberation movements of the 1960s, 1970s, and 1980s. And eventually, all four published distinguished books that confront, to some degree, the losses that attend postwar American Cath-olic identity.

In another sense, however, the term "generation" elides certain signifi-cant, even critical, distinctions. In Rodriguez's case, the most obvious of these distinctions is ethnicity. But the relationship of each writer to the "immigrant/postimmigrant" frame is also significant. For while Carroll's and Haraway's families of origin had already moved into the professional/managerial class, Rodriguez and his siblings comprise the first "generation" of their family to do so.

The ethnic and socioeconomic contexts of these moves contribute to divergent representations of the cross and of the Catholic Church in the writings of Carroll, Gordon, Haraway, and Rodriguez. Carroll's embrace of postwar American liberalism, for example, brought with it a fairly thorough-going rejection of the "Catholic grammar of suffering" and the reconfiguration of Jesus crucified as a triumphant, Christic hero. Through his political and ecclesiological conservatism, Rodriguez, too, attempts to escape the grief that shadows personal, cultural, and religious change in his life. But he finds such a refusal to grieve ultimately impossible to sustain and registers that impossibility, as we shall see, in a Jesus not triumphant but lighter than air. So much is this the case that by the early years of the new millennium, he has moved to a new place, a place in which contradictions are sustained and the crucifix is never out of sight.[2]

As yet another member of the Catholic "postwar generation," I have on many occasions turned with longing toward a Christic hero like Carroll's, a hero who will enable us to overcome our adversaries, who can keep ahead of those chips of heterogeneity that threaten our integrity. Yet I, a woman and the first member of my own working-class family to "go to college," have also come to know, in part at least, the futility of this narrative line. And so, in previous chapters, I have delineated the beginning of an alternative trajectory of the cross. This trajectory comes more fully into view in Richard Rodriguez's first two collections of autobiographical essays, *Hunger of Memory* and *Days of Obligation*, and culminates in the transformative embrace of contradiction and impurity inscribed in his most recent collection, *Brown*.[3]

HUNGER OF MEMORY

Richard Rodriguez first gained public recognition in the 1970s when, as a "minority" Ph.D. student at the University of California at Berkeley, he authored a series of articles and addresses opposing affirmative action and bilingual education. He subsequently achieved a national literary reputation with the publication, in 1982, of *Hunger of Memory: The Education of Richard Rodriguez*, a moving and maddening book in which Rodriguez takes strong positions regarding not only Catholicism but also his ethnicity, his class, and his skin color.[4] Rodriguez's first national television appearance followed soon after; since then, he has appeared well over a hundred times as a commentator or essayist on public television's *McNeil-Lehrer News Hour* (now *The News Hour with Jim Lehrer*) and other programs.[5]

Hunger of Memory is a collection of essays—"essays impersonating an autobiography"—written when Rodriguez was in his early thirties.[6] I have some notions about why he would describe them as "six chapters of sad, fuguelike repetition." The 1960s and 1970s, out of which we were then just emerging, were not, in fact, an easy time for all young people, whatever cultural historians may say about them. This was especially the case for young people like Rodriguez and me, groomed by our parents and teachers to be the first college graduates and professional/managerial members of our respective working-class families at a time when protest and resistance were the order of the day. My solution, in the short run, was more typical: dropping out of college (twice); teaching in little, artsy, community schools; living in rural communes; feeling confused.

Rodriguez, on the other hand, did what he was supposed to do. The child of working-class Mexican immigrants, Rodriguez graduated from one elite university (Stanford) and did graduate work at two others (Columbia and Berkeley). Eventually, though, he undertook his own form of resistance, refusing a plum job in the Yale English Department and then leaving the academy altogether because he believed his success was predicated on the unfair privileging of middle-class "minorities" under affirmative action. But a first-rate education is highly portable, as Rodriguez soon learned. He subsequently received a fellowship from the National Endowment for the Humanities to write his autobiography, *Hunger of Memory*. By the mid-1980s, he was more successful than most professors of English, even those at Yale, would ever be.

In the prologue to *Hunger of Memory*, Rodriguez identifies himself as a "middle-class American man. Assimilated."[7] The remainder of his autobiography comprises overlapping treatments of how this assimilation came about and what it might mean. Pivotal to the book is the brutal termination of Rodriguez's "enchantedly happy" Spanish-speaking childhood when his parents enrolled him in the first grade at Sacred Heart, the English-speaking Catholic school in their Anglo neighborhood in Sacramento.[8]

For a while after enrolling, Ricardo, known at school as "Rich-heard," made little progress. He was restored to happiness each night when he returned to the intimacy of home, however, an intimacy he associates with the "private" language spoken by his family. Then, one day, three of the nuns from Sacred Heart arrived at the door; they had come to ask Rodriguez's parents to encourage their children to speak English at home.

> Of course, my parents complied. What would they not do for their children's well-being? And how could they have questioned the Church's authority which those women represented? In an instant they agreed to give up the language (the sounds) that had revealed and accentuated our family's closeness. The moment after the visitors left, the change was observed. "*Ahora*, speak to us *en ingles*," my father and mother united to tell us.[9]

Others in addition to Rodriguez have written about the pain that attends such a change of language. In *Eloquent Obsessions*, the literary scholar Alice Yeager Kaplan examines the losses she endured when she underwent a similar linguistic shift, from English to French: "language is a home," she writes, "as surely as a roof over one's head is a home, and . . . to be without a language, or to be between languages, is as miserable in its way as to be without bread."[10] Yet at the time of her loss, Yeager Kaplan was older than Rodriguez—she moved to France as an adult—and had done so more or less freely.

However emotionally wrenching the extirpation of Spanish from the Rodriguez household must have been, in *Hunger of Memory* it signifies far more than linguistic homelessness. In most cases, language is intuitively associated with the public as well as private culture in which it is spoken. As a preschool Spanish-speaking child growing up in an Anglo neighborhood, however, Rodriguez came to think of Spanish as his family's private language and English the language of publicness. In Rodriguez's recollection, the linguistic isolation his family shared served to deepen their intimacy, and when he and his siblings were forced to speak English at home, an almost preverbal intimacy was irrevocably lost.

As the essay proceeds, Rodriguez renounces with something of a flourish the identification he made as a child between Spanish and familial intimacy. On the other side of an initial sadness, he tells us, is the realization that intimacy "cannot be held":

> With time would come the knowledge that intimacy would finally pass. . . . Intimacy is not trapped within words. It passes through words. It passes. The truth is that intimates leave the room. Doors close. Faces move away from the window. Time passes. Voices recede in the dark. Death finally quiets the voice. And there is no way to deny it. No way to stand in the crowd, uttering one's family language.[11]

At first, this passage seems to convey a profound engagement with mourning. Loss is inevitable, intimacy passes, and there is no way to avoid Death (with a capital *D*). On closer inspection, however, a rigidity can be discerned within it that, quite the contrary, tries to defend the speaker from feeling the pain of loss. Intimacy, we are warned, will finally pass. No other love will take its place. Finally? No other? This is the leaden language that signals, as Julia Kristeva tells us, a failed or incomplete mourning and a desire to return to the ambivalent love that is inscribed within it. It is also a language that is translated into new forms only with great difficulty. And sure enough, in this same chapter, even as Rodriguez renounces his childhood confusion between intimacy and his family's private language, he is warning other Latino writers and activists of the futility of wanting to speak their "familial" language in the public, that is to say, in the English-speaking sphere.[12]

There is something counterintuitive, even perverse, about designating a passage in a critically acclaimed literary work like *Hunger of Memory* leaden and defensive. As Kristeva also argues, writing, like religion, offers a privileged opportunity to work through the traumas of separation. *Hunger of Memory* thus doubtless initiates or extends the very process of mourning that the frozen language of the passage in question is meant to fend off. Yet as we shall see, *Hunger of Memory* is clearly marked by a series of strategies like this one, calculated to deny what Eric Santner describes as "the painful awareness that 'I' and 'you' have edges, and that inscribed within the space of this interval are the possibilities of misunderstanding, disappointment, even betrayal."[13] In particular, such denial is inscribed in what Rodriguez perceives as the unbridgeable distance between public and private, especially as it is manifested in the relationship between Anglo language and the languages and cultures of the "others." *Hunger of Memory* proves, in the end, to be almost as much a refusal to feel the pain of early losses as it is an engagement with them.

At first, Rodriguez's response to his linguistic amputation suggests that this is not the case. He does indeed feel and express anger at his parents for having enforced English in his home and links this anger to his own determination to succeed at school. Yet this anger is a half-measure at best. As Rodriguez notes, he also felt guilty for succeeding in the new world his parents and the nuns at Sacred Heart had forced upon him, for the betrayal of them that his transformation into an English speaker seemed to constitute. Guilt is a classic strategy for avoiding the pain of separation, a defense against the feelings that accompany not betraying but having been betrayed. Such a denial virtually guarantees the reappearance of those feelings at a later date.

THE SCHOLARSHIP BOY

But Rodriguez, as *Hunger of Memory*'s subtitle indicates, is less concerned with the traces of grit embedded in his recollections than with his experience of becoming educated. He had first begun to interrogate the implications of his education, of his ostensible assimilation into American culture, in the Reading Room of the British Museum in London where he went, as a young man, to research his Ph.D. dissertation in English Renaissance literature. Finding himself unable to endure the loneliness of the scholarly life he had been moving toward for many years, he begins reading books by "modern educational theorists," finally discovering Richard Hoggart's *The Uses of Literacy*. He resonates in particular with Hoggart's depiction of "the scholarship boy," the sensitive, high-strung, working-class child who does not manage a graceful transition from one world to another, for "success comes with special anxiety."[14] This child, Hoggart notes, can no longer identify with his parents, would do anything to please his teachers, and becomes quite ambitious.

In the midst of recalling his discovery of Hoggart's "scholarship boy," Rodriguez describes the "grandiose" reading program he himself undertook in elementary school.[15] By the fourth grade, although he did not yet enjoy reading, Rodriguez had intuited that books were the path to becoming an educated adult. So he undertook to read all the important adult books he could lay his hands on; by high school, he had read hundreds of them. With each, the procedure was the same: after completing a book, Rodriguez would woodenly record its title and theme in a specially designated notebook. Reading—in effect, consuming—was entirely what learning was about, the recording of information stored inside books. And although he mocks himself for having been merely a "bookish" reader and not a good one, he concludes that the "habit" of reading brought him the success he hoped it would.[16]

But when he encounters in *The Uses of Literacy* Hoggart's characterization of the "scholarship boy" as "piling up . . . knowledge and received opinions . . . [with] something of the blinkered pony" about him, Rodriguez balks. Hoggart's criticism is "more accurate than fair." The scholarship boy, Rodriguez argues, actually has no choice; education requires radical—in fact, total—self-reformation:

> as he struggles with an early homework assignment, [the scholarship boy] knows this too well. This is why he lacks self-assurance. He does not forget that the classroom is responsible for remaking him. He relies on his teacher, depends on all that he hears in the classroom and reads in his books. He becomes in every obvious way the worst student, a dummy mouthing the opinions of others. But he would not be so bad—nor would he become so successful, a scholarship boy—if he did not accurately perceive that the best synonym for primary "education" is "imitation."[17]

Then follows a clear statement of the conservative educational ideology that will reappear like a mantra throughout *Hunger of Memory*: "Radical educationists complain that ghetto schools 'oppress' students by trying to mold them, but the truer critique would be just the reverse. They oppress them because 'they change most students barely at all.'"[18] The lesson from the story of the scholarship boy, according to Rodriguez, is that education is necessarily an unglamorous, even "demeaning" process, one "never natural to the person one was before one entered the classroom."[19]

This assertion comprises a second pivotal moment in *Hunger of Memory*. The reader has been inclined to give Rodriguez's earlier emphatic statements the benefit of the doubt, if only because they are so well written. But now, seen in the context of Rodriguez's own puzzling admission of guilt for having done something he was, in fact, forced to do, this polemic emerges clearly as the reiteration of a defense against mourning, against feelings that accompany betrayal and loss. Education is the complete remaking of the student; the scholarship student alone knows the truth that being demeaned, being made into a machine, having the rough edges between "I" and "you" forced upon him with little empathy, is a favor teachers do for students.[20] How dreadful, then, could it have been that there was no empathic witness at home or at school who understood the losses Ricardo had suffered, who could help him make a transition from familial intimacy to the separation of adulthood? Worse than the loss Rodriguez sustained initially is his ongoing commitment to repressing the pain of that loss, his need to assert that it could have been no other way if he wanted to have a successful life in the world.[21]

As another "working-class scholarship student," albeit one from an English-speaking family, my experience was different from that of Rodriguez. There was, of course, a fair amount of "imitation" in my childhood, the necessary kind as well as the scandalous busywork inflicted upon working-class children by working-class teachers. But for me, fairly quickly, reading and writing also became a way of envisioning something else—upward mobility, perhaps, but also the possibility of fashioning a self in a world that was more than obedience and drudgery.

It seems that Rodriguez was less fortunate; for a long time, though perhaps not forever, Rodriguez defends himself from the trauma of his loss of childhood intimacy by repeating again and again in his writing the ideological mantra: it couldn't have been any other way. His intense opposition to bilingual education in particular is a displacement of that trauma onto other ethnics who have not been thus traumatized. For Rodriguez, students are either totally remade or not changed at all; immigrants are either assimilated or left behind. Indeed, this highly defended trauma is reiterated in the public/private binary that runs throughout *Hunger of Memory*. As he tells us repeatedly, for Rodriguez, public individuality can only be attained by renunciation of the private separateness that accompanies ethnic identity.[22]

The period that preceded the publication of *Hunger of Memory* was one of considerable change for Latinos in the United States. Lyndon Johnson's War on Poverty, which began in 1964, made federal grants directly available to groups of poor people. The 1965 Civil Rights Act, although focused primarily on African Americans, made the imposition of an English-language voting-rights requirement illegal as well. Also in 1965, revisions in federal immigration laws greatly increased the number of Spanish-speaking residents in the United States, and the first bilingual education programs were funded in 1967. These developments, along with the new anti-imperialist discourse and activism of the civil rights and antiwar movements, were part of a major reconfiguration of race and ethnicity in the United States.[23] For Mexican Americans, the rise of César Chavez and the United Farm Workers and the development of urban activist groups undergirded emergent Chicana/o political and cultural movements. Among Chicana/os and other Latina/os, trends toward cultural and linguistic assimilation were now actively resisted.[24]

Because Rodriguez takes emphatic positions in *Hunger of Memory* in opposition to affirmative action and bilingualism and in support of assimilation, Hispanic American scholars and activists have criticized him, sometimes bitterly.[25] Some find Rodriguez's writing marked by alienation and binary thinking, and they lament his inability to participate in several worlds at a time. Others believe his position on affirmative action to be fueled by identification with power and privilege. Still others accuse him of self-flagellation, self-pity, or "ephemeral archness."[26]

Yet some Hispanic writers find more value and complexity in Rodriguez than his ideological eruptions, seen in isolation, would warrant. Although continuing to indict Rodriguez for his neoconservatism, the Chicana critic Norma Alarcón also believes that his claims of total assimilation may not be as straightforward as they seem. Rather, his "imitation" may actually be a form of mimicry, the holding up of a rhetorical mirror to the aristocrats from whom he, the colonized, ostensibly learned his manners.[27] She compares his work to that of Trinh T. Min-Ha, the postcolonial critic, and Judith Butler, the feminist-psychoanalytic theorist, who write of a postmodern doubleness in which the outsider becomes insider and the insider outsider. "In the never-ending play of the rhetorical," Alarcón writes, "Rodriguez reveals his ethnicity because he is an American, and he reveals his Americanness because he is an ethnic."[28]

The philosopher and literary critic Henry Staten, in a close reading of *Hunger of Memory* that may be the best study of Rodriguez published to date, extends Alarcón's discernment of complexity.[29] Staten brings an extraordinary sensitivity to nuance in *Hunger of Memory*, in part, at least because he is, as he so delicately puts it, one of those "who exist or will exist in the penumbra of Chicano-Chicana identity," despite the "strange power" of being marked by the name of his only Anglo grandparent. He exists in relation to "the (per)formative power of the names *Mexican*, and then *Chicano*" without being named by them.[30]

While questioning Rodriguez's "absolute non-relation" to the name *Chicano*[31] and his bifurcation of "full public individuality" from the supposedly inherently private ethnic self,[32] Staten also stresses the self-deprecating irony throughout *Hunger of Memory* that destabilizes these binaries. He likewise questions the totalized discourse of some of the theorists of Chicano/Chicana identity who criticize Rodriguez. The notion of *chicanismo* that emerged in the United States in the 1960s, Staten argues, was a transposition of *indigenismo*, an official Mexican ideology that, after the "democratic" revolution of 1910–1920, asserted that the Indian inheritance was the root of the distinctive racial character and cultural greatness of Mexico.

Marginally democratic, the revolution consolidated a new capitalist Mexican ruling class[33] that used *indigenismo* in an effort to absorb the racially distinct Indian element into a homogenous *raza national* characterized by white European cultural traits and work habits suited to emerging Mexican industrialization. Conservative upper-class Mexicans who emigrated to the United States attempted after the revolution to force the concept of *La Raza* onto middle-class Mexican Americans who had lived in the American Southwest for generations. According to Staten, the *chicanista* identity of the 1960s, though it was fashioned to facilitate the political organization of poor Mexican Americans, nonetheless tends to continue this ideological process. Specifically, he believes that it "mystifies the sociopolitical bond that has historically been an instrument of hegemony for the Mexican ruling class over the very ethclass," as Staten terms it, "said to be the core of Chicano-Chicana identity," and that it obscures current racial and class divisions within the Mexican American community.[34]

Staten then demonstrates textually that Rodriguez's parents, although forced to take blue-collar jobs in the United States, were nonetheless historically linked to the Mexican upper class; this, in part, explains their willingness to live in an all-Anglo neighborhood and to facilitate their children's success by speaking English at home. Staten ties Rodriguez's refusal to identify as a Chicano and the attraction to wealth and privilege, which is apparent throughout his autobiographical writings, to this family background.[35] He also marks multiple locations throughout the text where Rodriguez, despite his refusal to conflate class differences within Chicano-Chicana/Mexican American identity, expresses "an intense connection with the most abjected Mexicans and longs to make contact with them."[36]

Staten also distinguishes helpfully between two frequently connected aspects of Rodriguez's work: his critique of affirmative action and his anti–bilingual education polemic. Quoting directly from *Hunger of Memory*, Staten demonstrates that Rodriguez attacks affirmative action from the left as a "liberal palliative" that, by supporting the most able among young ethnic and racial group members, neglects the (racially unspecific) American underclass. Rodriguez advocates instead the complete reform of elementary and secondary education, jobs and good housing for families, and three meals a day and safe neighborhoods for children. Many will find proportionate representation of ethnic/racial groups in American higher education also necessary and will regret Rodriguez's positing of an "either/or" here. Yet Staten's yoking of this far from neoconservative position to Rodriguez's "intense compassion for the plight of the dark skinned subalterns" significantly reshapes the conversation about him.[37] So does his suggestion that his Latino/a critics could have given Rodriguez credit for this correct, "if unoriginal," analysis but have not done so.[38]

CATHOLICISM AS FRAGILE CONNECTOR

According to Staten, Rodriguez's critics fail to factor his progressive stance on affirmative action into their evaluation of him because, for them, bilingual education is a far more significant issue, one that strikes at the very heart of Chicano/Chicana identity. But on the subject of bilingualism, Rodriguez's position is not left-leaning. For Rodriguez, the crucial attainment of full public individuality requires nothing less than assimilation, the abandonment of ethnic identity, because ethnic identity is inherently private. According to this line of reasoning, bilingual education deprives ethnic group members of publicness, the possibility of political and economic citizenship.

To explain this identification of ethnic identity with privacy, Staten turns to Rodriguez's "religious metaphysics":[39]

> This conclusion is motivated not by social analysis but by Rodriguez's religious metaphysics. Privacy is for him an unplumbable metaphysical depth. At its limit, it is the privacy of the Puritan, who stands alone before God. Only the Catholic church of his childhood, before its liberalization drove Rodriguez to Puritan solitude, could mediate between the individual's absolute privacy and the community of believers.[40]

Staten's invocation of Rodriguez's religion here is instructive, even if his interpretation of it is problematic. Rodriguez devotes an entire chapter of *Hunger of Memory* to his Catholicism and refers repeatedly to it throughout his writings. His Latina/o-Chicana/o critics tend either to reduce Catholicism to one of a series of more or less equivalent differences within his work or else use it as a synonym for Euro-Americanness in opposition to Indianness. Staten, however, intuits the centrality of Rodriguez's Christian faith but then accepts at face value Rodriguez's binarized construction of that faith as he never does the binaries in Rodriguez's representations of ethnicity. Thus, when Rodriguez, in the midst of another polemic, this time against the Vatican II renewal of the liturgy that, after all, robbed him of yet another beloved language, maintains that he has now "become like a Protestant Christian," Staten takes him literally; Rodriguez has moved into "Puritan solitude."

Undoubtedly, Rodriguez does at times deploy a Catholic/Protestant binary in his work, one that frequently depends on a dubious and highly metaphorical reading of each, certainly of "Protestants" or "Puritans."[41] Nevertheless, at other times he complicates that binary, recognizing in his increasingly "Protestant" self an unshakable Catholic materialism: the heavy gold crucifix he carried as an altar boy still protects him from the "Puritan" distrust of the material, he writes.[42] He also recognizes more nuance in the Catholicism of his childhood than Staten's Catholic-to-Puritan progression leaves room for.

In his second book, to be discussed later in this chapter, the same Irish nuns who taught Rodriguez in catechism class that tragedy is the essence of life also introduced him to American optimism in his secular studies without attempting to integrate the two. Staten's interest in the nuances of Rodriguez's ethnicity blinds him to the nuances of Rodriguez's Christianity.

The association Staten makes between Rodriguez's religion and his incoherent conflation of ethnicity and privacy is helpful, even if it is somewhat misconstrued. I do not believe that Rodriguez's "religious metaphysics" motivated him to any great degree to make what Staten calls his "amazing logical leap" from ethnicity to privacy.[43] Rather, the traumatic sundering of public from private in Rodriguez's childhood fueled his great love for Catholicism, not only before the council but after it as well. When, as Rodriguez notes, the intimacy of his family was ruptured for him in early grade school, at a time when everything seemed incompatible between "the two worlds of [his] life, the Church provided an essential link."[44] The church alone mediated between his public and private lives.

Far from legitimating the bifurcation of public from private, Catholicism constituted the one arena where Rodriguez dared lay down his defenses and risk a connection, however fragile, between his "private," feeling self and the world of adult publicness, which had presented itself to him as overwhelmingly unfeeling. Representations of Jesus on the cross and as the Sacred Heart connected the two spheres for him.[45] Nuns and priests carried names of familial intimacy—"Sister" and "Father"—yet the feelings that accompanied this intimacy took on great formality in the Catholic liturgy. Finally, the church was the locus outside the Rodriguez household where his parents were taken seriously. Within all this, Rodriguez himself enjoyed a secure situation, at least temporarily: altar boy and star pupil. Never mind that the (undeniable) ideological coherence and aesthetic pleasure afforded by the U.S. Catholicism of the 1950s was predicated on an extraordinarily narrow construal of the Christian faith and frequent repression of thought and creativity that dared extend beyond it. It nonetheless gave Rodriguez somewhere to sense the possibility of integration. In many respects, it functioned this way for me as well.

As I suggested previously, earlier unmourned losses are telescoped within Rodriguez's experience of losing his familial language when he started school. If my reading of *Hunger of Memory* is correct, then Rodriguez's turn to Catholicism comprises a double displacement of those unresolved early losses. Such displacements invariably disappoint. After a brief romance with liberal Catholicism during college, Rodriguez became increasingly disenchanted with the post–Vatican II renewal of the church. In particular, changes in the liturgy came to embody the loss of the unified Catholic world of his childhood. While in the Latin Mass the priest alone pronounced the words of the creed in the singular, "*Credo in unum Deum*," the post–Vatican II congregation prays it collectively, in the plural, "We believe in one God. . . . " For Rodriguez, this move obscures the far greater isolation Catholics suffer today than they did when their multiple solitudes were embodied in the priest's Latin "I."[46]

If Rodriguez had not felt betrayed by the changes put into play by the Second Vatican Council, he would have felt betrayed by some other aspect of the church. He makes evident the structural links between his loss of communal Catholicism and earlier losses when he assures us, once again, that it was his own doing. "And I will be uneasy knowing that the old faith was lost as much by *choice* as it was inevitably lost. My education may have made it inevitable that I would become a citizen of the secular city, but I have come to *embrace* the city's values; social mobility; pluralism; egalitarianism; self-reliance."[47]

As befits its distance from the original site of trauma, this assumption of responsibility, though still defensive, is more balanced than earlier ones; Rodriguez is learning to acknowledge his losses, but very slowly. Here the faith is lost only "as much by" his choice as by the inevitable. But how could Rodriguez have refused "embracing" pluralism or self-reliance once he was deposited in mid-twentieth-century middle-class America? And how would such a refusal have preserved the unity of Catholicism? In the late sixties, when Rodriguez was at Stanford flirting with liberal Protestantism, I joined an international Catholic women's movement called the Grail. At that time, Grail members still sometimes sang Gregorian chants and prayed the Office in common; by 1975, Catholicism was becoming more and more consciously marginal as we experimented with feminist and ostensibly Native American rituals. Some members who were unhappy with these developments went off seeking more explicitly Catholic situations, but their departure did not stop these changes. In point of fact, major components of the lives of American Catholic lay people had been situated in secular/industrial America for generations, but the ideological separatism of the institutional church obscured that reality.[48]

When assessing post–Vatican II changes in American Catholicism in *Hunger of Memory*, Rodriguez throws up defenses against loss, as he has done before. Yet the very fact that he once allowed himself to risk disappointment by experiencing, however briefly, a connection between his private and public life in the context of the Catholic Church suggests that the church will continue to be a locus of feeling for him. And loci where people risk feeling are potential loci of transformation. *Days of Obligation*, a collection of essays published ten years after *Hunger of Memory*, offers instances of just such transformation.

DAYS OF OBLIGATION

Respondents to *Hunger of Memory* refer occasionally to Richard Rodriguez's "metaphysics," a term that suggests the presence of an unchanging theoretical framework in his writing. But even before the first page of Rodriguez's second collection, *Days of Obligation: An Argument with My Mexican Father*, it is clear that something in his work has changed. Unlike the cover of *Hunger of Memory*, with its headshot of a solitary Rodriguez, this volume displays two Latino faces in obvious relation to one another, even if they are not happy about it. These faces embody the shift, signaled by Rodriguez's subtitle, from autobiography, that genre of the self, to the more relational "argument with my Mexican father."[49] A change is likewise indicated by the title, *Days of Obligation*. While also referring to Rodriguez's obligations to his Mexican heritage, the subtitle calls to mind the Roman Catholic practice of celebrating "holy days of obligation."[50]

In *Days of Obligation*, Rodriguez reconsiders a number of the positions he argued for strongly in *Hunger of Memory*.[51] He no longer assumes the identity of a middle-class American, "assimilated," as he once put it.[52] Indeed, Rodriguez's statement was always more complex than it appeared; the genuinely assimilated do not refer to their assimilation. Now, in *Days of Obligation*, Rodriguez struggles more consciously with the implications of his Mexican heritage. Specifically, the "argument" of his subtitle, which surfaces throughout the collection, is the conflict Rodriguez identifies within himself and in the world around him between a Mexican/Catholic sense of tragedy and an American/Protestant sense of optimism or comedy.

This "argument" is also one between a young man and an older one, Rodriguez in the past versus Rodriguez in the present, as well as between Rodriguez and his father. Since he believes that both participants in the debate possess wisdom, however, Rodriguez resists privileging the "old" man by refusing to conclude the collection with essays in favor of Catholic "tragedy," the position he is inclined toward at the time he is writing the book. Instead, he uses a reverse chronology, beginning with essays in which he is middle-aged and working back to his childhood and youth. He thus situates a prototypical deployment of the argument in his last chapter, "Nothing Lasts a Hundred Years":

> When I was fourteen and my father was fifty, we toyed with the argument that had once torn Europe, South from North, Catholic from Protestant, as we polished the blue DeSoto.
> "Life is harder than you think, boy."
> "You're thinking of Mexico, Papa."
> "You'll see."[53]

TRANSGRESSING BINARIES

In the "earlier" essays, especially the ones concerned with Catholicism, it sometimes appears that the argument over comedy and tragedy is still more a conflict between Rodriguez and others than within himself. Catholicism is a central theme or structuring element in four of the ten essays in *Days of Obligation* and surfaces intermittently in the rest. In one, the narrative of a visit to Tijuana is framed by the seven days of Holy Week, with Rodriguez accompanying a priest friend to Catholic services in poor rural villages and taking notes on the lot of poor Mexican illegals at the border. In another, he laments the secularization of the California missions and concludes that "our faith"—Catholicism—can no longer be found in them, but instead only in the California that the missions created.

Especially revealing is "The Latin American Novel." Here Rodriguez examines the relationship between Catholicism and evangelical Protestantism in Latin America. At first, binaries proliferate: Catholicism is communal, Protestantism the religion of the individual standing alone before God; Catholicism is a religion of villages, while Protestantism "taught Europe to imagine the self according to a new world of cities."[54] In this way, Rodriguez resists James Carroll's turn to story with his conviction that "Catholicism is just there, a way of life that need never come to a head. Catholicism never stands or falls on one decision. Catholicism isn't a novel." And again, "Despite the quantities of novels I have read, I find I do not believe in sudden shifts, revolutions of plot, reformations."[55] Indeed, Rodriguez writes essays, not fiction, in an increasingly poetic literary style that elicits the praise of some critics, the scorn of others.[56]

In this essay, flashbacks to Rodriguez's years in a Christian Brothers' high school put the sign of the cross into high relief once again. A glow-in-the-dark crucifix over his bed at home and another phallic crucifix "slung in (a visiting priest's) sash like a blunderbuss" establish continuities between contemporary Catholicism and the self-assured church of his childhood.[57]

Rodriguez's contempt for bilingualism, evident throughout *Hunger of Memory*, likewise continues in "The Latin American Novel," but this time it is the church rather than the education establishment that merits his scorn. Invited to speak on "multiculturalism" at a retreat for new Catholic pastors, he denounces the practice of parishes celebrating Mass in languages other than English. But in the attempt to win over his audience, Rodriguez transgresses the Catholic/Protestant binary. While he and the priests argue over multiculturalism, he says, Hispanic converts to evangelicalism, in Latin America and in the United States, are appropriating the best of the Catholic tradition. He cannot fathom the "apostasy" of the Filipino evangelicals who worship in his neighborhood, that they would abandon the "faith of their fathers":

> Yet, Fathers, how much they remind me of Catholics of the fifties, and of the prayer life of the Church which seemed eternal and ordinary. . . . For all of their obvious differences from Catholicism, I sense among evangelicals a longing for some lost Catholic village, some relief from loneliness. . . . The small Protestant Church revives the Catholic memory of the countryside. In the small evangelical church, people who are demoralized by the city turn to the assurance of community. In the small church, each soul has a first name again.[58]

Nor is this acknowledgment of the link between hyperindividualized urban Protestantism and communal village Catholicism the only change perceptible here. For in the midst of his presentation on Catholic "multiculturalism," Rodriguez's sophisticated defenses against disappointment by the church fall away; he becomes genuinely angry at the priests he is addressing. He believes they have abandoned their assigned task of imparting the "Catholic knowledge of union," so he undertakes to remind them of it. "We are Catholics, Fathers," he announces. This is something the respectful Rodriguez of the autobiography would never have said to a priest, just as his parents would never have refused the nuns' request to speak English at home.[59] In particular, his dismissal of a Mexican priest who defends celebrating the Mass in Spanish because it enables grandparents to pray with their grandchildren moves beyond irony to sarcasm and rage:

> Fine, I say (Asshole), have your Spanish masses and your Vietnamese masses. But realize the Church is setting itself against inevitability; the inevitable Americanization of the grandchildren. You are going to lose the grandchildren; in fact, you've lost them already. I'm beginning to suspect that you speak Spanish because in English you no longer believe. . . . A foreign language liturgy should be a mere strategy, a temporary appeasement.[60]

"PRIVATE LIVES WERE BECOMING PUBLIC"

This deviation from Rodriguez's previous controlled demeanor marks a significant shift in his stance toward the church. It is possible, of course, that the distressing situation registered in his session with the new pastors is the cause of this shift, as "The Latin American Novel" implies. But this situation—the vernacular Mass, priests who don't believe as they ought—is nothing new to Rodriguez. Long before *Days of Obligation*, he had lamented postconciliar Catholicism's ostensible squandering of the one, the true, and the beautiful. Something else, something more recent, must have precipitated this uncharacteristic outburst of grief and rage.

My choice for such a precipitating cause is a series of events in the life of the "older" Richard Rodriguez that is examined in "Late Victorians," an essay positioned toward the beginning of *Days of Obligation*.

On a Sunday in summer, ten years ago, I was walking home from the Latin Mass at St. Patrick's, the old Irish parish downtown, when I saw thousands of people on Market Street. It was the Gay Freedom Day parade—not the first, but the first I ever saw. Private lives were becoming public. There were marching bands. There were floats. Banners blocked single lives thematically into a processional mass, not unlike the consortiums of the blessed in Renaissance paintings, each saint cherishing the apparatus of his martyrdom: GAY DENTISTS, BLACK AND WHITE LOVERS, GAYS FROM BAKERSFIELD, LATINA LESBIANS. From the foot of Market Street they marched, east to west, following the mythic American path toward optimism. . . .

Five years later, another parade. Politicians waved from white convertibles. "Dykes on Bikes" revved up, thumbs-upped. But now banners bore the acronyms of death. AIDS. ARC. Drums were muffled as passing, plum-spotted young men slid by on motorized cable cars.[61]

The way this passage is constructed telegraphs the significance of the events it describes. In a clear invocation of the argument around which Rodriguez structures the collection, the "American" character of San Francisco's gay community—"following the mythic American path toward optimism"—is juxtaposed with the obvious pessimism inspired by the AIDS epidemic. Similarly, Rodriguez invokes *Days of Obligation*'s coded chronology: despite AIDS, despite those acronyms of death on the banners in the Gay Freedom Day Parade, an old man's pessimism does not necessarily trump a young man's optimism, he argues. Some things only a young man can know.[62]

"Late Victorians" braids together reflections on Rodriguez's life as a gay man in San Francisco's Castro district and on the death of his dear friend César, who dies of AIDS in the Castro. Sexuality seemed not to be a topic of interest in *Hunger of Memory*, except for the chapter in which Rodriguez addresses the sexual overtones of his Catholicism. "Late Victorians" serves as a coming-out story for Rodriguez, however; a careful reading of it brings gayness to the surface in his earlier book as well.[63] When Rodriguez writes in *Days of Obligation* that "to grow up homosexual is to live with secrets and within secrets," "Mr. Secrets," the concluding essay in *Hunger of Memory*, comes to mind, and the silence he examines there between himself and his family takes on new meaning.[64]

Because *Days of Obligation* acknowledges Rodriguez's Mexican heritage as *Hunger of Memory* does not, a convergence between Rodriguez's homosexuality and his ethnicity also becomes apparent in "Late Victorians." In a passage comparing and contrasting "barren" gays and materialistic yuppies, Rodriguez clearly associates being Latin with gayness; the Yuppies, he argues, have learned from the gays a new lifestyle, one marked by "the Mediterranean, the Latin, the Catholic, the Castro, the gay."[65] Neither is it entirely a coincidence that César, the man to whom Rodriguez became deeply attached, was Latino.[66]

This chain of qualifiers notwithstanding, connections between Rodriguez's gayness and his Catholicism are initially less obvious than those between his gayness and his Latino heritage. At the beginning of "Late Victorians," Rodriguez leaves the Latin Mass at St. Patrick's to follow the Gay Freedom Day Parade. Later, when he emerges from the solitude of his Victorian house to run errands in the Castro, he is recalled "by the prickly silhouette of St. Dominic's" but turns instead into the Pacific Heights Health Club.[67] San Francisco's gay community is, in many ways, a more credible terminus for Rodriguez's religious journey than the Puritanism he sometimes claims; the Castro, after all, is in itself an instance of the characteristically American, religio-utopian community.[68]

Yet once again it would be a mistake to compartmentalize these two dimensions of Rodriguez's life. I have already displayed the nexus between Rodriguez's ethnicity and the church that served as the only unifier of public and private in his early years.[69] Now a linkage between Rodriguez's Catholicism and his homosexuality becomes apparent. "Private lives were becoming public," he writes, referring both to the San Francisco gay community of the early 1980s and to the binary that undergirds *Hunger of Memory*. And "single lives" were being blocked into "a processional mass, not unlike the consortiums of the blessed in Renaissance paintings."[70] The communion of saints, at ever-greater risk in Rodriguez's mind since the Second Vatican Council, has suddenly been reconfigured, and it is marching through the city of St. Francis.

"THE LATIN, THE CATHOLIC, THE CASTRO, THE GAY"

For a while, however, the reader is less than certain about this restoration of the community of the Blessed. Upon first appearance, César, Rodriguez's friend, could serve as nothing more than one term in Rodriguez's repeated rhetorical polarization of optimistic Protestant individualism and pessimistic Catholic communalism. For César, as for many optimistic younger gay men who flock to the city, San Francisco was utopia: "Here César saw revolution, and he embraced it."[71] Rodriguez, on the other hand, assumes his old man's persona. Though he responds to spring, he has learned from his Mexican father and from his Irish nuns "to count on winter." After their friendship begins, he and César—"dear César," he calls him—move from restaurant to restaurant debating, Rodriguez on the side of limits, César defending freedoms.[72]

Victorian houses, in particular, figure Rodriguez's Catholic belief in limits and tragedy; once multigenerational loci of fecundity, they are now the habitats of gay men who decorate rather than populate them. Provoked by society's condemnation of the "sin against nature," the homosexual pursues redemption outside nature, "in artifice, in plumage, in lampshades, sonnets, musical comedy, couture, syntax, religious ceremony, opera, lacquer, irony."[73] Rodriguez recalls a straight friend's pity for the barren unrealness of "the poor darlings."[74] Even more than the feminist movement, he suggests, the gay male community has served as the paradigm for young urban professionals who reject childrearing and the work ethic in favor of comfort and glamour. Finally, Rodriguez seems to proffer that most repellent of arguments, the decimation of the Castro by AIDS as a punishment for sin. "As I regard this mirror, I imagine St. Augustine's meditation slowly hardening into syllogism, passing down through centuries to confound us: evil is the absence of good. . . . We have become accustomed to figures disappearing from our landscape. Does this not lead us to interrogate the landscape?"

It is difficult not to understand Rodriguez to be stereotyping gay men here, in a rejection of the gay community as brutal as his earlier attacks on unassimilated Chicanos. Yet Rodriguez clearly includes himself in this portrayal. Much of his own apartment in a late-Victorian house in the Castro is upended or reversed. The bedroom, with its convertible sleeper, is the public space where he receives visitors, while the library, open to the public in other settings, is the private space where he alone writes. Functionless twin green shutters hang on the inside of the bedroom, "turning (it) inside out."[75] At the top of his stairwell there hangs the vestige of the hinge from a gate that once must have kept infants from falling downstairs. Even Rodriguez's encounter with St. Augustine is as much a recording of his own self-scrutiny, the self-blame that some gay men entertained during the 1980s, as an indictment.

The invocation of Augustine is part of a citational chain put into play by Rodriguez in the opening paragraph of "Late Victorians"; there, Augustine's "cope of dust" figures human mortality, reiterating the Catholic binary of Rodriguez's tragedy/comedy argument. But something peculiar is going on with these signifiers, for in *Hunger of Memory*, Augustine figures precisely the opposite trajectory, weighing in as a "Protestant . . . more than a Catholic [church] father."[76] But now, San Francisco and its once Protestant gay community, by virtue of their playfulness, are "more Catholic than Protestant in [their] eschatological intuitions."[77] Further, gay-imitating Yuppies have rejected the North European work ethic in favor of "The Mediterranean, the Latin, the Catholic, the Castro, the Gay."[78] Rodriguez's apparently essentialized binaries are growing increasingly relational and contingent.

THE GOLD CRUCIFIX

The transgression of the binary here, and Rodriguez's inability from the outset to fully separate the terms of the binary, is an effect in his writing of the body and its concomitant sexuality. In one of the seemingly innumerable strands Rodriguez weaves throughout "Late Victorians," immediately following the Gay Freedom parade passage, a body—a suicide who has jumped from the Golden Gate Bridge—literally falls in front of Rodriguez out of the sky. Rodriguez could, of course, assimilate this jumper into the Catholic/tragedy pole of his argument, but he does not. Instead, he observes that San Francisco "toys with the tragic conclusion"; it supports tragedy and comedy as well.[79]

The conundrum of the irreducible body was already in evidence when Rodriguez's self-construal was at its most Protestant. In *Hunger of Memory*, the crucifix, which, by hanging over his bed and in his classroom, united his public and private lives, was nonetheless no unambiguous signifier. Rodriguez recalls the irony of hearing in eighth grade about the sins of the flesh:

> The priest told us how dangerous it was to look at our naked bodies, even while taking a bath—and I noticed that he made the remark directly under a near-naked figure of Christ on the cross.

The Church, in fact, excited more sexual wonderment than it repressed. I regarded with awe the "wedding ring" on a nun's finger, her black "wedding veil"—symbols of marriage to God. I would study pictures of martyrs—white-robed virgins fallen in death and the young, almost smiling, St. Sebastian, transfigured in pain. At Easter high mass I was dizzied by the mucous perfume of white flowers at the celebration of rebirth. At such moments, the Church touched alive some very private sexual excitement; it pronounced my sexuality important.[80]

This sense of the erotic was, in part, what made nineteenth-century American Protestants suspicious of Catholicism.[81] But for Rodriguez, even as he sees himself becoming more and more like a Protestant in the wake of the Second Vatican Council, there is still something about the sense of himself inscribed by erotic Catholic devotionalism that he will not—or cannot—abandon: "My upbringing has shaped in me certain attitudes which have not worn thin over the years. I am, for example, a materialist because I was brought up to believe in the central mystery of the Church—the redemptive Incarnation. (I carried the gold crucifix in church ceremonies far too often to share the distrust of the material still prevalent in modern Puritan America.)"[82]

Rodriguez subsequently subordinates the significance of this "attitude" to his belief in the "central tenets" of the faith, the Creed, but "Late Victorians" suggests that the gold crucifix, the irreducible body, may, in fact, have been a more central "tenet" than the younger Rodriguez was prepared to recognize. In particular, the death of César calls into question Rodriguez's ambivalent attachment to the binaries of the pre–Vatican II church. It likewise pushes him, in the last decade of the twentieth century, toward a Catholicism less monolithic and wider and more empathic than the one that, for many years, he was convinced had betrayed him.

THE MYSTICAL BODY OF CÉSAR

César was a privileged Latin American who arrived in the Castro, by way of Europe, in middle age. César's lifestyle—his hedonism, his love of the bathhouses, his death from AIDS—is Rodriguez's analogue for the trajectory of the childless Victorian house, the barrenness of the gay lifestyle. César had an "excellent mind," but he was "otherwise ruled by pulp . . . loved everything that ripened in time . . . found paradise at the baths,"[83] and had "no religion beyond aesthetic bravery."[84] He was emblematic of "men who pursued an earthly paradise," whose company Rodriguez had come to find "charming" despite his own wintry, pessimistic inclinations.[85]

Yet Rodriguez calls into question the unambiguous identification of César with secularism and American optimism by associating him with a series of religious and/or Catholic signifiers. Rodriguez may seem to be doing nothing more than exercising his usual irony shading into sarcasm when he calls César's desire to add the Castro to the gates of Jerusalem a "conceit"[86] or when he observes that "César could fashion liturgy from an artichoke."[87] But there is an undeniable change in tone when he describes César's discovery of "paradise" at the baths, "floating from body to body, open arms yielding to open arms in an angelic round." For an imagination as deeply Catholic as Rodriguez's, the absence of rejection, the welcome César speaks of as the men move from one cubicle to another around the bathhouse calls to mind nothing so much as a communion service. Likewise, César's best, ecstatic evening at the baths, in a pool with an antiques dealer "bawling out Nöel Coward songs," is wryly reminiscent of a baptism.

In a conversation with César about his experience at the baths, Rodriguez initially resists the transcendence of these associations. "But each went home alone?" he half asks, half rebuts. When César responds in words of undeniable religious resonance, he not only clarifies the nature of his experience at the baths but also implicitly calls into question Rodriguez's fantasy of familial and ecclesial fusion: "Each satisfied, dear, César corrected. And all the way home San Francisco seemed to him balanced and merciful. He felt weightlessness of being, the pavement under his step as light as air."[88] In this journey home from the baths, César is as weightless as Jesus transfigured on Mt. Tabor, or ascending, mysteriously, into heaven.

The overlapping of gay and straight, transcendent and mortal, inscribed in César's bathhouse transfiguration is sustained in the subsequent narrative of his death and those of innumerable other AIDS victims. It is, further, embodied there in another figuration of César as Christ, but, in this case, a crucified Christ, a Christ no longer in the air but in extremity. "It was not," Rodriguez tells us, "as in some Victorian novel . . . a matter of custards in covered dishes, steaming possets, *Try a little of this my dear.*" Nor was it as in some stereotypical gay lifestyle, with "issues of *Architectural Digest* strewn about the bed." No, Rodriguez assures us, "César experienced agony."[89]

One could quibble about this reading. Rodriguez himself might do so, since he moves rather quickly to characterize César, at his own funeral, as having had no religion, "improperly buried . . . unconvincingly resurrected in the conditional." However, the effect of César's death and of the deaths of other gay men in San Francisco is more compelling than are César's irregular religious credentials. In the face of death, in the face of the AIDS crisis, as with the death of Jesus, "a community was gathering over the city."[90] Rodriguez testifies about it in a manner not unlike that of a Protestant evangelical: "I have seen people caressing it, staring Death down. I have seen people wipe its tears, wipe its ass; I have seen people kiss Death on his lips, where once there were lips. . . . They walked Death's dog. They washed his dishes. They bought his groceries. They massaged his poor back. They changed his bandages. They emptied his bedpan."[91]

Rodriguez then goes beyond testifying. He signals the significance of the "saints of this city," as he calls them,[92] by ending "Late Victorians" as it began, with a service in one of the Catholic churches of San Francisco. Most Holy Redeemer functions for him here as the second of a pair of parentheses, as St. Patrick's was the first. But in this second church, Rodriguez does not participate in the Latin Mass, as he did at St. Patrick's. Rather, he participates in a ceremony in which a diverse group of volunteers —men and women, young, middle aged and old, straight and gay—come forward to be recognized for their service in an AIDS support group.

Rodriguez plays down the location of this event. "It might have been any of the churches or community centers in the Castro district, but it happened at Most Holy Redeemer." And we almost believe him, until his observation swells into a lament: "at a time in the history of the world when the Roman Catholic Church pronounced the homosexual a sinner." Ever the master of indirection, Rodriguez does not announce that the Catholicism that has bitterly disappointed him by failing to hold together his fragmented early self is in the process of being reconfigured. The intensity of his lament reveals it nonetheless.

Another signal of this reconfiguration is Rodriguez's portrayal of a participant in the recognition ceremony, a seventy-year-old gay man with iodine hair. Critics may accuse Rodriguez—probably have already accused him—of unkindness here. There is "something of the old dear about him," he writes, "wizened butterfly, powdered old pouf." Yet Rodriguez's identification with this old gay man, even if it is a negative one, is uncharacteristically revealing, devoid of irony or metaphor: "Certainly he is what I fear becoming." After which he clothes him in metaphors that can hardly be misunderstood: "And then he rises, this old monkey, with the most beatific dignity, to take his place in the company of the Blessed."[93] This, too, is a Christ figure—"and then he rises." Although Rodriguez is more indirect here than in his rage over bilingual masses, he is deeply present in both passages.

The words of reconfiguration, of transubstantiation, of promise that Rodriguez finally utters echo eerily the pivotal discourse of "it" examined in Mary Gordon's characterizations of the church in chapter 3.[94] The "it" that happened at Most Holy Redeemer clearly refers to the ceremony of recognition for AIDS volunteers, but now, other referents are emerging:

> So this is it—this, what looks like a Christmas party in an insurance office, and not as in Renaissance paintings, and not as we had always thought, not some flower-strewn, some sequined call of grease painted heroes gesturing to the stalls. A woman with a plastic candy cane pinned to her lapel. A Castro clone with a red bandanna exploding from his hip. A perfume counter lady with a Hermès scarf mantled upon her shoulder. A black man in a checkered sports coat. The pink-haired punkess with a jewel in her nose. Here, too, is the gay couple in middle age; interchangeable plaid shirts and corduroy pants. Blood and shit and Mr. Happy Face. These know the weight of bodies.[95]

Finally, Rodriguez has left behind, at least for the time being, the binarized trajectories that have defended him from loss for much of his life. "It" is not as in a Renaissance painting, that figure of the ornate, highly cultured, Tridentine Catholicism Rodriguez has clung to, nor in the flower-strewn, sequined caricature that protects him from full identification with the gay community, his use of "we" here notwithstanding. "It" may even look like that singularly secular and commercialized occurrence, a Christmas party in an insurance agency. "It" is none of these, however, but rather a ragtag communion of saints in clown gear—candy canes, red bandannas, and pink hair. For Rodriguez, inveterate denouncer of ecclesial informality and vernacularism, this is quite a realization.

Any doubts that this circuslike *ekklesia* figures a new vision of Catholicism for Rodriguez are soon laid to rest. For in the last sentence of the paragraph, Rodriguez, whose religious identity was formed by carrying the body of Jesus on a ceremonial cross at Catholic services, now recognizes the same marking on the AIDS Support Group volunteers. "These know the weight of bodies," he acknowledges. It may even have occurred to him, since those bodies have been smeared with blood and shit, that they are more substantial than the gold crucifix he himself once bore.

GAYNESS WITHIN THE PENUMBRA OF THE CROSS

"Late Victorians" is a wonderful piece of writing. In the face of the Catholic Church's increasing organization of itself around sexual prohibition and gender exclusion, the essay reconfigures the body of the crucified Christ as one of the most controversial forms of the sexual abject and the church as the community gathered to support AIDS victims in San Francisco.

These splendid accomplishments notwithstanding, "Late Victorians" does have a few little problems. Near the end, in conjunction with his paean to the company of the blessed, Rodriguez inserts some material that, I must admit, gives me pause. Men who had sought to order their lives around aesthetics have been "recalled to nature," he tells us. With AIDS, the gay community of San Francisco, once possessed of the freedom César had celebrated, now "consented to necessity—to all that the proud world had for so long held up to them, withheld from them, as 'real humanity.'"[96]

It may be that Rodriguez's allusion to the humanizing effects of AIDS on the gay community, and even his representation of the AIDS support group as the "company of the Blessed," are instances of the Catholic tendency to find redemption in massive evil.[97] A similar reference earlier to the homosexual finding "his redemption outside nature" seems to be leavened by the characteristic Rodriguez irony, but it is difficult to be certain.

There can be no doubt, however, that Rodriguez realizes something is not right with him. In the last line of "Late Victorians," he writes, "These [the bearers of bodies] learned to love what is corruptible, while I, barren skeptic, reader of St. Augustine, curator of the earthly paradise . . . I shift my tailbone upon the cold, hard pew."[98] His confession recalls an encounter just before César's death when César predicted that everyone else he knew might contract AIDS and die, but Rodriguez would be "spared"; he was "too circumspect." César's comment was meant to sound ironic, but Rodriguez knows better. His survival implies that he had held out for the "Catholic" side of the argument: "that the garden of earthly delights was, after all, only wallpaper." But Rodriguez concludes that his "unwillingness to embrace life" was a greater sin than any committed by his friends who were dying of AIDS.[99] This admission inevitably calls to mind other defensive postures— other refusals to mourn—in evidence throughout Rodriguez's work.

CONCLUSION: BROWN CATHOLICISM

With the 2002 publication of his third collection of essays, *Brown: The Last Discovery of America*, however, Rodriguez resolves whatever doubts "Late Victorians" may instill in his readers. Already in the 1990s Rodriguez had begun to oppose publicly the church's mistaken teaching on homosexuality. In an interview with Paul Crowley, S.J., published in 1995 in the Jesuit weekly *America*, Rodriguez calls the church's understanding of sexuality "primitive." When asked to tell of someone who is a moral example for him, he speaks of a retired Navy officer who is gay, drinks too much, ushers at his parish, takes communion to sick people, and is cheerful "at a time of despair in the rectory."[100] Rodriguez challenges the pope to witness for himself the moral seriousness of the gays and lesbians at Most Holy Redeemer in the Castro and predicts that the Vatican will one day apologize to gay people for its centuries of moral cowardice. To use the language of Julia Kristeva and Judith Butler, Rodriguez emphatically resists here the institutional church's efforts to expel the sexual abject from the Catholic cultural domain.

In *Brown*, however, Rodriguez moves from bridging particular binaries to proposing an entirely new interpretive frame by means of which to view contemporary culture in both its secular and ecclesial manifestations. At first blush, *Brown* appears to be concerned with the race of the Latino and other immigrant populations currently transforming the face of America. But if Rodriguez writes about race, he does so to undermine the essentialized notions of it that have long rung false to him. He chooses the color brown as the trope around which to construct his assault on racial and other essentialisms. "Brown, not in the sense of pigment, necessarily, but brown because mixed, confused, lumped, impure, unpasteurized, as motives are mixed, and the fluids of generation are mixed and emotions are unclear, and the tally of human progress and failure in every generation is mixed, and unaccounted for, missing in plain sight."

In each of the nine essays in *Brown*, Rodriguez brings together narrative, figuration, humor, sarcasm, recollection, reference, and analysis to produce a rhetorical form of this very idea, brownness.[101] In "The Third Man," for example, he begins by describing himself on a stage between a black speaker and a white speaker so as to interrogate the incommensurable categories that seem to separate them: race (blackness), culture (Hispanicity), and invisibility (whiteness). In the midst of this multifaceted riff, Rodriguez cuts to the problem of his friend Darrel's absolute certainty that he is black. As he does so, Rodriguez recalls seeing a certain blackbird. "Speaking of warblers," he writes,

> I saw a blackbird the other day—Avian American—he was sitting in the sun. Little patch of lawn. In this particular sun—or was it just the Fabergé of the moment—the blackbird appeared green, green as ink, and with gold tracery on the nib of his folded wing; the green of the gayest recesses of the swooniest forest of Fragonard.
> *Blackbirds are green*
> *Violets blue . . . So?*[102]

This passage is worth reading just for the hilariously satiric expression "Avian American," but the green blackbird drives home Rodriguez's objection to his friend's refusal to acknowledge mixture, complexity, within his racial identity. Darrel's blackness, we come to see, is as inviolate as a blackbird that is as "green as ink," as green as violets are blue.

Because of Rodriguez's use of an ornate literary style to represent the emerging complex character of American culture, *Brown* will be less accessible to some readers than its more linear predecessors. Rodriguez's style may also obscure the ways in which *Brown* confirms the vision of Catholicism introduced in "Late Victorians." In fact, it could appear that in *Brown* Catholicism is hardly a focus of attention at all, so preoccupied does Rodriguez seem to be with "the straight line, unstaunchable—the line separating black from white."[103] But in *Brown* the division between black and white is only one of a vast array of subjects that "forms at the border of contradiction,"[104] among which, also, is Rodriguez's beloved church. The reader who fails to recognize the constitutive place of Catholicism in Rodriguez's argument also forgets the critical role a sense of innocence plays in postconciliar Catholicism's self-defense against the losses of the modern period. The impurity that preoccupies Rodriguez spells the end of that innocence, and not only at the symbolic level. For within Rodriguez's turn to brown is the erotic, the miscegenation that creates possibilities that have never existed before.[105] Even more explicitly than in "Late Victorians," noninnocent—brown—sexuality complicates Rodriguez's vision of the church.

Although representations of Catholicism surface intermittently throughout *Brown*, Rodriguez addresses the church most explicitly in the final essay of the volume. From the outset, "Peter's Avocado" signals Rodriguez's religious preoccupations: its epigraph is drawn from Mark's Gospel: "Can't you see that nothing that goes into someone from outside can make that person unclean, because it goes not into the heart but into the stomach and passes into the sewer?"[106] Ultimately, the essay demonstrates that the church is no more exempt from the hermeneutic of brownness than any of the other linchpins of twenty-first-century culture. Its ostensibly secular subject, a request put to Rodriguez's friend to purchase an organic avocado for the friend's son, Peter, affords Rodriguez another opportunity to reflect on his overriding theme, impurity. A supposedly pure avocado becomes the platform from which to trace a long arc of impurities that emerge from multiple seemingly untainted polarities. Central among these is the whiteness of the ash-blond wife of Rodriguez's Hindu cousin; such purity, paradoxically, seemed to Rodriguez to pollute the brownness that others had considered polluted from the get-go. This particular impurity suggests others, such that Rodriguez is soon calling to mind confessing his sins to his "beloved" Father Edmund O'Neill in the parish church of his school years, among them, throwing a rock at Billy Walker "because I loved him."[107]

But 1950s Sacramento was no place for same-sex attraction; half a century later, Father O'Neill still disapproves of Rodriguez's lifestyle. And so the younger Rodriguez was embarrassed by his same-sex attraction as well as by his racial/cultural otherness; growing up, he "lived [his] life in fragments . . . [his] eyes looking one way, [his] soul another."[108] Even Rodriguez's interest in literature, which generated the very skills with which he now fashions his ornate "brown" argument, is a byproduct of this fragmented youth.

The ambivalence generated by a 1950s Catholic upbringing did not drive Rodriguez out of the church, however. When questioned today about his oxymoronic self-identification, "gay Catholic," Rodriguez assures the inquirer that, at least initially, being Catholic was no more a choice than being gay. Catholicism "was the air," he testifies; "it was the light." And so there arose "some little tug of war, some tension" within him, on which Rodriguez has come to depend. This tension is what Rodriguez means by brown, he tells us, and "by brown I mean love."[109]

Thereafter, "Peter's Avocado" is a deeply moving counterpoint of brownness, homosexuality, and Catholicism. The mixing of all the peoples of the earth, for Rodriguez, is not synonymous with "the poor shall inherit the earth," but it's close. The pregnant teenager from an earlier essay becomes for one moment the Virgin in a painting of the Annunciation. And Peter, having finally obtained his organic avocado, dreams of being able to reconcile irreconcilable substances. But Rodriguez himself awakens before the sun rises, in bed beside the lover he has never before acknowledged in print, and ponders his "brown paradox":

> The church that taught me to understand love, the church that taught me well to believe love breathes—also tells me that it is not love I feel, at four in the morning, in the dark, even before the birds cry.
> *Of every hue and caste am I.*

What I find most moving in this deeply moving essay, the final chapter in the final volume of Rodriguez's trilogy of exquisitely crafted autobiographical essays, is that it is precisely the crucifix that enables Rodriguez to sustain this tension, this "brown paradox." Even in the early years of his fragmentation, Rodriguez tells us, the crucifix was superimposed upon his every thought. But in more recent days, marked though they sometimes are by rage over his church's primitive sexual orthodoxies, Rodriguez does "not wish to live beyond a crucifix." Although the church was at first a given in his life, like the air, he later turned to it consciously because it was "established for losers, for a kingdom not of this world, a kingdom of fools."[110] Because of the understanding of loss inscribed in the crucifix, Rodriguez is able to sustain the apparent contradiction between his gayness and his Catholicism, as well as between his Hispanic, Indian, and Anglo inheritances. No matter what "those old men sitting in a row through centuries" may say, this crucifix does not represent guilt to Rodriguez, but love.[111] And so he continues.

In recent years, the Vatican has issued increasingly shrill prohibitions regarding sexuality and gender, especially homosexuality. While certain prohibited acts seemed once to be the crux of the matter, by the early twenty-first century, the institutional church finds sexual identities themselves an obstacle to the Christian life, at least if its rejection of even celibate gay priests is any indicator.[112] For the most part, these rejections emerge from a smooth, anything-but-brown discourse of "life" and the "natural law."[113] All of this supports Gene Burns's hypothesis that since Vatican II sexual ideology has come to bear greater weight in institutional Catholicism than the commonly held teachings of the Christian faith. In light of these developments, I find the display of the gay body by as widely recognized a Catholic as Richard Rodriguez and his explicit linkage of gay and other brown communities with the communion of saints and the body of Christ on the cross a moving and significant intervention in American Catholic discourse at the turn of the twenty-first century.

Conclusion

Blessed are those who mourn, for they shall be comforted.

—MATTHEW 5:4

$\mathcal{A}$lthough *Tracing the Sign of the Cross* opens with the celebration of the Roman Catholic Easter Vigil in 2003, my motivations for writing it go much farther back. They are linked in my mind with an almost paradigmatic exchange between my parents and me concerning our life in a small stucco house constructed just after World War II in a working-class suburb of Philadelphia. Like most children, I was given to occasional expressions of disappointment, even rage. My parents found these emotions difficult to comprehend. But we are so lucky, they would exclaim. We own our own house. Someday you'll be going to college.

And indeed, we were lucky, by very many standards, and certainly in contrast to the disease, deprivation, and early death that had assaulted their own families of origin. So I threw myself into the activities that composed a 1950s white working-class East Coast American Catholic childhood: street games, Girl Scouts, summer camp, piano lessons, the Mickey Mouse Club, and for me, most of all, our parish church and school. I was a good girl. I went to church a lot. By the sixth grade, I was first in my class. I was, it seemed, on the road to many of the great things my parents had in mind for me.

But I now suspect that my early and ongoing attachment to the Catholic faith was also an unconscious protest against this required optimism. For in the 1950s, before Vatican II, no matter how much neo-Thomism buttressed clear, bifurcated categories—truth/falsehood, clergy/lay, pure/impure— there was, still and always, the crucifix. At daily Mass. At Benediction. Hanging in every classroom. And every Friday afternoon throughout Lent, at the Stations of the Cross, carried from station to station by an acolyte and conveyed in the haunting melody of the Stabat Mater:

At the cross her station keeping
Stood the mournful Mother weeping
Close to Jesus to the last.

Adolescence being what adolescence is, with high school, it seems, I might have left this world behind, especially considering the years in question—1961 to 1965. And indeed, I look back on my time in high school as an experience of genuine liberation. I made splendid friends; I was challenged intellectually as I had never been before; and the Sisters of Notre Dame de Namur, who educated me, facilitated my first extended encounters with art and literature, especially poetry, and this made an enormous difference in my life.

In many ways, the keystone of all this for me was the Second Vatican Council (1962–1965) and the reforms it set in motion: no matter how much I loved the church, the tension between the nearly rote, industrial-strength Catholicism of my childhood and the modernization and upward mobility inscribed in the rest of my life was palpable. I thus relished the church's entrance into the "modern world." I rejoiced especially in the post–Vatican II liturgy, with its haunting, biblically based music. New forms of liturgical celebration expressed physically a Catholic openness to human wholeness and possibility that comported well with my family's expectations of a better life.

To this day, I recall these years with great satisfaction, but even as I do so, I have to admit that there is something about it all that does not compute. In many respects, I experienced the Second Vatican Council and the changes it set in motion as the most significant and inspiring events of my young adulthood, that is, of the years between 1960 and 1970. I experienced them this way even as the world around me was turning upside down — the civil rights movement, burgeoning opposition to the Vietnam War, the early stages of the women's liberation movement, and beneath them all, like the skull beneath the skin, the assassinations of John and Robert Kennedy and Martin Luther King Jr. This odd perspective says a good deal about my own psyche, of course, but it also suggests how tenaciously at least some of us in those days clung to the dream of a modern, idealized way of life, even as it disintegrated around us. "We Catholics," a Philadelphia friend once said, "were making our way into the modern world just as everyone else was exiting it."[1]

For some American Catholics, defenses against disintegration began to wobble in 1968 when Pope Paul VI, against wide expectations, confirmed the church's traditional condemnation of artificial contraception, presciently laying out the battle lines of the future. Some congregations of American Catholic Sisters had by then likewise slammed up against the limits of church renewal, as the bishops to whom they reported clamped down on them for implementing the very modernization Vatican II seemed to call for.[2] During this same period, I wasn't finding the long-awaited trip to college all that wonderful, though in classic American fashion, I understood my difficulties to be almost entirely personal, things I should try harder to overcome. Threatening this compartmentalization was the departure from religious life of literally thousands of Catholic sisters, some of whom had exerted considerable influence on my life. And then the postwar economic boom that had fueled the optimism and upward mobility of my own and many other American Catholic families began to wind down.

RECONSOLIDATION

By the early 1970s, a good number of American Catholics could hardly have avoided beginning to mourn these many losses. I suspect this was particularly the case for the thousands of priests and nuns who chose, quite bravely in some instances, to make new lives for themselves on or beyond the boundaries of the church.[3] A significant number of us, however, soldiered on. Some parishes established effective parish councils, though always subject to the pastor's veto. National groups such as Call to Action were formed to extend the council's vision of human dignity and liberation; some of them continue to this day. Even the successful student strike at Catholic University to protest the clearly retaliatory firing of the priest-theologian Charles Curran for resistance to the birth-control encyclical, *Humanae Vitae*, inspired hope that Vatican authoritarianism could be resisted.

My own way of preserving the dream of a liberal Catholicism in these years was to become increasingly taken up with the women's movement in the church. I was first introduced to religious feminism at Grailville, the U.S. center of the international laywomen's movement, the Grail. Beginning in the 1940s, the Grail had been active in liturgical and catechetical renewal and the formation of women leaders in the American church; then, in the 1970s, Grailville became a launching pad for feminist theology and spirituality. Many leading second-wave feminist theologians and ethicists, including Mary Daly, Rosemary Radford Ruether, Elisabeth Schüssler Fiorenza, Dorothee Soelle, Beverly Harrison, Judith Plaskow, Carol Christ, Phyllis Trible, and Katie Geneva Cannon, lectured and taught at Grailville during those years, and many of the next generation of women theologians and ethicists were introduced to the women's movement in church and synagogue at Grail programs.[4] As a member of the Grailville community from 1975 to 1979, I was deeply involved in these efforts, focusing especially on the development of Christian feminist worship forms, an extension of my earlier investment in the Vatican II liturgical renewal.[5] In those years, especially in the 1970s but also in the 1980s, I was strongly convinced of the significance, even the revelatory value, of feminist theology and the changes inscribed in it. I read feminist theology and spirituality, gave talks about them, led continuing-education programs on them, and wrote articles, reviews, and books about them.[6] Also during this period, I attended the first conference on the ordination of women in the Catholic Church, held in Detroit in 1975. My commitment to the ordination of Catholic women, inspired by this conference, would continue into the new millennium, when I served as a member of the board and ultimately as president of the national Women's Ordination Conference. I am still involved in that movement, if writing critical articles about it counts as involvement.[7]

In the beginning, I experienced feminist theology and activism as my part in the great revolution underway in church and society. And indeed, the growing inclusion of (some) women in business, government, church, and academy launched in those years comprises a significant change in American society, as evidenced, for example, by the accessions of Condoleezza Rice, an African American woman, to the office of U.S. Secretary of State, and Nancy Pelosi, a postimmigrant American Catholic woman, to the speakership of the U.S. House of Representatives. Yet today, thirty years later, I am struck by the extent to which the feminist theology and spirituality that I perceived as revolutionary preserved, at least in part, the optimistic liberal vision that had shaped my post–World War II American Catholic upbringing and especially my enthusiasm for Vatican II modernization.

Much has been written about the philosophical assumptions that underpin second-wave Christian feminist theology; its belief in an essential, rational, and ideal human being, one that presumably includes females as well as males; and the identification of women's, or feminist, experience with divine revelation and all that this construal excludes.[8] It is worth recalling, however, that the three most influential theologians in that first stage of second-wave Christian feminism, Mary Daly, Elizabeth Schüssler Fiorenza, and Rosemary Radford Ruether, were all Roman Catholics.[9] With regard to the feminist theology of Rosemary Radford Ruether, for example, poststructuralist feminist theologian Rebecca Chopp writes:

> In the horizon of how theology operated and adjudicated its claims, for example, Ruether's "foundational" moves were really no different from those of Karl Rahner. . . . The difference between Ruether and her male, modern counterparts had to do with whose experiences became normative, whose forms of rationality provided the evaluative norms, and what material from the past got selected to form the Great Tradition.[10]

The optimistic liberal Vatican II vision of the "dignity of the human person" was preserved and extended in these formative second-wave Catholic feminist theologies, no matter how radical some of us perceived those theologies to be.

All this notwithstanding, fractures began to emerge in the second-wave feminist edifice fairly early on. Already in the 1970s, African American women began to detail the ways in which they were excluded from second-wave feminist discourse, if not activism.[11] And for Catholic feminists, the publication of *Inter Insignores*, the 1976 papal encyclical rejecting the possibility of the ordination of Catholic women, was surely a sign of things to come. But few of us were ready to accept Vatican denial of our inclusion in the very vision of the human Vatican II had so recently inspired in us. And we were not the only ones. For many American Catholics, conservatives and liberals alike, opposing or supporting Catholic teaching on sexuality and gender was a powerful defense against the decline of a church that was once at the center of our lives.

TRACING THE SIGN OF THE CROSS AS "WORKING THROUGH"

Initial fractures in my own second-wave feminist vision had as much to do with class as with race or papal intransigence. One of the more memorable episodes in the shaking of my feminist foundations occurred in 1984, by which time I was living in New York City. I had joined a newly formed feminist liturgy group. Participants, many of them connected in some way with Union Theological Seminary, were explaining why they had come. The well-dressed woman sitting next to me was there, she told us, because "men write history and women don't." In total violation of the rules—everyone was entitled to express her "experience" without rebuttal—I replied, "well, you can't be thinking of my working-class father when you say that; he hardly spoke in sentences."

Not long after, I began graduate studies in religion, hoping to achieve some insight into an increasingly fissiparous world. And indeed, I came away from my years of study grateful for, but also chastened by, the difficult readings of church and society that I encountered there. But it was no coincidence that that early fracture in my feminist fortifications, at a women's liturgy group across from Union Seminary, sent me back to the very working-class parents whose efforts to defend me from loss had necessarily failed. I invested much of the two decades after that feminist gathering in tracing the fractures in postwar American Catholic optimism, the many efforts to efface them, and their intermittent painful engagement.

Tracing the Sign of the Cross is the outcome of those years of excavation. As I look back, I am particularly struck by the key role the writings of James Carroll played in my research. In many respects, the vision of American Catholicism inscribed in James Carroll's fiction and memoirs is a deeply troubling one. But the fantasized conquests of Carroll's Christic heroes—Michael Maguire, Terry Mullen, Colman Brady—hold at bay the losses of the American Catholic community and not Carroll's losses only.

As a longtime church-reform activist, I identify easily with Carroll's enraged responses, and those of a number of his heroes, to the relentless disappointments of the last thirty years, especially those related to sexuality and the roles of women and gays. Carroll is like a favorite Irish cousin, or somebody we went to school with, and the conflict between his benign liberalism and his determination to defeat the enemy is our conflict too. And the erotic/homosocial struggle between adversaries marks more than Carroll's fiction; it carries over, with little variation, into his popular journalistic jeremiads against the Vatican and the hierarchy.

Initially, Mary Gordon's work seemed to extend the baseline established in the writing of James Carroll. Gordon's early fiction is populated with characters from the same postimmigrant pool of American Catholics that Carroll draws from. And the contradictions that stud Carroll's fiction are not far removed from the conflicts Gordon's early heroines experience.

But Mary Gordon is a more complicated Catholic than Jim Carroll. She is, to begin with, a girl, and a smart girl at that, to which must also be added her ethnic Jewish identity. This means that while Carroll can project his conflicts outward, onto external adversaries, Gordon's conflicts are more internal. By the 1990s, her writings reflect this complexity, with traces of the racial and sexual other marbling her previously bedrock Catholicism. And though her journalism is uneven, reflecting at times a nostalgia that rarely marks her fiction, Gordon does not flinch from ethical complexity when she discusses clergy sex abuse, a subject that often inspires the abandonment of nuance and even mercy.

These differences notwithstanding, it is also true that Gordon and Carroll occupy strikingly similar worlds. Gordon may in fact write one article on clergy sex abuse for every seven that Carroll writes, but they are both still preoccupied with the topic, as are too many of the rest of us post–Vatican II American Catholics.[12] The wars over sexuality and gender roles have been an effective diversion from American Catholic losses since Vatican II precisely because they do such a stellar job of capturing our attention.

But even the most preoccupying of diversions can become wearisome. My own weariness with endless internecine struggle was, in large part, what led me at a certain stage of my work to seek allies working in the field of secular feminist theory. The fact that the potential ally who most appealed to me, Donna J. Haraway, turned out to be yet another product of postimmigrant American Catholicism ought not to overshadow the very real aid her work accorded me. Paolo Smaldone's heterogenous Eucharist and even Maria Meyers's permeable sliver of land bring representations of Catholicism a long way beyond neo-Thomist rigidity, but something about Haraway's genetically altered rodent wearing a crown of thorns—now pictured on the wall of my study next to the bronze crucifix—anneals the Catholic/Christian tradition to our technoscientifically altered world in a totally new way. And I will never again hear an ostensible innocent argument—for "life," or "choice"—without remembering Haraway's portrayals of fetuses embedded in multiple diverse communities of practice and especially those postborn fetuses of the Brazilian Nordeste drowning in their own diarrhea.

Beyond these specific interventions, engagement with Donna Haraway's writing has functioned as a kind of circuit breaker in my work, making it possible to conceive my overall project in a new way, by positioning my reading of Richard Rodriguez at the end. I have to confess that at an earlier point, I found it difficult to imagine Richard Rodriguez's construal of the church as an end point to my investigation of mourning and the inability to mourn in post–Vatican II American Catholicism. In those days, the liberal/conservative binary held a good deal more meaning for me than it does now, and Rodriguez's austere Augustinian Catholicism and his opposition to bilingualism, among other things, led me to consign him to the latter part of the binary.

But since the publication of *Brown* in 2002, the liberal/conservative binary as well as a number of others simply no longer apply to Rodriguez's work. By this I do not mean to suggest that with *Brown* Rodriguez has created a transcendent category within which all differences happily disappear. The church's "primitive" teaching on sexuality is as much a source of grief for Rodriguez in *Brown* as it was in *Days of Obligation*. And, like Carroll and Gordon, Rodriguez has clear opinions about the clergy sex-abuse crisis. But he seems not to feel the need that so many liberal, white, middle-class American Catholics seem to feel to subsume the entire contemporary church into those tragic events, despite the fact that the church's response to the crisis has had especially destructive implications for gay Catholics. Instead, Rodriguez has put considerable energy in recent years into addressing the plight of immigrants in the United States, something that his apparent commitment to immigrant assimilation in *Hunger of Memory* should have made unlikely.

That this concern for immigrants is part and parcel of Rodriguez's identity as an American Catholic becomes clear in the title of an interview with him conducted by Sandip Roy of the Pacific New Service in 2006: "In Immigration Fight, Catholic Church Finds Its Moral Voice."[13] For many, the clergy sex-abuse crisis finally proved that the institutional church is as evil—as corrosive, xenophobic, absolutist, and sorry—as they long suspected it to be. For Rodriguez, however, in the struggle for justice for immigrants in the United States, the Catholic Church, "with this long tradition of honoring poverty, of seeing poverty as this blessed state . . . has found its voice."

The attention Rodriguez has come to pay to the church's role in the immigration debate is a good deal more than a move to a new journalistic focus. Rather, Rodriguez understands the church's renewed concern for immigrants to be an expression of repentance on the bishops' part for their failure to protect another helpless segment of their community.[14] This introduction of the possibility of repentance and forgiveness into the clergy sex-abuse controversy resonates palpably with Rodriguez's determination in *Brown* to maintain the crucifix at the center of the Catholic faith. This is the same crucifix that helped earlier generations of immigrant Catholics find meaning in their suffering and deprivation. That Rodriguez, a member of a sexual minority much vilified by the official church, is able to understand the bishops' actions as an expression of repentance constitutes a powerful instance, in my estimation, of the "working through" of loss that communal healing demands. What better place to arrive, at the end of my interrogation of the dashed hopes and unmourned losses of postimmigrant American Catholics, than this vision of a renewed church welcoming outsiders of all nationalities, ethnicities, and even—dare we dream it?—sexual persuasions.

In the introduction to this volume, I suggested the hope that art, literature, and religion itself might function as transferential regions within which to engage and work through the pain of loss. After struggling for years to interpret representations of sexuality, mourning, and resistance to mourning in the writings of four gifted members of my own postwar generation of American Catholics, I am persuaded that this hope is not without foundation. Rodriguez, Gordon, Haraway, and even somewhat Carroll are not alone in having worked through certain painful losses to such an extent that they find themselves in a new place. As I carried out this project, I too saw my understanding of the church and my place in it change. For a number of

American Catholics, the clergy sex-abuse crisis—or the election of Joseph Ratzinger, the church's doctrinal watchdog, as the new pope—was the final, unforgivable blow. A friend who pastors an American Baptist congregation in Seattle says that the majority of his new members are former Catholics. These events confirmed my sense of myself as a Catholic, however. Conservative Catholics have long advocated cutting the church back to the faithful few. Some believe the new pope chose the name Benedict in memory of the monastic founder who presided over a similar retraction, in his case, of Roman civilization. But my engagement with the deeply moving texts discussed in this volume have confirmed the deep meaning, for me, of being a Roman Catholic.

Beyond the decision to remain a Catholic, I have also decided to stop fighting the internecine Catholic battles in which I have participated for much of my adult life. In a certain sense, in the short run at least, my fellow activists and I have lost. We have no leverage in the governance structure of the Catholic Church. Increasing numbers of Catholic women are choosing to be ordained by an organization that prepares women for ordination, Roman Catholic Womenpriests, launched by the ordination of a group of European Catholic women on a boat on the Danube in 2002; others are being ordained by small faith communities or by various schismatic Catholic groups.

However, my more than twenty years of involvement with congregationally governed Protestant denominations have helped me understand what small sectarian religious groups do: they splinter. "Four Baptists, three churches," as the saying goes. The point of being Catholic, for me, is to be connected with a vast cloud of witnesses extending both back in time and across space. When I was a schoolgirl, a favorite hymn celebrated the three hundred million voices that made up the church. Today, that number is more than a billion.

With this in mind I have become increasingly drawn to Catholicism in what is now called the Global South. I still believe that the Catholic Church is making a mistake to exclude women from ordination; this refusal, and related sexual prohibitions and gender exclusions, risk driving away a significant percentage of the white ethnic Catholics whose forebears built the American church, at least on the East Coast.

But Catholicism is not the same everywhere. The scholar of global Christianity Lamin Sanneh argues that the Catholic Church, simply by allowing women to play a secondary leadership role in its liturgy, raises women's social status in majority Muslim countries. This is so even if such a practice falls far short of what many American Catholics desire.[15] Here in the United States, the religious congregation that educated me, the Sisters of Notre Dame de Namur, has been declining for decades for lack of new members, but in the Global South, their numbers are growing steadily. They now anticipate that within twenty years, an absolute majority of the congregation will be from Africa and Latin America. Perhaps these Catholic women of the Global South are deluded by patriarchy, or perhaps a life of independence and service appeals to them as it did American Catholic women two and three generations ago.

As for me, I am sending my money, such as it is, to support the construction of a series of photovoltaic grids that these sisters are having constructed in the villages they serve, in the Democratic Republic of Congo and Nigeria. These grids will generate electricity for schools and hospitals and eventually for local families; the electricity will also fuel the purification of water in these villages, freeing women and girls to go to school instead of hauling water long distances every day. John Paul II, the pope who dashed the hopes of so many American Catholics, also spearheaded the tremendous growth of Catholicism in Africa and other parts of the Global South. I try to hold both of these realities in my heart at the same time, even as I teach global theologies to a new generation of Protestant and Catholic (and a few Buddhist) ministers.

None of this eliminates the death of that particular dream of a liberal American Catholicism that inspired many of us when John Kennedy and John XXIII were in office. I, too, find the current state of the church, especially the mediocrity, or worse, of much of the American hierarchy disheartening. And I know now that there will be no end to this mourning. The Catholic Church is not going to become the heroic institution I once anticipated. Whatever we American Catholics make of our church, we will do so in the interstices between the polarized positions that have occupied us for too long, especially those related to sexuality and gender roles. I join with others to fashion this modest church of the future because I continue to find the Catholic tradition, rooted in the transformation of suffering and loss, a source of encouragement and hope in my life. Like Richard Rodriguez, I am grateful to spend my life within the shadow of the crucifix.

NOTES

Introduction

1. For a more detailed discussion of the U.S. Catholic clergy sex-abuse crisis and the American Catholic inability to mourn, see Marian Ronan, "The Clergy Sex Abuse Crisis and the Mourning of American Catholic Innocence," *Pastoral Psychology* 56, no. 3 (January 2008): 321–339.

2. The Boston Globe, *Betrayal: The Crisis in the Catholic Church* (Boston: Little, Brown, 2002).

3. The John Jay College of Criminal Justice, "The Nature and Scope of the Problem of Sexual Abuse of Minors by Catholic Priests and Deacons in the United States," The United States Conference of Catholic Bishops, March 2004, available online at http://www.usccb.org/nrb/johnjaystudy/, accessed May 2, 2008. See especially "Executive Summary."

4. John T. McGreevy, *Catholicism and American Freedom: A History* (New York: Norton, 2003), 289.

5. A previous round of revelations of Catholic clergy sex abuse by priests began in 1984 and 1985, with the case of Rev. Gilbert Gauthe, a priest of the diocese of Lafayette, Louisiana; it was followed by a number of other high-profile cases, including those of Rev. Bruce Ritter of Covenant House and Rev. James Porter. See Philip Jenkins, *Pedophiles and Priests: Anatomy of a Contemporary Crisis* (New York: Oxford University Press, 1996), 34–38. Yet it was possible to get the impression from the power of the response to the new round of revelations beginning in 2002 that such events had not occurred. In Ronan, "The Clergy Sex Abuse Crisis," 333, I connect the massive increase in attention to clergy sex abuse in January 2002 to the media's need to find another high-profile issue to fill the gap created by diminishing attention to the attack on the World Trade Center and the Pentagon, which had taken place four months earlier.

6. Elisabeth Schuessler Fiorenza, *In Memory of Her: A Feminist Theological Reconstruction of Christian Origins* (New York: Crossroads, 1983), 285–334.

7. Two of the most widely hailed conciliar documents, "The Pastoral Constitution on the Church in the Modern World" and "The Declaration on Religious

Freedom," strongly support this impression. See *The Documents of Vatican II, with Notes, and Comments by Catholic, Protestant, and Orthodox Authorities*, ed. Walter M. Abbott (New York: Guild Press, America Press, Association Press, 1966), 675–696, 199–308.

8. Gene Burns, *The Frontiers of Catholicism: The Politics of Ideology in a Liberal World* (Berkeley: University of California Press, 1992).

9. Burns, a sociologist, is concerned with Roman Catholic ideology. Roman Catholic theology inflects "faith and morals" somewhat differently. In *Pastor Aeternus*, Vatican Council I describes the pope as infallible when he defines a doctrine concerning morals as well as faith that are to be upheld by the universal church. But Vatican I was ambiguous about the subject matter that can be infallibly defined, and different kinds of obligations attend to different subject matters; while a definition concerning revelation must be believed with an assent of faith, "matters that are not revealed [e.g., teachings about the natural law] require acceptance, yet not strictly an assent of faith; furthermore . . . since there has never been a clear instance when infallibility was exercised about a matter of 'morals,' theologians disagree whether the Council intended 'morals' to mean: a person's fundamental option, or basic principles of morality, or universal precepts of the natural law, or specific commandments." John T. Ford, "Infallibility," *The New Dictionary of Theology*, ed. Joseph Komonchak et al. (Wilmington, Del.: Michael Glazier, 1987), 518–519.

10. "The natural law, present in the heart of each man and established by reason, is universal in its precepts and its authority extends to all men. . . . Application of the natural law varies greatly; it can demand reflection that takes account of various conditions of life according to places, times, and circumstances. Nevertheless, in the diversity of cultures, the natural law remains as a rule that binds men among themselves and imposes on them, beyond the inevitable differences, common principles. . . . The natural law is *immutable* [emphasis in original] and permanent throughout the variations of history; it subsists under the flux of ideas and customs and supports their progress. . . . The natural law provides revealed law and grace with a foundation prepared by God and in accordance with the work of the Spirit." *Catechism of the Catholic Church* (Mahwah, N.J.: Paulist Press, 1994), 475.

11. Some would argue that Catholic social teaching (on issues such as the death penalty, war, the environment, etc.) carries as much or even more weight than Catholic sexual teaching. However, Burns demonstrates that church statements on social issues fall below sexual teaching in the Catholic ideological hierarchy; they are intentionally vague and rarely enforced. Burns, *Frontiers*, 201–202. However, for a comparison between Catholic sexual and social teaching that finds a larger number of loopholes and thus *more* nuance in the latter, see Christine Gudorf, "To Make a Seamless Garment, Use a Single Piece of Cloth," *Cross Currents* 34, no. 4 (Winter 1984–1985): 473–491.

12. "Vatican Stands Firm on Women Priests," *BBC News World Edition* (January 27, 2003), available online at http://news.bbc.co.uk/2/hi/europe/2699101.stm, accessed January 29, 2008.

13. Michelle Dillon, *Catholic Identity: Balancing Faith, Reason, and Power* (New York: Cambridge University Press, 1999).

14. I take it as a commentary on the postwar American Catholic conviction of the superiority of the Middle Ages that I do not remember a time when I did not know the title of James Walsh's book on the thirteenth century though I am sure I never read it: James Joseph Walsh, *The Thirteenth, Greatest of Centuries* (New York: Fordham University Press, 1946 [1907]).

15. James Hennessey, "Leo XIII's Thomistic Revival: A Political and Philosophical Event," in *Celebrating the Medieval Heritage: A Colloquy on the Thought of Aquinas and Bonaventure*, ed. David Tracy, supplement, *The Journal of Religion* 54 (1978): 89–90.

16. David Schultenover, *A View from Rome: On the Eve of the Modernist Crisis* (New York: Fordham University Press, 1993), 1–3.

17. Michael J. Coughlan, *The Vatican, the Law, and the Human Embryo* (Iowa City: Iowa University Press, 1990), 11–25.

18. In 2008, on the eve of Pope Benedict XVI's first visit to the United States, 52 percent of Americans surveyed and 74 percent of American Catholics rated the pope favorably, through three in ten said they did not know this pope well enough to respond. Pew Center for the People and the Press, "On Eve of Visit, Pope Benedict Still Unknown to Many Americans," available online at www.people-press.org/reports/display.php3?ReportID=408, accessed April 10, 2008.

19. Eric Santner, *Stranded Objects: Mourning, Memory, and Film in Postwar Germany* (Ithaca, N.Y.: Cornell University Press, 1990), 29, 7–9.

20. See, for example, William Parsons, Diane Jonte-Pace, and Susan Henking, *Mourning Religion* (Charlottesville: University of Virginia Press, 2008).

21. Sigmund Freud, "Mourning and Melancholia," in *The Standard Edition of the Complete Psychological Works of Sigmund Freud*, ed. James Strachey (London: The Hogarth Press, 1953–1974), 14:237–259.

22. Anahid Kassabian and David Kazanjian, "Melancholic Memories and Manic Politics: Feminism, Documentary, and the Armenian Diaspora," in *Feminism and Documentary*, ed. Diane Waldman and Janet Walker (Minneapolis: University of Minnesota Press, 1999), 207.

23. Alexander Mitscherlich and Margarete Mitscherlich, *The Inability to Mourn: Principles of Collective Behavior* (New York: Grove Press, 1975).

24. Kassabian and Kazanjian, "Melancholic Memories," 202–223.

25. Ibid., 208–209.

26. Ibid., 210.

27. Julie Byrne, "Roman Catholics and Immigration in Nineteenth-century America," in *Divining America: Religion in American History: Essays by Leading Scholars*, available online at http://nationalhumanitiescenter.org/tserve/nineteen/nkeyinfo/nromcath.htm, accessed March 8, 2008.

28. James T. Fisher, "Catholicism Ascendant: American Popular Culture in the 1950s," *Culturefront* 7, no. 4 (Winter 1998–1999): 58–60, 75–76.

29. James Terence Fisher, *The Catholic Counterculture in America* (Chapel Hill: University of North Carolina Press, 1989), 80–81, draws on Jay Dolan's discussion in *Catholic Revivalism* of the Catholic gospels of "acceptance" and of "success." Fisher himself favors the term the "Catholic grammar of suffering," though he also uses Dolan's term "the gospel of acceptance" (80ff.). See Jay P. Dolan, *Catholic Revivalism* (Notre Dame, Ind.: University of Notre Dame Press, 1978).

30. In *Catholic Counterculture*, 81–82, Fisher discusses Orsi's *Madonna of 115th Street* as a classic example of the Catholic grammar of suffering. See Robert A. Orsi, *The Madonna of 115th Street: Faith and Community in Italian Harlem, 1880–1950* (New Haven, Conn.: Yale University Press, 1985).

31. Discussed in Fisher, *Catholic Counterculture*, 75–76.

32. Ibid.

33. Ibid., 81.

34. Ibid.

35. Fisher nuances the role of ritual in the gradual transformation of the Catholic grammar of suffering, however, suggesting that ritualization helped to make possible the movement beyond suffering to glory—in effect, providing a container where the increasingly less prominent preoccupation with suffering could be stored. Ibid., 80.

36. Ibid., 82.

37. William M. Halsey, *The Survival of American Innocence: Catholicism in an Era of Disillusionment, 1920–1940* (Notre Dame, Ind.: University of Notre Dame Press, 1980).

38. Ibid., 2. For a study of the Boston Catholic bourgeoisie in the early twentieth century that in some respects complements Halsey's work, see Paula M. Kane, *Separatism and Subculture: Boston Catholicism, 1900–1920* (Chapel Hill: University of North Carolina Press, 1994).

39. Daniel A. Dombrowski and Robert Deltete, *A Brief, Liberal, Catholic Defense of Abortion* (Urbana: University of Illinois Press, 2000), 58.

40. Quoted in ibid.

41. Ibid.

42. Mark A. Massa, *Anti-Catholicism in America: The Last Acceptable Prejudice* (New York: Crossroads, 2003), 77–85.

43. Philip Jenkins, *The New Anti-Catholicism: The Last Acceptable Prejudice* (New York: Oxford University Press, 2003), 43–45; David H. Bennett, *The Party of Fear: From the Nativist Movement to the New Right in American History* (Chapel Hill: University of North Carolina Press, 1988), 219.

44. Jenkins, *Anti-Catholicism*, 44.

45. After emancipation, African Americans were subjected to far more extreme sexual vilification than white ethnic immigrant American Catholics, with African American men regularly portrayed as rapists and lynched and African American women portrayed as Jezebels and sexually assaulted.

46. Santner, *Stranded Objects*, 9.

47. For another examination of the modern as a fantasy of innocence, see Jane Flax, "The End of Innocence," in *Feminists Theorize the Political*, ed. Judith Butler and Joan W. Scott (New York: Routledge, 1992), 445–463.

48. Julia Kristeva, *The Powers of Horror: An Essay in Abjection* (New York: Columbia University Press, 1982).

49. Iris Marion Young, *Justice and the Politics of Difference* (Princeton, N.J.: Princeton University Press, 1990), 144.

50. Diane Jonte-Pace, *Speaking the Unspeakable: Religion, Misogyny, and the Uncanny Mother in Freud's Cultural Texts* (Berkeley: University of California Press, 2001), 110.

51. Jenkins, *Anti-Catholicism*, 54–66.

52. Ibid., 64–65.

53. George Weigel, "A Crossroad for the Catholic Church," *Washington Post* (February 3, 2004).

54. Daniel J. Wakin, "Bishops Open a New Drive Opposing Contraception," *New York Times*, November 13, 2003.

55. Jonte-Pace, *Speaking the Unspeakable*, 144.

56. Ibid.

57. James Carroll, *An American Requiem: God, My Father, and the War That Came Between Us* (Boston: Houghton Mifflin, 1996).

58. Mary Gordon, *The Shadow Man* (New York: Random House, 1996).

59. Mary Gordon, *The Rest of Life* (New York: Viking, 1993).

60. Mary Gordon, *Pearl* (New York: Pantheon, 2005).

61. Donna J. Haraway, "Ecce Homo, Ain't (Ar'n't) I a Woman, and Inappropriate/d Others: The Human in a Posthumanist Landscape," in *Feminists Theorize the Political*, 86–100; *Modest_Witness@SecondMillenium.FemaleMan©_Meets_Oncomouse™: Feminism and Technoscience* (New York: Routledge, 1997).

62. Richard Rodriguez, *Hunger of Memory: The Education of Richard Rodriguez* (New York: Bantam Books, 1982).

63. Richard Rodriguez, *Days of Obligation: An Argument with My Mexican Father* (New York: Penguin Books, 1992).

64. Ibid., 26–47.

65. Richard Rodriguez, *Brown: The Last Discovery of America* (New York: Penguin Books, 2002).

1. Skating Ahead of the Cracks

1. "James (P.) Carroll," in *Contemporary Literary Criticism* 38, ed. Daniel G. Marowski (Detroit, Mich.: Gale Publications, 1986).

2. For a discussion of the Catholic gospel of suffering, see the introduction, 10–11; see also James T. Fisher, *The Catholic Counterculture in America* (Chapel Hill: University of North Carolina Press, 1989), 75–76.

3. In 1997, Carroll received a National Book Award for *An American Requiem*.

James Carroll, *An American Requiem: God, My Father, and the War That Came Between Us* (Boston: Houghton Mifflin, Mariner Books, 1996).

4. In an interview, James O'Gara, the former editor of *Commonweal* and, like James Carroll's father, a postimmigrant Catholic from Chicago, noted that his own years in a minor (high-school level) Catholic seminary in Chicago in the 1930s ought not to be taken for more than they were. The seminary, he suggested, was a time-honored way for intelligent working-class boys to get an education in those days. James O'Gara, interview, Catonsville, Md., June 13, 1997.

5. Carroll, *An American Requiem*, 52, 33.

6. Ibid., 32.

7. Robert A. Orsi, *The Madonna of 115th Street: Faith and Community in Italian Harlem, 1880–1950* (New Haven, Conn.: Yale University Press, 1985), 219–231.

8. Donna J. Haraway, *Simians, Cyborgs, and Women: The Reinvention of Nature* (New York: Routledge, 1991), 191–192.

9. Carroll, *An American Requiem*, 57.

10. Ibid., 64.

11. Ibid., 44. In Carroll's 1984 novel, *Prince of Peace*, one of the main characters, Maguire, had, when he was a prisoner of war in Korea, "disciplined himself to look for crosses everywhere—in the plaster cracks, in the weave of his palm mat, in the shadows cast by the stockade grilles." James Carroll, *Prince of Peace* (Boston: Little, Brown and Company, 1984), 288.

12. Carroll, *An American Requiem*, 47.

13. Ibid., 44.

14. Jansenism is a heresy initiated in the seventeenth century by Cornelius Janssen, the Catholic bishop of Ypres, France, which taught a doctrine of justification by faith and predestination, quite like those of the Protestant Reformers. Its pessimistic view of life and, in particular, of sexuality, permeated French Catholicism for centuries after its official condemnation by the Catholic Church. The Irish clergy, many of whom were trained in French seminaries because of British suppression of Catholicism in Ireland, were strongly influenced by Jansenism and carried it to the United States in the great emigrations. See Peter Occhiogrosso, *The Joy of Sects: A Spirited Guide to the World's Religious Traditions* (New York: Doubleday, 1996), 327.

15. Carroll, *An American Requiem*, 22. Carroll's reflections in this regard shed light on my father's older brother, who in 1937 left St. Charles Borromeo Seminary in Philadelphia after being ordained to the diaconate and spent the rest of his life selling tickets in a bus station. That St. Charles did not award secular degrees for many years, thus rendering Uncle Hubert's eleven years of philosophy, theology, and classical languages practically useless, was no doubt part of the problem. But his entrance into the seminary upon the death of his mother when he was fourteen must have been another part.

16. Ibid., 214.

17. Orsi, *The Madonna of 115th Street*, 219–231.

18. Carroll, *An American Requiem*, 92.

19. Because there is an ongoing debate about whether the term "American-ism" corresponds with any actual theological position, scholars sometimes call it "a phantom heresy." Hecker's relationship to it, too, is murky; the most questionable "Americanist" material was contained in the introduction to a French translation of Hecker's autobiography written not by Hecker but by a liberal French cleric after Hecker's death. Philip Gleason, "The New Americanism in American Catholic History," *U.S. Catholic Historian* 11 (Summer 1993): 3–4.

20. Carroll, *An American Requiem*, 243–245.

21. Carroll later suspects that his father's support of the war was less unambiguous than it had seemed while the war was in progress; like Robert McNamara, he may have opposed the war to the government leaders who were making American policy but maintained a loyal silence in public. Since Carroll did not know this, it had no effect on his attitude toward his father at the time, however.

22. "No more war! War never again!" Carroll, *An American Requiem*, 160.

23. Ibid., 6.

24. Ibid., 11.

25. Ibid., 48.

26. James Terence Fisher, *The Catholic Counterculture in America, 1933–1962* (Chapel Hill: The University of North Carolina Press, 1989), 223.

27. Hopkins himself experienced conflict between being a priest and being a poet, destroying a number of his poems when he entered the Society of Jesus. His later poems survived, however, and fortunately so; they had a significant influence on several generations of American Catholics. In *Prince of Peace*, 44, Durkin, the pro-tagonist, goes from his old New York neighborhood to New York University, where he "fell under the spell of Gerard Manley Hopkins." When I was a high-school fresh-man in 1961, Hopkins's poetry strongly influenced me as well, but I had no idea at the time that many other young Catholics were being similarly influenced.

28. James Carroll, *Forbidden Disappointments* (Rahway, N.J.: Paulist/Newman, 1974).

29. James Carroll, *Feed My Lambs: A Guide for Parents Who Want to Prepare Their Children for the Eucharist and Penance* (Dayton, Ohio: Pflaum Publishers, 1967); James Carroll, *Tender of Wishes: The Prayers of a Young Priest* (Paramus, N.J.: Newman Press, 1970); James Carroll, *Wonder and Worship* (Paramus, N.J.: Paulist/ Newman, 1970); James Carroll, *Prayers from Where We Are: Suggestions About the Possibility of Prayer Today* (Dayton, Ohio: Pflaum Publishers, 1970); James Carroll, *Elements of Hope* (Paramus, N.J.: Paulist Press, 1971); James Carroll, *Contemplation: Liberating the Ghost of the Church, Churching the Ghost of Liberation* (Paramus, N.J./Kansas City, Mo.: Paulist Press/National Catholic Reporter, 1972); James Car-roll, *A Terrible Beauty: Conversions in Prayer, Politics, and Imagination* (Paramus, N.J.: Paulist/Newman, 1973); James Carroll, *The Winter Name of God* (New York: Sheed and Ward, 1975).

30. Carroll, *An American Requiem*, 206.

31. "James (P.) Carroll," in *Contemporary Authors: A Bio-bibliographical Guide to Current Writers in Fiction, General Nonfiction, Poetry, Journalism, Drama, Motion*

Pictures, Television, and Other Fields, ed. Frances Carol Locher (Detroit, Mich.: Gale Research Co., 1979), 79.

32. Carroll, *An American Requiem,* 15.

33. Ibid., 267.

34. For a discussion of differences between the Catholic hierarchy and the Reformers in the sixteenth century as refracted through the issue of sacrifice, see Nancy Jay, *Throughout Your Generations Forever: Sacrifice, Religion, and Paternity* (Chicago: University of Chicago Press, 1992), 112–127.

35. There is no necessary connection between marriage and parenthood, of course, nor is Carroll clear about whether the ontological priesthood of parenthood is biological or whether one can join this privileged class by adopting a child as well.

36. Carroll, *An American Requiem,* 268. Also, in Carroll's novel, *Prince of Peace,* after the birth of his daughter, the narrator, Frank Durkin, observes, "I have referred already to the 'ontological change' that traditional theology claims as an effect of ordination, a notion I had dismissed as meaningless. But . . . that arcane phrase described what had happened to me. . . . She taught me in that first encounter that the most radical separation of all is between people who have brought children into the world and those who haven't." Carroll, *Prince of Peace,* 303.

37. Andrew Greeley, "Why Do Catholics Stay in the Church? Because of the Stories," *New York Times Magazine* (July 10, 1994).

38. For example, Leslie Tentler and Margaret Susan Thompson concluded their workshop "Gender and the Construction of Catholic Memory" by attributing the unity of contemporary Catholicism to the shared Catholic practice of going to Mass. Leslie Tentler and Margaret Susan Thompson, "Gender and the Construction of Catholic Memory," Workshop, Engendering American Catholic Studies (Notre Dame, Ind., September 29–October 1, 1995). Similarly, 80 percent of American Catholics polled in a Gallup survey published in 1999 identify the sacraments as the element of greatest importance in being a Catholic, a position I am emotionally inclined to agree with. The survey included white and Hispanic Catholics but not African Americans. William V. D'Antonio, "The American Catholic Laity," *National Catholic Reporter* (October 29, 1999).

39. Ann Taves, *The Household of Faith: Roman Catholic Devotions in Mid-nineteenth-century America* (Notre Dame, Ind.: Notre Dame University Press, 1986).

40. Standardization and centralization of worship were not limited to Catholicism, but their effects varied according to context. Jenna Weissman Joselit notes that discouraging the old worship practices of the earlier, smaller, "unsanitary" Eastern European *chevras* was part of the program of the big Orthodox synagogues built in New York City in the first third of the twentieth century. These "undesirable" practices included noisy praying aloud, *davaning* (swaying while worshipping), making public donations during the Torah reading, and *shnuddering,* the auctioning of communal honors during the service, a practice that was so embedded in the financing of synagogues that it took forty years to extinguish it. Jenna Weisman Joselit, "Bigger

and Better Orthodox Synagogues," in *New York's Jewish Jews*, ed. Jenna Weisman Joselit (Bloomington: Indiana University Press, 1990), 25–53.

41. Carroll, *An American Requiem*, 100–101.

42. Ibid., 103.

43. James Carroll, *Madonna Red* (Boston: Bantam Books, 1976).

44. James Carroll, *Fault Lines* (New York: Dell Publishing Company, 1980).

45. Carroll, *Prince of Peace*, 98, 133, 531.

46. James Carroll, *The City Below* (Boston: Houghton Mifflin, 1994).

47. Carroll, *An American Requiem*, 266.

48. Though sometimes I think it was the exquisite minor key of the melody rather than the words that made me love it. Anonymous, 12th C., "Jesus Christ Is Risen," E. C. Schirmer Music Co., 1943. William F. Lynch, S.J., *Christ and Apollo: The Dimensions of the Literary Imagination* (Notre Dame, Ind.: University of Notre Dame Press, [1960] 1975).

49. Lynch, *Christ and Apollo*, 49.

50. Then again, perhaps he knew it very well. According to William Birmingham, former co-editor of *Cross Currents*, Lynch was a strong and conscious Platonist. William Birmingham, telephone conversation, November 29, 1999.

51. Carroll, *Prince of Peace*, 122.

52. James Carroll, *Mortal Friends* (Boston: Little, Brown and Co., 1978).

53. Webster Schott, "Maguire the Mettlesome Priest," review of *Prince of Peace* by James Carroll, *New York Times Book Review* (November 4, 1984); Thomas Filbin, review of *The City Below* by James Carroll, *The Hudson Review* 47, no. 3 (Winter 1995): 653–654.

54. Carroll, *An American Requiem*, 44.

55. Ibid.

56. Taves, *The Household of Faith*, 8–9.

57. Carroll, *An American Requiem*, 22.

58. Ibid., 166.

59. Ibid., 180.

60. The classic text on this subject is Gayle Rubin, "The Traffic in Women: Notes on the Political Economy of Sex," in *The Second Wave: A Reader in Feminist Theory*, ed. Linda Nicholson (New York: Routledge, 1997), 27–62.

61. Quoted in Eve Kosofsky Sedgwick, *Between Men: English Literature and Male Homosocial Desire* (New York: Columbia University Press, 1985), 3.

62. Although a father-son relationship—between J. Edgar Hoover and an FBI agent—does figure in Carroll's 1989 novel *Firebird*, the relationship is less central than in these earlier works. James Carroll, *Firebird* (New York: E. P. Dutton, 1989).

63. Sedgwick, *Between Men*.

64. Ibid., 21.

65. Carroll, *Prince of Peace*, 515.

66. Carroll, *The City Below*, 308–309.

67. Carroll, *An American Requiem*, 101.

68. Sedgwick, *Between Men*, 216.

69. See, for example, James Carroll, "Why Dissident Catholics Stay," *Boston Globe* (May 14, 1996); and "Abortion Complexity," *Boston Globe* (April 23, 1996).

70. Janet R. Jakobsen, *Working Alliances and the Politics of Difference: Diversity and Feminist Ethics* (Bloomington: Indiana University Press, 1998), 58–97.

71. Carroll, *The City Below*, 404.

72. Carroll, *An American Requiem*, 254.

73. Ibid., 279.

74. James Uebbing, review of *An American Requiem* by James Carroll, *Commonweal* 123, no. 13 (July 12, 1996): 25–26.

75. Ed Block, "A Cold War Story," review of James Carroll's *Secret Father*, *America* 190, no. 1 (January 1, 2004), available online at http://www.americamagazine.org/content/article.cfm?-id=3367, accessed May 2, 2008.

76. James Carroll, "The Silence," *New Yorker* (April 7, 1997).

77. Carroll, *An American Requiem*, 217.

78. Carroll, "The Silence," 59.

79. Ibid., 60.

2. Flowers, and Dirt, and a Few Stones

1. James Carroll, *Tender of Wishes: The Prayers of a Young Priest* (Paramus, N.J.: Newman Press, 1970).

2. Alma Bennett, *Mary Gordon* (New York: Twayne Publishers, 1996), 9; Richard Rodriguez, *Hunger of Memory: The Education of Richard Rodriguez* (New York: Bantam Books, 1982), 162.

3. Bennett, *Mary Gordon*, 67–68.

4. James Hennessey, "Leo XIII's Thomistic Revival: A Political and Philosophical Event," and Gerald McCool, "Twentieth-century Scholasticism," in *Celebrating the Medieval Heritage*, ed. David Tracy, Supplement to *The Journal of Religion* 54 (1978): 89–90, 203.

5. Other interpretations of the neo-Thomist Revival include Arnold Sparr, *To Promote, Defend, and Redeem: The Catholic Literary Revival and the Cultural Transformation of American Catholicism, 1920–1960* (New York: Greenwood Press, 1989); and Peter Huff, *Allen Tate and the Catholic Revival: Trace of the Fugitive Gods* (New York: Paulist Press, 1996).

6. William M. Halsey, *The Survival of American Innocence: Catholicism in an Era of Disillusionment, 1920–1940* (Notre Dame, Ind.: University of Notre Dame Press, 1980), 171.

7. Mary Gordon, "The Irish Catholic Church," in *Once a Catholic: Prominent Catholics and Ex-Catholics Reveal the Influence of the Church on Their Lives and Work*, ed. Peter Occhiogrosso (Boston: Houghton Mifflin, 1987), 69.

8. F. E. Peters, *Ours: The Making and Unmaking of a Jesuit* (New York: Penguin Books, 1981), 175.

9. Quoted in Hennessey, "Leo XIII's Thomistic Revival," 195.

10. Mary Gordon, *Final Payments* (New York: Ballantine, 1978), 64.

11. Julia Kristeva, *The Powers of Horror: An Essay in Abjection* (New York: Columbia University Press, 1982), 1–31 and throughout. The American feminist theorist Judith Butler also utilizes the concept of the abject: in *Bodies That Matter*, the sexual other, the abject, is repeatedly expelled to or beyond the boundaries of the social/cultural domain in the building up of the sexed body. That is to say, the body itself is constructed from the repeated recognition of what it ostensibly could never be, the repellent sexual other. Butler also includes race in her construal of the abject, as I do here. Judith Butler, *Bodies That Matter: On the Discursive Limits of Sex* (New York: Routledge, 1993), 1–23.

12. Gordon, *Final Payments*, 2.

13. Mary Gordon, *The Company of Women* (New York: Ballantine, 1980).

14. Mary Gordon, *Men and Angels* (New York: Ballantine, 1985).

15. Mary Gordon, *The Other Side* (New York: Viking, 1989).

16. Disidentification is a failure of imitation, a repetition that does not repeat exactly, thus permitting the return of something that is meant to be excluded. Butler, *Bodies That Matter*, 37, 45, 83, 213, 214, 220.

17. Bennett, *Mary Gordon*, 114.

18. Gordon, *Final Payments*, 298.

19. Gordon, "The Irish Catholic Church," 75.

20. Mary Gordon, *The Rest of Life* (New York: Viking, 1993).

21. Quoted in Bennett, *Mary Gordon*, 148.

22. Quoted in ibid.

23. Ibid., 148–164.

24. The Paracletists are a fictional religious order descended, perhaps, from another such fictional order, J. F. Powers's "Clementines." Mary Gordon, "The Priestly Comedy of J. F. Powers," in *Good Boys and Dead Girls and Other Essays* (New York: Penguin Books, 1991), 99.

25. Gordon, *The Rest of Life*, 16.

26. Ibid.

27. Ibid., 24.

28. Ibid., 25.

29. Ibid., 33.

30. Ibid., 29.

31. Ibid.

32. Ibid., 70.

33. For a discussion of Gordon's manipulation of autobiographical material across literary genres, see Bennett, *Mary Gordon*, 181. For a discussion of the autobiographical mode in fiction, see Leigh Gilmore, *The Limits of Autobiography: Trauma and Testimony* (Ithaca, N.Y.: Cornell University Press, 2001).

34. Gordon, *The Rest of Life*, 35.

35. Bennett, *Mary Gordon*, 158.

36. For example, there is not the least hint of sexual impropriety between Father Cyprian and the women who surround him in *The Company of Women* (which is not to suggest that their relationships are in no sense sexual). Similarly, Vincent

McNamara in *The Other Side* emphatically resists the advances of an elderly woman in a nursing home where he lives temporarily.

37. Gordon, *The Rest of Life*, 10.

38. Ibid., 213.

39. Bennett, *Mary Gordon*, 154.

40. In *The Other Side*, Ellen McNamara does have a Jewish socialist friend, but she is a minor character. Gordon, *The Other Side*, 126. And the title story of *Temporary Shelter*, Gordon's 1988 collection of short stories (New York: Ballantine), includes a father figure, a Jewish convert to Catholicism, whose daughter and another child, as adults, are the main characters in Gordon's 2005 novel *Pearl* (New York: Pantheon).

41. Vincent McNamara also returns to Ireland to bring his wife's elderly mother back to New York. This trip is filled with shame and secrecy, however, and not nearly so central to *The Other Side* as Paola's is to "The Rest of Life." Gordon, *The Other Side*, 16–34.

42. Gordon, *The Rest of Life*, 255–256.

43. Ibid., 256–257.

44. Ibid., 257.

45. Ibid.

46. Ibid., 195.

47. Ibid., 255.

48. Ibid., 199.

49. Robert Anthony Orsi, *The Madonna of 115th Street: Faith and Community in Italian Harlem, 1880–1950* (New Haven, Conn.: Yale University Press, 1985), 227 and throughout.

50. Gordon, *The Rest of Life*, 252.

51. Ibid., 24.

52. Mary Gordon, "Getting Here from There: A Writer's Reflections on a Religious Past," in Gordon, *Good Boys and Dead Girls*, 31–33.

53. Gordon, *The Rest of Life*, 257.

54. Mark Chaves, *Ordaining Women: Culture and Conflict in Religious Organizations* (Cambridge, Mass.: Harvard University Press, 1997).

55. Gordon, *The Rest of Life*, 257.

56. Patrick H. Samway, S.J., "An Interview with Mary Gordon," *America* 170 (May 14, 1994): 14.

57. Mary Gordon, *The Shadow Man* (New York: Random House, 1996).

58. Ibid., xvi.

59. Ibid., 93–94.

60. Ibid., 10.

61. Ibid.

62. Ibid., 29.

63. Ibid., 105.

64. Ibid., 201.

65. Ibid.

66. Gordon, *The Rest of Life*, 256–257.

67. Gordon, *The Shadow Man*, 245–246.

68. Ibid., 269.

69. Ibid., 261.

70. Ibid., 269.

71. Ibid.

72. Fisher, *The Catholic Counterculture in America*, 82.

73. Gordon, *The Shadow Man*, 189.

74. Ibid., 268.

75. Mary Gordon, *Spending* (New York: Scribner, 1998); and *Pearl*. Since 2000, Gordon has also published *Joan of Arc* (New York: Viking, 2000), *Seeing Through Places: Reflections on Geography and Identity* (New York: Scribners, 2001), *The Stories of Mary Gordon* (New York: Pantheon, 2006), and many articles.

76. I suggested, for example, that a series of paintings by the protagonist of *Spending*, Monica Szabo, of the postcrucifixion Christ in postcoital exhaustion rather than death extends Gordon's earlier efforts to reintegrate the body into the bedrock Jansenist Catholicism of her, and my, youth. Ronan, "A Sliver of Dry Land," 90.

77. Gordon, *Pearl*, 292.

78. Ibid., 270.

79. Ibid., 320.

80. Ibid., 321.

81. Ibid., 356.

82. Ibid., 354.

83. Mary Gordon, "Women of God," *Atlantic Monthly* (January 2002). Available online at http://www/theatlantic.com/doc/200201/gordon, accessed May 7, 2008.

84. Mary Gordon, "The Feminist Rosary: Rediscovering a Subversive Prayer," *Boston College Magazine* (Fall 2003). Available online at http://bcm.bc.edu/issues/fall_2003/features.html, accessed May 2, 2008.

85. Mary Gordon, "The Priestly Phallus," *Studies in Gender and Sexuality* 5, no. 1 (2004): 103–111; "Unholy Orders," review of *Our Fathers: The Secret Life of the Catholic Church in an Age of Scandal* by David France, *New York Times* (January 25, 2004), available online at http://query.nytimes.com/gst/fullpage.html?res=9C00E6D61E30F936A15752C0A9629C8B63, accessed May 2, 2008.

86. Gordon is particularly incensed by the so-called "zero-tolerance" policy of the American Catholic bishops, which she considers primarily a "preemptive strike against American litigiousness." Gordon, "The Priestly Phallus," 111.

87. On this subject, for example, James Carroll published twelve newspaper columns in 2002 alone, the first year of renewed attention to American Catholic clergy sex abuse. His book, *Toward a New Catholic Church: The Promise of Reform* (Boston: Mariner Books, 2002), also addresses the crisis at some length—no mean feat, since the book must have been substantially completed before the revelations of early 2002.

88. Gordon, "Unholy Orders."

89. Gordon, "The Priestly Phallus," 108.

90. Gordon might respond here that the nuance belongs to David France; she likes his book very much and reports meticulously on its achievements. But not all reviewers would praise an author whose "very lack of final judgment allows him a delicacy of tone that neutralizes the blood-in-the-water instinct that has been too closely associated with the pedophile scandal" or whose "method allows us to . . . make important distinctions among the priests and their victims." Gordon, "Unholy Orders."

91. Gordon, "Women of God."

3. The Passion of Oncomouse™

1. Sonya Andermahr, Terry Lovell, and Carol Wolkowitz, eds., *A Concise Glossary of Feminist Theory* (New York and London: Arnold, 1997), 1–4.

2. And perhaps to Aquinas's turn to Avicenna and Aristotle as well. Mary Gordon, *Men and Angels* (New York: Ballantine Books, 1985); Mary Gordon, *The Rest of Life* (New York: Viking, 1993). For a discussion of Gordon's use of these non-Catholic and/or non-Irish characters, see chapter 2, 55, 57–66.

3. Donna J. Haraway, "Manifesto for Cyborgs: Science Technology and Socialist Feminism in the 1980s," *Socialist Review* 80 (1985): 65–108. This article was later anthologized in Haraway's American Book Award–winning collection, *Simians, Cyborgs, and Women: The Reinvention of Nature* (New York: Routledge, 1991), 149–182, under the title of "A Cyborg Manifesto: Science, Technology and Socialist Feminism in the Late Twentieth Century."

4. Ibid., 149, 163.

5. Ibid., 154.

6. Donna J. Haraway, *Modest_Witness@Second.Millennium.FemaleMan©_ Meets_Oncomouse: Feminism and Technoscience* (New York: Routledge, 1997), 9.

7. Ibid., 10.

8. Figuration also plays a significant role in the Hebrew scriptures; the figure of Hagar in the book of Genesis prefigures and fulfills the figures of Moses and the Suffering Servant of Second Isaiah, for example.

9. Haraway's first book, a revision of her Yale Ph.D. dissertation, includes no tropes or arguments related to Christianity; furthermore, it includes no references of any kind to Haraway's personal life, except in the acknowledgments and the dedication. Donna J. Haraway, *Crystals, Fabrics, and Fields: Metaphors of Organicism in Twentieth-century Developmental Biology* (New Haven, Conn.: Yale University Press, 1976).

10. *Primate Visions* is Haraway's massive "history of the modern sciences and popular cultures emerging from accounts of the bodies and lives of monkeys and apes." Donna J. Haraway, *Primate Visions: Gender, Race, and Nature in the World of Modern Science* (New York: Routledge, 1989), 1.

11. Ibid., 9.

12. Ibid.

13. Haraway, *Simians, Cyborgs, and Women*, 71. See also 2, 82–83, 158, 175–176.

14. Ibid., 3.

15. Ibid., 189, 191, 193, 195.

16. Haraway, "A Cyborg Manifesto," 150.

17. Ibid., 151, 155, 163.

18. Ibid., 173.

19. Donna J. Haraway, "*Ecce Homo*, Ain't (Ar'n't) I a Woman, and Inappropriate/d Others: The Human in a Posthumanist Landscape," in *Feminists Theorize the Political*, ed. Judith Butler and Joan W. Scott (New York: Routledge, 1992), 86–100.

20. Ibid., 86.

21. Ibid., 87.

22. James T. Fisher, *The Catholic Counterculture in America* (Chapel Hill: University of North Carolina Press, 1989), 81; Robert A. Orsi, *The Madonna of 115th Street: Faith and Community in Italian Harlem, 1880–1950* (New Haven, Conn.: Yale University Press, 1985), 202–204.

23. Sharon V. Betcher, "Putting My Foot (Prosthesis, Crutches, Phantom) Down: Considering Technology as Transcendence in the Writings of Donna Haraway," Scholarly Presentation, Annual Meeting of the American Academy of Religion, Orlando, Florida, November 1998, 1.

24. Jill Marsden, "Virtual Sexes and Feminist Futures: The Philosophy of 'Cyberfeminism,'" *Radical Philosophy* 78 (July/August 1996): 6, 9, and throughout.

25. "Standpoint Epistemologies," in *A Concise Glossary of Feminist Theory*, ed. Sonya Andermahr, Terry Lovell, and Carol Wolkowitz (New York: Routledge, 1997), 211.

26. Haraway, *Simians, Cyborgs, and Women*, 190.

27. Marsden, "Virtual Sexes," 9.

28. Ibid., 12.

29. Marsden also finds contradictory Haraway's opposition to the Enlightenment idea of progress while calling at the same time for a "progressive" politics. Ibid., 13, 14.

30. Betcher, "Putting My Foot . . . Down," 27.

31. Marsden, "Virtual Sexes," 14.

32. Haraway, "*Ecce Homo*," 88.

33. For an examination of anti-Judaism in Christian and post-Christian feminist writings, see Katharina von Kellenbach, *Anti-Judaism in Feminist Religious Writings* (Atlanta, Ga.: Scholars Press, 1994).

34. Haraway, "*Ecce Homo*," 86.

35. Ibid. Emphasis mine.

36. Ibid., 90.

37. Joan Wallach Scott, "Women's History," in *American Feminist Thought at Century's End: A Reader*, ed. Linda S. Kauffman (Cambridge, Mass.: Blackwell, 1993), 241.

38. Betcher, "Putting My Foot . . . Down," 27.

39. Haraway, "A Cyborg Manifesto," 148.

40. Haraway, "*Ecce Homo*," 87.

41. Haraway, "A Cyborg Manifesto," 155–165.

42. Haraway, "*Ecce Homo*," 87.

43. Ibid.

44. Haraway, *Modest_Witness*, 43.

45. Ibid., 71.

46. Ibid.

47. For another use of the figure of a mouse to represent serious twentieth-century issues and events, see Art Spiegelman, *Maus: A Survivor's Tale* (New York: Pantheon Books, 1997).

48. The panopticon is a building arranged so that all parts of the interior can be viewed from a single point. Michel Foucault uses the design of the panopticon in his study of the origins of modern techniques of incarceration, *Discipline and Punish: The Birth of the Prison*, trans. A. M. S. Sheridan Smith (Harmondsworth: Penguin, 1977), 206–216.

49. Haraway, *Modest_Witness*, 78.

50. Ibid., 125.

51. Ibid., 127.

52. Haraway, "Situated Knowledges," 16.

53. See the introduction to this book, 11–12, for connections between William Halsey's work on American Catholic innocence and optimism and my own analysis of the American Catholic inability to mourn in the last third of the twentieth century.

54. Haraway, *Modest_Witness*, 41.

55. Ibid., 157.

56. Ibid., 191.

57. Ibid., 294.

58. Ibid., 191–192; bell hooks, *Yearning* (Boston: Southend Press, 1990).

59. Donna J. Haraway, "Cyborgs at Large: Interview with Donna Haraway," in *Technoculture*, ed. Constance Penley and Andrew Ross (New York: Routledge, 1991), 9–10. This phrasing came from one of Haraway's interviewers, Constance Penley, but Haraway did not disagree and, in fact, completed Penley's sentence for her.

60. Haraway, *Modest_Witness*, 192.

61. Ibid., 186.

62. Ibid., 198.

63. Ibid., 202.

64. Ibid., 207.

65. Ibid., 211.

66. Ibid.

67. Many thanks to Tania Oldenhage for offering the clear and insightful summary of my argument that underpins this paragraph.

68. Haraway, *Modest_Witness*, 44, 169, 178.

69. Ibid., 43.

70. Ibid., iv. Emphasis mine.

71. Ibid., 151.

72. Haraway, "The Actors Are Cyborg," 9.

73. Haraway, *Modest_Witness*, 133.

74. Ibid., 10.

75. Ibid., 203.

76. I am reminded here of a secular Jewish couple I was friendly with in New York in the 1980s. Their older son returned from a postcollege year in Israel practicing a high level of Jewish religious observance and refusing to eat in their house unless they began doing so as well. "He's got us by the short hairs," his mother said. They ultimately installed another sink, refrigerator, and set of cabinets in their kitchen in order to keep kosher.

77. Haraway, *Modest_Witness*, 205, does acknowledge the influence of Catholic liberation theology on Scheper-Hughes's book.

78. Karen Trimble Alliaume, "The Risks of Repeating Ourselves: Reading Feminist/Womanist Figures of Jesus," *Cross Currents* 48, no. 2 (Summer 1998): 198–217.

79. Haraway, *Modest_Witness*, 47.

4. The Company of the Blessed

1. *Random House Unabridged Dictionary*, 2nd ed., ed. Stuart Berg Flexner (New York: Random House, 1987), 795.

2. Richard Rodriguez, *Brown: The Last Discovery of America* (New York: Penguin Books, 2002), 224.

3. Richard Rodriguez, *Hunger of Memory: The Education of Richard Rodriguez* (New York: Bantam Books, 1982), and *Days of Obligation: An Argument with My Mexican Father* (New York: Penguin Books, 1992).

4. Reviews of *Hunger of Memory* appeared in the *Christian Science Monitor* (June 24, 1983); *New York Times* (February 28, 1982); *New York Times Book Review* (February 6, 1983); *San Francisco Review of Books* 7 (Summer 1982): 11; *Texas Observer* (July 2, 1982); *Texas Observer* (June 18, 1982); and *Washington Post* (March 21, 1983). Reviews cited in Sabine Marinic, *Contemporary Autobiographies in the Mexican American Borderland: Richard Rodriguez in Perspective* (MA thesis, University of Salzburg, 1996), 143.

5. Between 1991 and 2006, 161 essays by Richard Rodriguez were featured on "The McNeil-Lehrer News Hour" and its successor program, "The News Hour with Jim Lehrer." Rodriguez also appeared as a panelist on those shows another twenty-one times during that period. Lexis-Nexis Research Database.

6. Rodriguez, *Hunger of Memory*, 7.

7. Ibid., 3.

8. Ibid.

9. Ibid., 21.

10. Alice Yeager Kaplan, "On Language Memoir," in *Eloquent Obsessions: Writing Cultural Criticism*, ed. Marianna Torgovnik (Durham, N.C.: Duke University Press, 1994), 59–70.

11. Rodriguez, *Hunger of Memory*, 39.

12. Ibid., 271.

13. Eric Santner, *Stranded Objects: Mourning, Memory, and Film in Postwar Germany* (Ithaca, N.Y.: Cornell University Press, 1990), 2.

14. Rodriguez, *Hunger of Memory*, 48.

15. Ibid., 61.

16. Ibid., 64.

17. Ibid., 67. In the nineteenth century, American Catholics showed a marked preference for imitation over instruction in the education of children. Colleen Mc-Dannell, *The Christian Home in Victorian America, 1840–1900* (Bloomington: Indiana University Press, 1986), 147.

18. Rodriguez, *Hunger of Memory*, 68.

19. Ibid.

20. In his argument for the positive value of "the swift and sure punishment meted out to parochial school miscreants" during his childhood, James T. Fisher employs a tone not unlike the tone employed by Rodriguez here. James Terence Fisher, "Clearing the Streets of the Catholic Lost Generation," in *Catholic Lives, Contemporary America*, ed. Thomas Ferraro (Durham, N.C.: Duke University Press, 1998), 84.

21. In "Tropology of Hunger: The Miseducation of Richard Rodriguez," Norma Alarcón hypothesizes a connection between Rodriguez's rage at his parents' betrayal and his attempted bifurcation of private Spanish and public English. In *The Ethnic Canon: History, Institutions, and Interventions*, ed. David Palumbo-Liu (Minneapolis: University of Minnesota Press, 1995), 149.

22. For critiques of the liberal bourgeois notion of the public sphere, see Jürgen Habermas, "Further Reflections on the Public Sphere," 423–461, and Nancy Fraser, "Rethinking the Public Sphere: A Contribution to the Critique of Actually Existing Democracy," 109–142, both in *Habermas and the Public Sphere*, ed. Craig Calhoun (Cambridge, Mass.: The MIT Press, 1992).

23. Anthony M. Stevens-Arroyo, "The Emergence of Social Identity Among Latino Catholics: An Appraisal," in *Hispanic Catholic Culture in the U.S.*, ed. Jay P. Dolan and Allan Figueroa Deck (Notre Dame, Ind.: University of Notre Dame Press, 1994), 102–108.

24. Moises Sandoval, "The Organization of a Hispanic Church," in *Hispanic Catholic Culture in the U.S.*, 131.

25. According to Alice Yeager Kaplan, *Hunger of Memory* is actually a compilation of the speeches Rodriguez gave during the 1970s in opposition to affirmative action, bilingual education, and Chicano nationalism. Yeager Kaplan, "On Language Memoir," 61.

26. Tomás Rivera, "Richard Rodriguez's *Hunger of Memory* as Humanistic Antithesis," *MELUS* 11, no. 4 (Winter 1984): 5–13; Norma Alarcón, "Tropology of Hunger: The 'Miseducation' of Richard Rodriguez," 140–152; Victor Perera, review of *Days of Obligation: An Argument with My Mexican Father* by Richard Rodriguez, *The Nation* 256, no. 2 (January 18, 1993): 63; Rosaura Sánchez, "Calculated Mus-

ings: Richard Rodriguez's Metaphysics of Difference," in Palumbo-Liu, *The Ethnic Canon: Histories, Institutions, and Interventions*, 165.

27. For a discussion of mimicry in relation to colonialism, see Homi Bhabha, "Of Mimicry and Man: The Ambivalence of Colonial Discourse," *October* 28 (1984): 125–133.

28. Alarcón, "Tropology," 147–148. Also, for Hispanic Americans who praise Rodriguez because of his opposition to bilingualism and affirmative action, see Linda Chavez, "Hunger of Memory: The Metamorphosis of a Disadvantaged Child," *American Educator* 6, no. 3 (Fall 1982): 14–16; Yolanda DeMola, "The Language of Power," *America* 160 (April 22, 1989): 364–365.

29. Henry Staten, "Ethnic Authenticity, Class, and Autobiography: The Case of *Hunger of Memory*," *PMLA* 113, no. 1 (January 1998): 103–116.

30. Ibid., 114.

31. Ibid.

32. Ibid., 109.

33. The PRI, the political party that emerged triumphant after the revolution, remained in power in Mexico through the 1990s; responsibility is attributed to the PRI for the massacre of Indians in Chiapas in 1997. Trina Kleist, "Pain of Massacre Remains," *San Francisco Chronicle* (December 22, 1998).

34. Staten, "Ethnic Authenticity," 107.

35. Initially unschooled as I was in Mexican and Mexican American social history, my own awareness of Rodriguez's class position was triggered only by his nostalgia for the pre–Vatican II liturgy. When he speaks of the joy of hearing Mozart or Bach sung at Mass in his parish church in Sacramento, I know that, in this respect at least, we grew up in different worlds. For in the parish church I attended during and for a while after the council, Mozart was either never sung or was sung in a version so bastardized that Rodriguez himself might have preferred to it the post–Vatican II "folk music" he despises. Rodriguez, *Hunger of Memory*, 95.

36. Staten, "Ethnic Authenticity," 111.

37. Ibid., 108.

38. Ibid., 109. In a footnote, Staten singles out Juan Bruce-Novoa as one important theorist of Chicano/Chicana identity who defends Rodriguez. Bruce-Nova has, Staten writes, "consistently objected to what he calls 'truncating definitions of the ethnicity that treat it as a monological absolute.'" For Bruce-Novoa, voices such as Rodriguez's are "'representative of the conflicting plurality' within the Chicano-Chicana community." Ibid., 114.

39. Sánchez, "Calculated Musings," 153, likewise attributes a metaphysics to Rodriguez.

40. Staten, "Ethnic Authenticity," 109.

41. It seems unlikely that Puritans were characterized by any more, or even as much, "solitude" as midcentury Catholics, if by solitude Rodriguez means the destruction of family and community ties, much of which was, after all, brought on by modernization. Likewise, members of some contemporary Protestant congregations—Black and Chinese ones, for example—are more intimately linked to one

another, in my experience, than Catholics during the late 1940s and early 1950s, when Rodriguez and I were children. Rodriguez's Catholic/Puritan binary is really, I think, a way of talking about his own feelings of isolation and the possibility that he is more isolated now than he was as a child.

42. Rodriguez, *Hunger of Memory*, 101.

43. Staten, "Ethnic Authenticity," 103–116.

44. Rodriguez, *Hunger of Memory*, 82.

45. Ibid., 77.

46. Ibid., 105–106.

47. Ibid., 107.

48. Paula M. Kane, *Separatism and Subculture: Boston Catholicism, 1900–1920* (Chapel Hill: University of North Carolina Press, 1994).

49. For a study of autobiography in the American Protestant context that in some respects supports Rodriguez's description of himself as a "Puritan," see Daniel B. Shea, *Spiritual Autobiography in Early America* (Princeton, N.J.: Princeton University Press, 1968).

50. Attendance at the Eucharistic liturgy is required of Roman Catholics on holy days of obligation. Sunday is the foremost day of obligation; Christmas, Epiphany, the Ascension of Jesus into Heaven, Corpus Christi, the Immaculate Conception, the Assumption, and the feasts St. Joseph, Saints Peter and Paul, and All Saints are others, although national bishops' conferences reshape the list somewhat. *The Catechism of the Catholic Church* (Mahwah, N.J.: The Paulist Press, 1994), 525.

51. Sánchez, "Calculated Musings," 158, characterizes *Days of Obligation* as a rebuttal of criticism leveled at *Hunger of Memory*.

52. Richard Rodriguez, *Hunger of Memory*, 3.

53. Rodriguez, *Days of Obligation*, 292.

54. Ibid., 176. With this binary, Rodriguez shows himself to be unaware of the distinctly urban strategy of the foremost shock troops of the Catholic Reformation, the Society of Jesus. Thomas M. Lucas S.J., *Landmarking: City, Church, and Jesuit Urban Strategy* (Chicago: Loyola Press, 1997).

55. Rodriguez, *Days of Obligation*, 182, 192.

56. Perera, for example, dislikes the "crowded mesh" of Rodriguez's prose style. Perera, "*Days of Obligation*," 65.

57. Rodriguez, *Days of Obligation*, 184–185.

58. Ibid., 198.

59. Ibid., 196.

60. Ibid., 195–196.

61. Ibid., 26–27.

62. Ibid., 26.

63. But by identifying "Late Victorians" as a coming-out story, we may collude in Rodriguez's purported assimilation; to some, the stress on the closet is characteristic of English-speaking discussions of gayness but not of those concerning gayness in Latin cultures. Emilie L. Bergmann and Paul Julian Smith, eds., *Entiéndes? Queer Readings, Hispanic Writings* (Durham N.C.: Duke University Press, 1995), 1.

64. Rodriguez, *Days of Obligation*, 30.

65. Ibid., 37.

66. Staten, "Ethnic Authenticity," 115, n. 18.

67. Rodriguez, *Days of Obligation*, 37–38.

68. Frances Fitzgerald includes the Castro in her study of four U.S. utopian communities in which individuals attempt to "reinvent" themselves. The others are Jerry Falwell's Liberty Baptist community; Sun City, Arizona; and Rajneeshpuram in the Pacific Northwest. Frances Fitzgerald, *Cities on a Hill: A Journey Through Contemporary American Culture* (New York: Simon and Schuster, 1981), 25–119.

69. See this chapter, 115–119.

70. Rodriguez, *Days of Obligation*, 26.

71. Ibid., 28.

72. Ibid., 29.

73. Ibid., 32.

74. Ibid., 36.

75. Ibid., 34.

76. Rodriguez, *Hunger of Memory*, 109.

77. Rodriguez, *Days of Obligation*, 35.

78. Ibid., 37.

79. Ibid., 28.

80. Rodriguez, *Hunger of Memory*, 84.

81. For a discussion of the associations between Catholicism and sexuality as perceived by scandalized nineteenth-century American Protestants, see Jenny Franchot, *Roads to Rome: The Antebellum Protestant Encounter with Catholicism* (Berkeley: University of California Press, 1994), 190–193.

82. Rodriguez, *Hunger of Memory*, 102.

83. Rodriguez, *Days of Obligation*, 42.

84. Ibid., 44.

85. Ibid., 41.

86. Ibid., 29.

87. Ibid., 42.

88. Ibid., 43.

89. Ibid., 42.

90. Ibid., 45.

91. Ibid.

92. Ibid.

93. Ibid., 46.

94. See chapter 2.

95. Rodriguez, *Days of Obligation*, 46–47.

96. Ibid., 45.

97. A striking instance of this is the foreword to Elie Wiesel's *Night*, in which Francois Mauriac compares a Jewish boy hanged at Auschwitz to Christ crucified and proposes the state of Israel as the resurrection of the Holocaust's dead. François Mauriac, foreword to Elie Weisel, *Night* (New York: Bantam Books, 1982), x–xi.

98. Rodriguez, *Days of Obligation*, 47.

99. Ibid., 43.

100. Paul Crowley, S.J., "An Ancient Catholic: An Interview with Richard Rodriguez," *America* 173, no. 8 (September 23, 1998): 8–10.

101. Rodriguez acknowledges that the rhetorical complexity of the book is intended to represent brownness: "All these brown facts of my life, I've tried to record in some way, rhetorically, through a brown style." Suzy Hansen, "The Browning of America," *Salon.com*, April 27, 2002, available online at http://dir.salon.com/story/books/int/2002/04/27/rodriguez/index.html, accessed May 2, 2008.

102. Rodriguez, *Brown*, 137.

103. Ibid., xi.

104. Ibid.

105. Hansen, "The Browning of America."

106. Rodriguez, *Brown*, 193.

107. Ibid., 203.

108. Ibid., 206.

109. Ibid., 224, 225.

110. Ibid., 224.

111. Ibid.

112. In 1998, David Garrick, a Holy Cross priest on the faculty at the University of Notre Dame, had his priestly faculties suspended at the basilica on the Notre Dame campus after revealing in the student newspaper that he was gay but celibate. Patricia Lefevere, "N.D. Priest Resigns Over Policy on Gays," April 10, 1998. Available online at http://natcath.org/NCR_Online/archives2/1998b/041098/041098d.htm, accessed May 7, 2008. And in February 2006, the new head of the Congregation for the Doctrine of the Faith, Cardinal William Levada, stated that the homosexual priest "makes it difficult for people to see the priest as representing Christ, the bridegroom of his bride, the church." Cindy Wooden, "Doctrinal Chief: Openly Gay Priests Make It Tough to Represent Christ," *The Catholic Voice* 44, no. 5 (March 6, 2006): 6. In each case, priestly celibacy, that is, the actual sexual behavior of the priest, seems to be irrelevant.

113. Committee for Pro-life Activities of the National Conference of Catholic Bishops, *Living the Gospel of Life: A Challenge to American Catholics* (Washington, D.C.: United States Catholic Conference, 1996).

Conclusion

1. Mary E. Gindhart, personal conversation, around 1995.

2. See, for example, Anita Caspary, *Witness to Integrity: The Crisis of the Immaculate Heart Community of Los Angeles* (Collegeville, Minn.: Liturgical Press, 2003).

3. Though he is not American, I find particularly moving the memoir/reflection by French moral theologian Jacques Pohier, who left the Dominicans after being forbidden to preach, teach, or publish because of his opposition to the French

hierarchy's position on abortion: Jacques Pohier, *God—in Fragments* (New York: Crossroads, 1986).

4. Janet Kalven, *Women Breaking Boundaries: A Grail Journey, 1940–1995* (Albany: State University of New York Press, 1999), 209–214.

5. Linda Clark, Marian Ronan, and Eleanor Walker, *Image-breaking, Image-building: A Handbook for Creative Worship with Women of Christian Tradition* (New York: The Pilgrim Press, 1981).

6. See, for example, Susan Cady, Marian Ronan, and Hal Taussig, *Sophia: The Future of Feminist Spirituality* (San Francisco: Harper and Row, 1986).

7. Marian Ronan, "Ethical Challenges Confronting the Roman Catholic Women's Ordination Movement in the Twenty-first Century," *Journal of Feminist Studies in Religion* 23, no. 3 (November 2007): 149–169.

8. Sheila Greeve Davaney, "The Limit of the Appeal to Women's Experience," in *Shaping New Visions: Gender and Values in American Culture*, ed. Clarissa Atkinson et al. (Ann Arbor: UMI Research Press, 1987), 31–50; Rebecca S. Chopp, "Theorizing Feminist Theology," in *Horizons in Feminist Theology: Identity, Tradition, and Norms*, ed. Rebecca S. Chopp and Sheila Greeve Davaney (Minneapolis: Augsburg Fortress, 1997), 215–231; Ellen Armour, *Deconstruction, Feminist Theology, and the Problem of Difference* (Chicago: University of Chicago Press, 1999), 11–38.

9. With the publication of *Beyond God the Father* (Boston: Beacon Press, 1973), of course, Daly declared herself no longer a Catholic. But, as Beverly Wildung Harrison argues convincingly, Daly went on thinking like a Catholic and, in fact, like a neo-Thomist. Harrison, "The Power of Anger in the Work of Love," in *Making the Connections: Essays in Feminist Social Ethics*, ed. C. S. Robb (Boston: Beacon Press, 1985), 3–19, 269–270, n. 3, 5.

10. Chopp, "Theorizing Feminist Theology," 217.

11. The Combahee River Collective, "A Black Feminist Statement," in *The Second Wave: A Reader in Feminist Theology*, ed. Linda Nicholson (New York: Routledge, 1997), 63–70. Groundbreaking womanist, that is to say, black Christian feminist, contributions to this critique include Katie G. Cannon, *Black Womanist Ethics* (Atlanta, Ga.: Scholars Press, 1988); and Jacquelyn Grant, *White Women's Christ and Black Women's Jesus: Feminist Christology and Womanist Response* (Atlanta, Ga.: Scholars Press, 1989).

12. I include myself in this observation, though I leave it to the reader to decide whether writing about the clergy sex-abuse crisis as an instance of the American Catholic inability to mourn constitutes participation in the Catholic sex/gender wars or an attempt to change the subject. Marian Ronan, "The Clergy Sex Abuse Crisis and the Mourning of American Catholic Innocence," *Pastoral Psychology* 56, no. 3 (January 2008): 321–339.

13. Sandip Roy, "In Immigration Fight, Catholic Church Finds Its Moral Voice—An Interview with Richard Rodriguez." *Pacific News Service: New America Media* (March 31, 2006). Available online at http://news.pacificnews.org/news/view_article .html?article_id=046ab604367717a3a7d40507d4ba7bd5, accessed May 2, 2008.

14. Ibid.

15. Lamin Sanneh, "Why Is Christianity, the Religion of the Colonizer, Growing So Fast in Africa?" Santa Clara, Calif.: Ignatian Center for Jesuit Education, Santa Clara University, 2005.

Abbott, Walter M., ed. *The Documents of Vatican II, with Notes and Comments by Catholic, Protestant, and Orthodox Authorities*. Trans. Joseph Gallagher. New York: Guild Press, America Press, Association Press, 1966.

Alarcón, Norma. "Chicana Feminist Literature: A Re-vision Through Malintzin/or Malintzin: Putting Flesh Back on the Object." In *This Bridge Called My Back: Writings by Radical Women of Color*, ed. Cherrie Moraga and Gloria Anzaldúa, 182–190. New York: Kitchen Table: Women of Color Press, 1981.

———. "Tropology of Hunger: The 'Miseducation' of Richard Rodriguez." In *The Ethnic Canon: Histories, Institutions, and Interventions*, ed. David Palumbo-Liu, 140–152. Minneapolis: University of Minnesota Press, 1995.

Allitt, Patrick. *Catholic Intellectuals and Conservative Politics in America, 1950–1958*. Ithaca, N.Y.: Cornell University Press, 1993.

Almaguer, Tómas. "Chicano Men: A Cartography of Homosexual Identity and Behavior." *differences: A Journal of Feminist Cultural Studies* 3, no. 2 (1991): 75–100.

Andermahr, Sonya, Terry Lovell, and Carol Wolkowitz, eds. *A Concise Glossary of Feminist Theory*. New York: Arnold, 1997.

Anonymous. "Jesus Christ is Risen." E. C. Schirmer Music Company, 1943.

Armour, Ellen. *Deconstruction, Feminist Theology, and the Problem of Difference*. Chicago: University of Chicago Press, 1999.

Beckwith, Sarah. *Christ's Body: Identity, Culture, and Society in Late Medieval Writing*. New York: Routledge, 1993.

Bennett, Alma. "Conversations with Mary Gordon." *South Carolina Review* 28 (Fall 1995): 3–36.

———. *Mary Gordon*. Twayne's United States Authors Series. New York: Twayne Publishers, 1996.

Bergmann, Emilie L., and Paul Julian Smith, eds. *Entiéndes? Queer Readings, Hispanic Writings*. Durham, N.C.: Duke University Press, 1995.

Betcher, Sharon V. "Putting My Foot (Prosthesis, Crutches, Phantom) Down: Considering Technology as Transcendence in the Writings of Donna Haraway." Paper presented at the Feminist Theory and Religious Reflection section, annual meeting of the American Academy of Religion. Orlando, Fla., November 1998.

Bhabha, Homi. "Of Mimicry and Man: The Ambivalence of Colonial Discourse." *October* 28 (1984): 125–133.

Bianchi, Eugene, and Peter McDonough. "Jesuit Sexualities: Personal Crisis, Corporate Dilemma." Roundtable, the Annual Meeting of the American Academy of Religion, San Francisco, November, 1997.

Block, Ed. "A Cold War Story." *America* 190, no. 1 (January 5, 2004): 16–18.

Boys, Mary C. "The Cross: Should a Symbol Betrayed Be Redeemed?" *Cross Currents* 44, no. 1 (Spring 1994): 5–27.

Brien, Dolores Elise. "The Catholic Revival Revisited." *Commonweal* 106 (December 21, 1979): 714–716.

Brock, Rita Nakashima. *Journeys by Heart: A Christology of Erotic Power*. New York: Crossroads, 1992. Originally published in 1988.

Brown, Alden V. *The Grail Movement and American Catholicism*. Notre Dame, Ind.: The University of Notre Dame Press, 1989.

Brown, Joanne Carlson, and Rebecca Parker. "For God So Loved the World?" In *Christianity, Patriarchy, and Abuse*, ed. Joanne Carlson Brown and Carole R. Bohn, 1–30. Cleveland, Ohio: The Pilgrim Press, 1989.

Brown, Karen McCarthy. *Mama Lola*. Berkeley: University of California Press, 1991.

Burns, Gene. *The Frontiers of Catholicism: The Politics of Ideology in a Liberal World*. Berkeley: University of California Press, 1992.

Butler, Judith. *Bodies That Matter: On the Discursive Limits of Sex*. New York: Routledge, 1993.

——, and Joan W. Scott, eds. *Feminists Theorize the Political*. New York: Routledge, 1992.

Bynum, Caroline Walker. *Fragmentation and Redemption: Essays on Gender and the Human Body in Medieval Religion*. New York: Zone Books, 1992.

——. *Holy Feast and Holy Fast: The Religious Significance of Food to Medieval Women*. Berkeley: University of California Press, 1987.

——. *Jesus as Mother: Studies in the Spirituality of the High Middle Ages*. Berkeley: University of California Press, 1982.

——. "'And Woman His Humanity': Female Imagery in the Religious Writing of the Later Middle Ages." In *Gender and Religion: On the Complexity of Symbols*, ed. Caroline Walker Bynum et al., 257–288. Boston: Beacon Press, 1986.

Cady, Susan, Marian Ronan, and Hal Taussig. *Sophia: The Future of Feminist Spirituality*. San Francisco: Harper and Row, 1986.

Cahill, Lisa Sowle. "Presidential Address: Feminist Ethics and the Challenge of Cultures." *CTSA Proceedings* 48 (1993): 65–83.

Cain, Maureen. "Realist Philosophy and Standpoint Epistemologies or Feminist Criminology as a Successor Science." In *Feminist Perspectives in Criminology*, ed. Loraine Gelsthorpe and Allison Morris, 124–140. Philadelphia: Open University Press/Milton Keynes, 1990.

Calhoun, Craig, ed. *Habermas and the Public Sphere*. Cambridge, Mass.: The MIT Press, 1992.

Cannon, Katie G. *Black Womanist Ethics*. Atlanta, Ga.: Scholars Press, 1988.

Carroll, James. "Abortion Complexity." *Boston Globe* (April 23, 1996).

——. "An American Requiem." Public Address. The Free Library of Philadelphia Rebuilding the Future Series. Main Library, Free Library of Philadelphia, April 29, 1997.

——. *An American Requiem: God, My Father, and the War That Came Between Us.* Boston: Houghton Mifflin, 1996.

——. *The City Below.* Boston: Houghton Mifflin, 1994.

——. *Contemplation: Liberating the Ghost of the Church, Churching the Ghost of Liberation.* Paramus, N.J.: Paulist Press, in cooperation with the National Catholic Reporter, 1972.

——. *Elements of Hope.* Paramus, N.J.: Paulist Press, 1971.

——. *Family Trade.* Boston: Little, Brown, 1982.

——. *Fault Lines.* New York: Dell Publishing Company, 1980.

——. *Feed My Lambs: A Guide for Parents Who Want to Prepare Their Children for the Eucharist and Penance.* Dayton, Ohio: Pflaum Publishers, 1967.

——. *Firebird.* New York: E. P. Dutton, 1989.

——. *Forbidden Disappointments.* Rahway, N.J.: Paulist/Newman, 1974.

——. *Madonna Red.* Boston: Bantam Books, 1976.

——. *Mortal Friends.* Boston: Little, Brown, 1978.

——. *Prayers from Where We Are: Suggestions About the Possibility of Prayer Today.* Dayton, Ohio: Pflaum Publishers, 1970.

——. *Prince of Peace.* Boston: Little, Brown, 1984.

——. "The Silence." *New Yorker* (April 7, 1997).

——. *Tender of Wishes: The Prayers of a Young Priest.* Paramus, N.J.: Newman Press, 1970.

——. *A Terrible Beauty: Conversions in Prayer, Politics, and Imagination.* Paramus, N.J.: Paulist/Newman, 1973.

——. *Toward a New Catholic Church: The Promise of Reform.* Boston: Mariner Books, 2002.

——. "Why Dissident Catholics Stay." *Boston Globe* (May 14, 1996).

——. *The Winter Name of God.* New York: Sheed and Ward, 1975.

——. *Wonder and Worship.* Paramus, N.J.: Paulist/Newman, 1970.

Caspary, Anita. *Witness to Integrity: The Crisis of the Immaculate Heart Community of Los Angeles.* Collegeville, Minn.: Liturgical Press, 2003.

Catechism of the Catholic Church. Mahwah, N.J.: The Paulist Press, 1994.

Chaves, Mark. *Ordaining Women: Culture and Conflict in Religious Organizations.* Cambridge, Mass.: Harvard University Press, 1997.

Chavez, Linda. "Hunger of Memory: The Metamorphosis of a Disadvantaged Child." *American Educator* 6, no. 3 (Fall 1982): 14–16.

Chopp, Rebecca S. "Theorizing Feminist Theology." In *Horizons in Feminist Theology: Identity, Tradition, and Norms,* ed. Rebecca S. Chopp and Sheila Greeve Davaney, 215–231. Minneapolis, Minn.: Augsburg Fortress, 1997.

Christ, Carol, and Judith Plaskow, eds. *Womanspirit Rising: A Feminist Reader in Religion.* San Francisco: Harper and Row, 1979.

Clark, Linda, Marian Ronan, and Eleanor Walker. *Image-breaking, Image-building: A Handbook of Creative Worship with Women of Christian Tradition*. New York: The Pilgrim Press, 1981.

Cole, Susan, Marian Ronan, and Hal Taussig. *Wisdom's Feast: Sophia in Study and Celebration*. 2nd ed. Kansas City, Mo.: Sheed and Ward, 1996. Originally published in 1989.

Committee for Pro-Life Activities of the National Conference of Catholic Bishops. *Living the Gospel of Life: A Challenge to American Catholics*. Washington, D.C.: United States Catholic Conference, 1996.

Cooper-Clark, Diana. "An Interview with Mary Gordon." *Commonweal* 20 (May 9, 1980): 270–273.

Cross, Robert D. *The Emergence of Liberal Catholicism in America*. Chicago: Quadrangle Paperbacks, 1968. Originally published in 1958.

Crowley, Paul, S.J. "An Ancient Catholic: An Interview with Richard Rodriguez." In *Catholic Lives, Contemporary America*, ed. Thomas J. Ferraro, 259–265. Durham, N.C.: Duke University Press, 1998.

Cruz-Malavé, Arnaldo. "Toward an Art of Transvestism: Colonialism and Homosexuality in Puerto Rican Literature." In *Entiéndes? Queer Readings, Hispanic Writings*, ed. Emilie L. Bergmann and Paul Julian Smith, 137–167. Durham, N.C.: Duke University Press, 1995.

Daly, Mary. *Beyond God the Father*. Boston: Beacon Press, 1973.

——. "Sin Big." *New Yorker* (February 6 and March 4, 1996).

D'Antonio, William V. "The American Catholic Laity." *National Catholic Reporter* (October 29, 1999).

Davaney, Sheila Green. "The Limit of the Appeal to Women's Experience." In *Shaping New Visions: Gender and Values in American Culture*, ed. Clarissa Atkinson et al., 31–50. Ann Arbor, Mich.: UMI Research Press, 1987.

Davies, Michael. *The New Mass*. Devon, Penn.: Augustine Publishing Company, 1977.

DeLaura, David. Review of *The New Religious Humanists*, edited by Gregory Wolfe. *Commonweal* 125, no. 5 (March 13, 1998): 18–19.

DeMola, Yolanda. "The Language of Power." *America* 160 (April 22, 1989): 364–365.

Derrida, Jacques. *Margins of Philosophy*. Chicago: University of Chicago Press, 1982. Originally published in 1972.

Díaz-Stevens, Ana Maria. *Oxcart Catholicism on Fifth Avenue: The Impact of the Puerto Rican Migration Upon the Catholic Archdiocese of New York*. Notre Dame, Ind.: University of Notre Dame Press, 1993.

Dimond, Karen Eileen, ed. *Addresses and Resources from the November, 1993 Reimagining Conference. Church and Society* 84, no. 5 (May/June 1994).

Dolan, Jay P. *The American Catholic Experience: A History from Colonial Times to the Present*. Garden City, N.Y.: Doubleday and Company, 1985.

——, and Allan Figueroa Deck, eds. *Hispanic Catholic Culture in the United States*. Notre Dame, Ind.: University of Notre Dame Press, 1994.

Edelman, Lee. "Tearooms and Sympathy, or the Epistemology of the Water Closet." In *Nationalisms and Sexualities*, ed. Andrew Parker et al., 263–284. New York: Routledge, 1991.

Farina, John. "General Introduction." In *Isaac T. Hecker, The Diary: Romantic Religion in Antebellum America*, 3–78. New York: Paulist Press, 1988.

Ferraro, Thomas J., ed. *Catholic Lives, Contemporary America*. Durham, N.C.: Duke University Press, 1998.

Filbin, Thomas. Review of *The City Below* by James Carroll. *Hudson Review* 47, no. 3 (Winter 1995): 653–654.

Fisher, James T. *The Catholic Counterculture in America, 1933–1962*. Chapel Hill: University of North Carolina Press, 1989.

——. "Clearing the Streets of the Catholic Lost Generation." In *Catholic Lives, Contemporary America*, ed. T. Ferraro, 76–103. Durham, N.C.: Duke University Press, 1998.

Fitzgerald, Frances. *Cities on a Hill: A Journey Through Contemporary American Culture*. New York: Simon and Schuster, 1981.

Fitzgerald, Kathleen, and Claire Breault, eds. *Whatever Happened to the Good Sisters: A Collection of Real Life Stories*. Mystic, Conn.: Whale's Tale Press, 1992.

Fitzpatrick, Joseph P. "Faith and Stability Among Hispanic Families: The Role of Religion in Cultural Transition." In *Families and Religions: Conflict and Change in Modern Society*, ed. William V. D'Antonia and Joan Aldous, 221–242. Beverly Hills, Calif.: Sage Publications, 1983.

Flax, Jane. "The End of Innocence." In *Feminists Theorize the Political*, ed. J. Butler and J. Scott, 445–463. New York: Routledge, 1992.

Foucault, Michel. *Discipline and Punish: The Birth of the Prison*, trans. A. M. S. Sheridan Smith. Harmondsworth: Penguin, 1977.

Franchot, Jenny. *Roads to Rome: The Antebellum Protestant Encounter with Catholicism*. Berkeley, Calif.: University of California Press, 1994.

Fraser, Nancy. "Rethinking the Public Sphere: A Contribution to the Critique of Actually Existing Democracy." In *Habermas and the Public Sphere*, ed. Craig Calhoun, 109–142. Cambridge, Mass.: The MIT Press, 1992.

Freud, Sigmund. "Mourning and Melancholia." In *The Standard Edition of the Complete Psychological Works of Sigmund Freud*, ed. James Strachey, 14:237–259. London: The Hogarth Press, 1953–1974.

Fulkerson, Mary McClintock. *Changing the Subject: Women's Discourses and Feminist Theology*. Minneapolis, Minn.: Fortress Press, 1994.

"Georgetown to Place Crucifixes." *National Catholic Reporter* (March 6, 1998).

Giles, Paul. *American Catholic Arts and Fiction*. Cambridge: Cambridge University Press, 1992.

Gilmore, Leigh. *The Limits of Autobiography: Trauma and Testimony*. Ithaca, N.Y.: Cornell University Press, 2001.

Gleason, Philip. "American Catholics and the Mythic Middle Ages." In *Keeping the Faith: American Catholicism Past and Present*, ed. Philip Gleason, 11–34. Notre Dame, Ind.: University of Notre Dame Press, 1987.

————. "The New Americanism in Catholic Historiography." *U.S. Catholic Historian* 11 (Summer 1993): 1–18.

Goldberg, Jonathan. "Bradford's 'Ancient Members' and 'A Case of Buggery Amongst Them.'" In *Nationalisms and Sexualities*, ed. Andrew Parker et al., 60–76. New York: Routledge, 1991.

Gordon, Mary. *The Company of Women*. New York: Ballantine, 1980.

————. "The Feminist Rosary: Rediscovering a Subversive Prayer." *Boston College Magazine* (Fall 2003). Available online at http://bcm.bc.edu/issues/fall_2003/features.html (accessed May 7, 2008).

————. *Final Payments*. New York: Ballantine, 1978.

————. *Good Boys and Dead Girls and Other Essays*. New York: Penguin, 1991.

————. "The Irish Catholic Church." In *Once a Catholic: Prominent Catholics and Ex-Catholics Reveal the Influence of the Church on Their Lives and Work*, ed. Peter Occhiogrosso, 65–78. Boston: Houghton Mifflin, 1987.

————. *Joan of Arc*. New York: Viking, 2000.

————. *Men and Angels*. New York: Ballantine Books, 1985.

————. "My Mother is Speaking from the Desert." *New York Times Magazine* (March 19, 1995).

————. *The Other Side*. New York: Viking, 1989.

————. *Pearl*. New York: Pantheon, 2005.

————. "The Priestly Phallus." *Studies in Gender and Sexuality* 5, no. 1 (2004): 103–111.

————. *The Rest of Life*. New York: Viking, 1993.

————. *Seeing Through Places: Reflections on Geography and Identity*. New York: Scribner, 2001.

————. *The Shadow Man*. New York: Random House, 1996.

————. *Spending*. New York: Scribner, 1998.

————. *The Stories of Mary Gordon*. New York: Pantheon, 2006.

————. *Temporary Shelter*. New York: Ballantine, 1988.

————. "Unholy Orders." Review of *Our Fathers: The Secret Life of the Catholic Church in an Age of Scandal* by David France. *New York Times* (January 25, 2004). Available online at query.nytimes.com/gst/fullpage.html?res=9C00E6D6 1E30F936A15752C0A9629C8B63&sec=&spon=&pagewanted=2 (accessed May 8, 2008).

————. "Women of God." *Atlantic Monthly* (January 2002). Available online at http://www/theatlantic.com/doc/200201/gordon (accessed May 7, 2008).

Graham, Robert A. "Introduction to the Declaration on the Relationship of the Church to Non-Christian Religions." In *The Documents of Vatican II with Notes and Comments by Catholic, Protestant and Orthodox Authorities*, ed. S.J. Walter M. Abbott, 656–659. New York: Guild Press, America Press, Association Press, 1966.

Grant, Jacquelyn. *White Women's Christ and Black Woman's Jesus: Feminist Christology and Womanist Response*. Atlanta, Ga.: Scholars Press, 1989.

Greeley, Andrew. "Why Do Catholics Stay in the Church? Because of the Stories." *New York Times Magazine* (July 10, 1994): 38–41.

Green, Sadie. "My Life Would Have Had an Altogether Different Shape Without It." *Sinister Wisdom* 52 (Spring/Summer 1994): 90–95.

Groden, Michael, and Martin Kreiswirth, eds. *The Johns Hopkins Guide to Literary Theory and Criticism*. Baltimore, Md.: The Johns Hopkins University Press, 1994.

Gudorf, Christine E. "To Make a Seamless Garment, Use a Single Piece of Cloth." *Conscience* 17, no. 3 (Autumn 1996): 10–21.

Habermas, Jürgen. "Further Reflections on the Public Sphere." In *Habermas and the Public Sphere*, ed. C. Calhoun. 423–461. Cambridge, Mass.: The MIT Press, 1992.

Halsey, William M. *The Survival of American Innocence: Catholicism in an Era of Disillusionment, 1920–1940*. Notre Dame, Ind.: University of Notre Dame Press, 1980.

Hansen, Suzy. "The Browning of America." *Salon.com* (April 27, 2002). Available online at http://dir.salon.com/story/books/int/2002/04/27/rodriguez/index.html (accessed May 7, 2008).

Haraway, Donna J. "The Actors Are Cyborgs, Nature Is Coyote, and the Geography Is Elsewhere: Postscript to 'Cyborgs at Large.'" In *Technoculture*, ed. Constance Penley and Andrew Ross, 21–26. Minneapolis: University of Minnesota Press, 1991.

——. *Crystals, Fabrics, and Fields: Metaphors of Organicism in Twentieth-century Developmental Biology*. New Haven, Conn.: Yale University Press, 1976.

——. "Cyborgs at Large: Interview with Donna Haraway." In *Technoculture*, ed. Constance Penley and Andrew Ross, 295–337. New York: Routledge, 1991.

——. "*Ecce Homo*, Ain't (Ar'n't) I a Woman, and Inappropriate/d Others: The Human in a Posthumanist Landscape." In *Feminists Theorize the Political*, ed. J. Butler and J. Scott, 86–100. New York: Routledge, 1992.

——. "Manifesto for Cyborgs: Science Technology and Socialist Feminism in the 1980s." *Socialist Review* 80 (1985): 65–108.

——. *Modest_Witness@SecondMillenium.FemaleMan©_Meets_Oncomouse™: Feminism and Technoscience*. New York: Routledge, 1997.

——. *Primate Visions: Gender, Race, and Nature in the World of Modern Science*. New York: Routledge, 1989.

——. "The Promise of Monsters: A Regenerative Politics for Inappropriate/d Others." In *Cultural Studies*, ed. Lawrence Grossberg et al., 295–337. New York: Routledge, 1992.

——. *Simians, Cyborgs, and Women: The Reinvention of Nature*. New York: Routledge, 1991.

Harrison, Beverly. "The Power of Anger in the Work of Love." In *Making the Connections: Essays in Feminist Social Ethics*, ed. Carol S. Robb, 3–19. Boston: Beacon Press, 1985.

Hawthorn, Jeremy. *A Concise Glossary of Contemporary Literary Theory*. New York: Arnold Publishing, 1998.

Hennessey, James. "Leo XIII's Thomistic Revival: A Political and Philosophical Event." In *Celebrating the Medieval Heritage: A Colloquy on the Thought of Aquinas and Bonaventure*, 185–195. Supplement, *The Journal of Religion* 54 (1978).

hooks, bell. *Yearning*. Boston: Southend Press, 1990.

Hopkins, Gerard Manley. *Gerard Manley Hopkins: Poems and Prose*. Ed. W. H. Gardner. New York: Penguin, 1953.

Hordern, William E. *A Layman's Guide to Protestant Theology*. New York: Macmillan, 1968. Originally published in 1955.

Horton, Anore. "Gendered Uses of Religion in the Construction of Community, Culture, and Class." Religion and Culture Colloquium, Center for the Study of American Religions at Princeton University. Princeton, N.J., February 11, 1994.

Huff, Peter. *Allen Tate and the Catholic Revival: Trace of the Fugitive Gods*. New York: Paulist Press, 1996.

Hunt, Mary E., and Frances Kissling. "The New York Times Ad: A Case Study in Religious Feminism." *Journal of Feminist Studies in Religion* 3, no. 1 (Spring 1987): 115–128.

Jakobsen, Janet R. *Working Alliances and the Politics of Difference*. Bloomington: Indiana University Press, 1998.

"James (P.) Carroll." In *Contemporary Authors: A Bio-bibliographical Guide to Current Writers in Fiction, General Nonfiction, Poetry, Journalism, Drama, Motion Pictures, Television, and Other Fields*, vols. 81–84, ed. Frances Carol Locher. Detroit, Mich.: Gale Research Co., 1979.

"James (P.) Carroll." In *Contemporary Literary Criticism*, vol. 38, ed. Daniel G. Marowski. Detroit, Mich.: Gale Publications, 1986.

Jay, Nancy. *Throughout Your Generations Forever: Sacrifice, Religion, Paternity*. Chicago: The University of Chicago Press, 1992.

Johnson, Elizabeth A. *She Who Is: The Mystery of God in Feminist Theological Discourse*. New York: Crossroads Publishing Co., 1992.

Jones, Arthur. "Out of the Pews and Against the Grain." *National Catholic Reporter* (July 30, 1999). Available online at www.natcath.com/NCR_Online/archives/073099/073099g.htm (accessed May 8, 2008).

Joselit, Jenna Weisman. "Bigger and Better Orthodox Synagogues." In *New York's Jewish Jews*, ed. Jenna Weisman Joselit, 25–53. Bloomington: Indiana University Press, 1990.

Julian of Norwich. *Showings*. Trans. Edmund Colledge and James Walsh. New York: Paulist Press, 1978.

Julius, Anthony. *T. S. Eliot, Anti-Semitism, and Literary Form*. New York: Cambridge University Press, 1995.

Kane, Paula. *Separatism and Subculture: Boston Catholicism, 1900–1920*. Chapel Hill: University of North Carolina Press, 1994.

Kalven, Janet. *Women Breaking Boundaries: A Grail Journey, 1940–1995*. New Paltz: State University of New York Press, 1999.

Kaplan, Alice Yeager. "On Language Memoir." In *Eloquent Obsessions: Writing Cultural Criticism*, ed. Marianna Torgovnik, 59–70. Durham, N.C.: Duke University Press, 1994.

Kassabian, Anahid, and David Kazanjian. "Melancholic Memories and Manic Politics: Feminism, Documentary, and the Armenian Diaspora." In *Feminism and Documentary*, ed. Diane Waldman and Janet Walker, 202–223. Minneapolis: University of Minnesota Press, 1999.

Katzenstein, Mary Fainsod. *Faithful and Fearless: Moving Feminist Protest Inside the Church and Military*. Princeton, N.J.: Princeton University Press, 1998.

Kaup, Monica. "The Architecture of Ethnicity in Chicano Literature." *American Literature* 69, no. 2 (June 1997): 361–397.

Kellenbach, Katharina von. *Anti-Judaism in Feminist Religious Writings*. Atlanta, Ga.: Scholars Press, 1994.

Kirp, David L. "Beyond Assimilation: Review of *Days of Obligation* by Richard Rodriguez." *New York Times Book Review* (November 22, 1992): 42.

Kleist, Trina. "Pain of Massacre Remains." *San Francisco Chronicle* (December 22, 1998).

Kole, Randall. "How to Find Your Own Style." *San Francisco Chronicle* (September 29, 1999).

Kristeva, Julia. *The Powers of Horror: An Essay in Abjection*. Trans. Leon S. Roudiez. New York: Columbia University Press, 1982.

Lacayo, Richard. Review of *Days of Obligation: An Argument with My Mexican Father* by Richard Rodriguez. *Time* (January 25, 1993) 69–70.

Lampe, Philip E. "Hispanic Heterogeneity." In *Hispanics in the Church: Up from the Cellar*, ed. P. Lampe, 7–24. San Francisco: International Scholars Publications, 1994.

——. "The Practice of Religion Among Hispanics." In *Hispanics in the Church: Up from the Cellar*, ed. P. Lampe, 53–70. San Francisco: International Scholars Publications, 1994.

Lears, T. J. Jackson. *No Place of Grace: Antimodernism and the Transformation of American Culture, 1880–1920*. New York: Pantheon Books, 1981.

Lefevere, Patricia. "Notre Dame Priest Resigns Over Policy on Gays." *National Catholic Reporter* (April 10, 1998). Available online at http://natcath.org/NCR_Online/archives2/1998b/041098/041098d.htm (accessed May 8, 2008).

Lentricchia, Frank, and Thomas McLaughlin, eds. *Critical Terms for Literary Study*. Chicago: University of Chicago Press, 1990.

Levitt, Laura S. *Jews and Feminism: The Ambivalent Search for Home*. New York: Routledge, 1997.

Lorde, Audré. "The Erotic as Power." In *Sister Outsider—Essays and Speeches*, by A. Lorde, 53–59. Freedom, Calif.: The Crossing Press, 1984.

Lucas, Thomas M., S.J. *Landmarking: City, Church, and Jesuit Urban Strategy*. Chicago: Loyola Press, 1997.

Lynch, William F. *Christ and Apollo: The Dimensions of the Literary Imagination.* Notre Dame, Ind.: University of Notre Dame Press, 1975. Originally published in 1960.

Marinic, Sabine. *Contemporary Autobiographies in the Mexican American Borderland: Richard Rodriguez in Perspective.* MA thesis, University of Salzburg, 1996.

Marsden, Jill. "Virtual Sexes and Feminist Futures: The Philosophy of 'Cyberfeminism.'" *Radical Philosophy* 78 (July–August 1996): 6–16.

Mauriac, François. Foreword to *Night*, by Elie Wiesel. New York: Bantam Books, 1982.

May, Henry Farnham. *The End of American Innocence: A Study of the First Years of Our Own Time, 1912–1917.* New York: Franklin Watts, 1964.

McBride, James. "Response to Building Bodies." Transgressive Performances in Religion Panel, Annual Meeting of the American Academy of Religion, San Francisco, November, 1997.

McCarthy, Colman. Review of *An American Requiem: God, My Father, and the War That Came Between Us* by James Carroll. *Washington Monthly* 28, no. 8 (July–August, 1996): 57.

McCarthy, Timothy G. *The Catholic Tradition: The Church in the Twentieth Century.* 2nd ed. Chicago: Loyola Press, 1998.

McCool, Gerald. "Twentieth-century Scholasticism." In *Celebrating the Medieval Heritage: A Colloquy on the Thought of Aquinas and Bonaventure*, 198–221. Supplement, *The Journal of Religion* 54 (1978).

McDade, John. "Catholic Theology in the Postconciliar Period." In *Modern Catholicism, Vatican II and After*, ed. Adrian Hastings, 422–433. New York: Oxford University Press, 1991.

McDannell, Colleen. *The Christian Home in Victorian America, 1840–1900.* Bloomington: Indiana University Press, 1986.

McGoldrick, Monica. "Irish Families." In *Ethnicity and Family Therapy*, ed. Monica McGoldrick et al., 310–339. New York: The Guilford Press, 1982.

McLaughlin, Eleanor. "Feminist Christologies, Redressing the Tradition." In *Reconstructing the Christ Symbol*, ed. Maryanne Stevens, 118–149. Mahwah, N.J.: Paulist Press, 1993.

McLaughlin, Thomas. "Figurative Language." In *Critical Terms for Literary Study*, ed. F. Lentricchia and T. McLaughlin, 80–90. Chicago: University of Chicago Press, 1990.

——. "Introduction." In *Critical Terms for Literary Study*, ed. F. Lentricchia and T. McLaughlin, 1–8. Chicago: University of Chicago Press, 1990.

Meeks, Wayne A. "The Man from Heaven in Johannine Sectarianism." In *The Interpretation of John*, ed. John Ashton, 141–173. Philadelphia, Penn.: Fortress Press, 1986.

Michaels, Walter Benn. "Race Into Culture: A Critical Genealogy of Cultural Identity." *Critical Inquiry* 18 (Summer 1992): 655–685.

"A Model Necklace." *The Voyager's Collection* [TWA In Flight Sales Catalogue] (October 1999).

Moi, Toril. "The Missing Mother: The Oedipal Rivalries of René Girard." *Diacritics* 12 (1982): 21–31.

Mosqueda, Lawrence J. *Chicanos, Catholicism, and Political Ideology.* Lanham, Md.: University Press of America, 1986.

Murray, John Courtney. "Introduction to 'Dignitatis Humanae.'" In *The Documents of Vatican II, with Notes and Comments by Catholic, Protestant, and Orthodox Authorities,* ed. W. Abbott, 672–674. New York: Guild Press, America Press, Association Press, 1966.

Nelson, Claude. "A Response to 'The Declaration on the Relationship of the Church to Non-Christian Religions.'" In *The Documents of Vatican II, with Notes and Comments by Catholic, Protestant, and Orthodox Authorities,* ed. W. Abbott, 669–671. New York: Guild Press, America Press, Association Press, 1966.

Nicholson, Linda, ed. *The Second Wave: A Reader in Feminist Theory.* New York: Routledge, 1997.

Nygren, Anders. *Agape and Eros.* Trans. Philip S. Watson. New York: Harper Torchbook, 1953.

O'Brien, David J. *Isaac Hecker: An American Life.* New York: Paulist Press, 1992.

Occhiogrosso, Peter, ed. *Once a Catholic: Prominent Catholics and Ex-Catholics Reveal the Influence of the Church on Their Life and Work.* Boston: Houghton Mifflin, 1987.

——. *The Joy of Sects: A Spirited Guide to the World's Religious Traditions.* New York: Doubleday, 1996.

Orsi, Robert. *The Madonna of 115th Street: Faith and Community in Italian Harlem.* New Haven, Conn.: Yale University Press, 1985.

——. "'Mildred is it fun to be a cripple?' The Culture of Suffering in Mid-twentieth-century American Catholicism." In *Catholic Lives, Contemporary America,* ed. T. Ferraro, 19–64, Durham, N.C.: Duke University Press, 1998.

——. "Questions of Identity and Authority." Unpublished response to panelists, Roman Catholic Studies Group, Meeting of the American Academy of Religion, Philadelphia, Penn., November 1995.

——. *Thank You, St. Jude: Women's Devotions to the Patron Saint of Hopeless Causes.* New Haven, Conn.: Yale University Press, 1996.

Padovano, Anthony. "World Moves on but Rome Resists." *National Catholic Reporter* (September 10, 1999).

Palumbo-Liu, David, ed. *The Ethnic Canon: Histories, Institutions, and Interventions.* Minneapolis: University of Minnesota Press, 1995.

Parker, Andrew, "Introduction." In *Nationalisms and Sexualities,* ed. Andrew Parker et al., 1–18. New York: Routledge, 1991.

Paz, Octavio. *The Labyrinth of Solitude: Life and Thought in Mexico.* New York: Grove Press, 1961.

Perera, Victor. Review of *Days of Obligation: An Argument with My Mexican Father* by Richard Rodriguez. *The Nation* 256, no. 2 (January 18, 1993): 63–65.

Peskowitz, Miriam. "Engendering Jewish History." In *Judaism Since Gender,* ed. Miriam Peskowitz and Laura S. Levitt, 17–39. New York: Routledge, 1997.

Peters, F. E. *Ours: The Making and Unmaking of a Jesuit*. New York: Penguin, 1981.

Plaskow, Judith. *Standing Again at Sinai: Judaism from a Feminist Perspective*. San Francisco: Harper and Row, 1990.

Pohier, Jacques. *God—in Fragments*. New York: Crossroads, 1986.

Portes, Alejandro. Review of *Days of Obligation: An Argument with My Mexican Father* by Richard Rodriguez. *New Republic* (April 26, 1993): 38–41.

Pratt, Minnie Bruce. "Identity: Skin Blood Heart." In *Yours in Struggle: Three Feminist Perspectives on Anti-Semitism and Race*, ed. Elly Bulkin et al., 11–63. Brooklyn: Long Haul Press, 1984.

Review of *Hunger of Memory* by Richard Rodriguez. *Christian Science Monitor* (June 24, 1983).

Review of *Hunger of Memory* by Richard Rodriguez. *New York Times* (February 28, 1982).

Review of *Hunger of Memory* by Richard Rodriguez. *New York Times Book Review* (February 6, 1983).

Review of *Hunger of Memory* by Richard Rodriguez. *San Francisco Review of Books* 7 (Summer 1982): 11.

Review of *Hunger of Memory* by Richard Rodriguez. *Texas Observer* (June 18, 1982).

Review of *Hunger of Memory* by Richard Rodriguez. *Washington Post* (March 21, 1983).

"Richard Rodriguez." In *Contemporary Authors: A Bio-bibliographical Guide to Current Writers in Fiction, General Nonfiction, Poetry, Journalism, Drama, Motion Pictures, Television, and Other Fields*, vol. 110, ed. Hal Roach. Detroit, Mich.: Gale Research Co., 1984.

Rivera, Tomás. "Richard Rodriguez's *Hunger of Memory* as Humanistic Antithesis." *MELUS* 11, no. 4 (Winter 1984): 5–13.

Rodriguez, Richard. *Brown: The Last Discovery of America*. New York: Penguin, 2002.

——. *Days of Obligation: An Argument with My Mexican Father*. New York: Penguin, 1992.

——. "Homosexuality." Essay presented on the McNeil-Lehrer News Hour. Lexis Nexis Transcript 4363, June 24, 1992.

——. *Hunger of Memory: The Education of Richard Rodriguez*. New York: Bantam Books, 1982.

Ronan, Marian. "The Clergy Sex Abuse Crisis and the Mourning of American Catholic Innocence." *Pastoral Psychology* 56, no. 3 (January 2008): 321–339.

——. "Donna Haraway's Catholic Trickster." Paper presented at the Tri-regional Meeting of the American Academy of Religion/Society for Biblical Literature, Boston, April, 1995.

——. "Ethical Challenges Confronting the Roman Catholic Women's Ordination Movement in the Twenty-first Century." *Journal of Feminist Studies in Religion* 23, no. 3 (November 2007): 149–169.

——. "From the Margins to the Universe." *Cross Currents* 42 (Spring 1992): 103–110.

——, ed. *The Grail Prayer Book*. Loveland, Ohio: The Grail, 1975.

———. "The Liturgy of Women's Lives: A Call to Celebration." *Cross Currents* 38, no. 1 (1988): 17–31.

———. "Reclaiming Women's Experience: A Review of Selected Christian Feminist Theologies." *Cross Currents* 48 (Summer 1998): 218–29. Available online at www.crosscurrents.org/ronan.htm (accessed May 8, 2008).

———. "A Sliver of Dry Land." *U.S. Catholic Historian* 23, no. 3 (Summer 2005): 71–92.

———. "Sometimes the Accidents Become the Substance." Review of *Allen Tate and the Catholic Revival* by Peter Huff. *Cross Currents* 48, no. 1 (Spring 1998): 128–132. Available online at http://crosscurrents.org/bookss98b.htm (accessed May 7, 2008).

Roy, Sandip. "In Immigration Fight, Catholic Church Finds Its Moral Voice: An Interview with Richard Rodriguez." *New American Media* (March 31, 2006). Available online at news.newamericamedia.org/news/view_article.html?article_id=046ab604367717a3a7d40507d4ba7bd5.

Rubin, Gayle. "The Traffic in Women: Notes on the Political Economy of Sex." In *The Second Wave: A Reader in Feminist Theory*, ed. L. Nicholson, 27–62. New York: Routledge, 1997.

Rubin, Miri. *Corpus Christi: The Eucharist in Late Medieval Culture*. Cambridge: Cambridge University Press, 1991.

Rudy, Kathy. *Beyond Pro-life and Pro-choice: Moral Diversity in the Abortion Debate*. Boston: Beacon Press, 1996.

Rycroft, Charles. *A Critical Dictionary of Psychoanalysis*. Totowa, N.J.: Littlefield, Adams and Co., 1973.

Samway, Patrick H. "An Interview with Mary Gordon." *America* 170, no. 17 (May 14, 1994): 12–15.

———. Review of *An American Requiem: God, My Father, and the War That Came Between Us*. *America* 174, no. 19 (June 8, 1996): 24–25.

Sánchez, Marta E. "Caliban: The New Latin American Protagonist of *The Tempest*." *Diacritics* 6, no. 1 (Spring 1976): 54–61.

———. "La Malinche at the Intersection: Race and Gender in *Down These Mean Streets*." *PMLA* 113, no. 1 (January 1998): 117–128.

Sánchez, Rosaura. "Calculated Musings: Richard Rodriguez's Metaphysics of Difference." In *The Ethnic Canon: Histories, Institutions, and Interventions*, ed. D. Palumbo-Liu, 153–174. Minneapolis: University of Minnesota Press, 1995.

Sandoval, Moises. "The Organization of a Hispanic Church." In *Hispanic Catholic Culture in the U.S.*, ed. Jay P. Dolan and Allan Figueroa Deck, 131–165. Notre Dame, Ind.: University of Notre Dame Press, 1994.

Sanneh, Lamin. "Why Is Christianity, the Religion of the Colonizer, Growing So Fast in Africa?" Santa Clara Lecture, Santa Clara University, May 11, 2005.

Santner, Eric. *Stranded Objects: Mourning, Memory, and Film in Postwar Germany*. Ithaca, N.Y.: Cornell University Press, 1990.

Schott, Webster. "Maguire the Mettlesome Priest." Review of *Prince of Peace* by James Carroll. *New York Times Book Review* (November 4, 1984).

Schultenover, David. *A View from Rome: On the Eve of the Modernist Crisis.* New York: Fordham University Press, 1993.

Schüssler Fiorenza, Elisabeth. *In Memory of Her: A Feminist Theological Reconstruction of Christian Origins.* New York: Crossroads Publishing Co., 1983.

——. *Jesus: Miriam's Child, Sophia's Prophet.* New York: Continuum, 1994.

Scott, Joan Wallach. "Women's History." In *American Feminist Thought at Century's End: A Reader,* ed. Linda S. Kauffman, 234–257. Cambridge, Mass.: Blackwell, 1993.

Sedgwick, Eve Kosofsky. *Between Men: English Literature and Male Homosocial Desire.* New York: Columbia University Press, 1985.

Seidman, Naomi. "Elie Wiesel and the Scandal of Jewish Rage." *Jewish Social Studies* 3, no. 1 (Fall 1996): 1–19.

Shea, Daniel B. *Spiritual Autobiography in Early America.* Princeton, N.J.: Princeton University Press, 1968.

Sheed, Wilfred. "Mary Gordon: Final Payments." In *The Good Word and Other Words.* New York: Penguin, 1980.

Shuter, Bill. "The Confessions of Richard Rodriguez." *Cross Currents* 45, no. 1 (Spring 1995): 95–105.

Smith, Paul Julian, and Emilie L. Bergmann. "Introduction." In *"Entiéndes?" Queer Readings, Hispanic Writings,* ed. Paul Julian Smith and Emilie L. Bergmann, 1–13. Durham, N.C.: Duke University Press, 1995.

Sparr, Arnold. *To Promote, Defend, and Redeem: The Catholic Literary Revival and the Cultural Transformation of American Catholicism, 1920–1960.* New York: Greenwood Press, 1989.

Spiegelman, Art. *Maus: A Survivor's Tale.* New York: Pantheon Books, 1986.

Spivak, Gayatri Chakravorty. "'In a Word': Interview." In *The Second Wave: A Reader in Feminist Theory,* ed. L. Nicholson, 358–378. New York: Routledge, 1997.

——. "Translator's Preface." In *Of Grammatology,* by Jacques Derrida, ix–xc. Baltimore, Md.: The Johns Hopkins University Press, 1974.

"Standpoint Epistemologies." In *A Concise Glossary of Feminist Theory,* ed. Sonya Andermahr et al. New York: Routledge, 1997.

Staten, Henry. *Eros in Mourning: From Homer to Lacan.* Baltimore, Md.: The Johns Hopkins University Press, 1995.

——. "Ethnic Authenticity, Class, and Autobiography: The Case of *Hunger of Memory.*" *PMLA* 113, no. 1 (January 1998): 103–116.

——. *Wittgenstein and Derrida.* Lincoln: University of Nebraska Press, 1984.

Stavans, Ilan. Review of *Days of Obligation: An Argument with My Mexican Father,* by Richard Rodriguez. *Commonweal* 120, no. 6 (March 26, 1993): 20–23.

Steinfels, Peter. "The Crisis of Liberal Catholicism." *Commonweal* 126, no. 20 (November 19, 1999): 30–39.

Stevens-Arroyo, Anthony M. "The Emergence of Social Identity Among Latino Catholics: An Appraisal." In *Hispanic Catholic Culture in the U.S.,* edited by Jay P. Dolan and Allan Figueroa Deck, 77–130. Notre Dame, Ind.: University of Notre Dame Press, 1994.

Sullivan, Andrew. "Virtually Normal." In *Catholic Lives, Contemporary America*, ed. Thomas J. Ferraro, 171–186. Durham, N.C.: Duke University Press, 1998.

Sumrall, Amber Cover, and Patricia Vecchione, eds. *Bless Me, Father: Stories of Catholic Childhood*. New York: Penguin, 1994.

———. *Catholic Girls: Stories, Poems, and Memoirs*. New York: Penguin, 1992.

Taves, Ann. *The Household of Faith: Roman Catholic Devotions in Mid-nineteenth Century America*. Notre Dame, Ind.: Notre Dame University Press, 1986.

Taylor, Mark Klein. *Remembering Esperanza: A Cultural-Political Theology for North American Praxis*. Maryknoll, N.Y.: Orbis Books, 1990.

Tentler, Leslie, and Margaret Susan Thompson. "Gender and the Construction of Catholic Memory." Workshop at the Engendering American Catholic Studies Conference, Cushwa Center for the Study of American Catholicism, Notre Dame, Ind., September 29–October 1, 1995.

Tracy, David, ed. *Celebrating the Medieval Heritage: A Colloquy on the Thought of Aquinas and Bonaventure*. Supplement, *The Journal of Religion* 54 (1978).

Trible, Phyllis. *Texts of Terror: Literary-Feminist Readings of Biblical Narratives*. Philadelphia, Penn.: Augsburg Fortress, 1984.

Trimble Alliaume, Karen. "Re(as)sembling the Body of Christ: Reading the Eucharist as a Seduction." Paper presented at the Roman Catholic Studies Panel, Annual Meeting of the American Academy of Religion, Philadelphia, Penn., November 1996.

———. "Re(as)sembling Christ: Feminist Christology, Identity Politics, and the Imagination of Christian Communities." Ph.D. diss., Duke University, 1999.

———. "The Risks of Repeating Ourselves." *Cross Currents* 48, no. 2 (Summer 1998): 198–217. Available online at http://www.crosscurrents.org/alliaume.htm (accessed May 7, 2008).

Tweed, Thomas. *Our Lady of the Exile: Diasporic Religion at a Cuban Shrine in Miami*. New York: Oxford University Press, 1997.

Uebbing, James. Review of *An American Requiem* by James Carroll. *Commonweal* 123, no. 13 (July 12, 1996): 25–26.

Walker, Williston, et al. *A History of the Christian Church*. 4th ed. New York: Charles Scribners' Sons, 1985.

Weakland, Rembert. "Liturgy and Common Ground." *America* 180, no. 5 (February 20, 1999): 7–11.

Wendell, Susan. *The Rejected Body: Feminist Philosophical Reflections on Disability*. New York: Routledge, 1996.

Williams, Delores. *Sisters in the Wilderness: The Challenge of Womanist God-Talk*. Maryknoll, N.Y.: Orbis Books, 1993.

Wolfe, Gregory, ed. *The New Religious Humanists: A Reader*. New York: The Free Press, 1998.

Wooden, Cindy. "Doctrinal Chief: Openly Gay Priests Make It Tough to Represent Christ." *Catholic Voice* 44, no. 5 (March 6, 2006): 6.

INDEX

abjection, 15–17, 19, 33, 54, 132, 159n. 11
abortion, 16, 17
affirmative action, 107, 115
African Americans, 11, 98–99, 152n. 45
AIDS crisis, 17, 20–21, 122–24, 128–29;
  death of César, 20; humanizing
  effects of, 131; self-blame for, 125–26.
  See also gayness
Alarcón, Norma, 113–14, 166n. 21
Alexander VI, 6
Alliaume, Karen Trimble, 104
allies, 79–80; feminist, 80–81
ambiguity, 4–5, 63–66
ambivalence, 57–58, 83–85, 102, 134–35
America, 48, 132
Americanism, 155n. 19
American Requiem, An: God, My
  Father, and the War That Came
  Between Us (Carroll), 18–19, 24, 34;
  Christic hero, 36–39; movement
  toward mourning in, 46–49
annunciation, 91, 102, 104
anti-Catholicism, 14, 16
anticommunism, 25, 31, 66–70
anti-Semitism, 10, 48–49, 52–53; of
  Gordon's father, 66–70; as racism, 71
appropriation, 87–88, 95, 102–3
Aquinas, St. Thomas, 6, 13, 53
Armenian genocide, 8
assimilation, 107–12, 119
Association for the Rights of Catholics
  in the Church, 2

Auerbach, Eric, 81–82
Augustine, St., 13, 125–26

Badham, Paul, 13
Baltimore Catechism, 6, 53
Becker, Canon, 54
Benedict XVI, 146, 151n. 18
Bennett, Alma ("Immaculate Man"),
  57
Berrigan, Daniel, 31, 33
Betcher, Sharon, 85
Between Men: English Literature and
  Male Homosocial Desire (Kosofsky
  Sedgwick), 43
bilingual education, 112, 113, 115–16, 121
binaries, 67, 83; Catholic/Protestant,
  116, 119–22; liberal/conservative, 144;
  private/public, 109–10, 112, 117–18,
  123–24; tragedy/comedy, 119–20, 126
Black Women's Empowerment Pro-
  gram (NAACP), 98–99
blasphemy, 83
Block, Ed, 48
body, 127–29; as irreducible, 126–27; reconfiguration of, 129–30; resistance
  to mourning losses of, 87. *See also*
  fetus
Boniface ("Immaculate Man"), 58–
  61
Bonner, Eleanor, 11
Boston, Archdiocese of, 1–2
Boston Globe, 1–2

cyborg, figure of, 20, 80, 89; as tool for understanding Catholicism, 81–83; troubling aspects of, 85–88

Cyprian, Father (*Men and Angels*), 55

Daly, Mary, 141, 171n. 9

Days of Obligation: An Argument with My Mexican Father (Rodriguez), 106, 119–20, 122–23, 124; binaries in, 120–22

Death Without Weeping (Scheper-Hughes), 99–100, 102–4

Derrida, Jacques, 89

devotional practices, 35–36, 104, 127

differential literacies, 91–92

diffraction, 101–104; noninnocent, 94–97

Dillon, Michelle, 5

discourse, materiality of, 103

disidentification, 51, 56, 67–68, 72, 76, 159n. 16

displacement, 54, 75, 112, 117–18

Dolan, David (*Fault Lines*), 42–43

Dolan, Jay, 10, 152n. 29

Dooley, Tom, 25

"Drama of Life Before Birth, The" (Nillson), 97, 98

Eagleton, Terry, 1

Easter Vigil, 1

"*Ecce Homo*, Ain't (Ar'n't) I a Woman, and Inappropriate/d Others: The Human in a Posthumanist Landscape" (Haraway), 20, 84–85, 87–89

economic success, 9–11

education: assimilation and, 110–15; as imitation, 111, 113, 166n. 17

Edward, Sister Anne (*Prince of Peace*), 41–42, 43

ekklesia of women, 2

Eloquent Obsessions (Kaplan), 108

erotic triangle, 43–44, 51, 143

Eucharist, 19, 34, 65, 144

European revolutions, 5

evil, redemption found in, 131

ex-Catholic identity, 73

excommunication: for abortion, 13; of gay celibate priests, 136, 170n. 112; of priests, 140; threats against Catholic lawmakers, 5; of women priests, 5

external ethics, 87, 95

father figures: impermeability of, 19, 53, 55–57, 59–61, 64, 70–72; as polarized, 67–68, 69–70

Fault Lines (Carroll), 37, 42–43

FBI agent, figure of, 25

Feeney, Leonard, 67

Female Man, The (Russ), 92

FemaleMan© (*Modest Witness*), 92

feminist-standpoint epistemology, 85

feminist theology and activism, 2, 140–41

feminist theory, secular, 143–44

Ferdinand and Isabella, 6

fetus, 13, 94, 96–100; Brazilian infant mortality rate, 99–100, 144; reclining nude cartoons, 97–98

figural realism, Christian, 81–83, 93, 101

figuration: in Hebrew scripture, 162n. 8; postmodernity as crisis of, 84–85

Final Payments (Gordon), 52, 54–55, 56, 72, 83

Fiorenza, Elisabeth Schüssler, 2, 141

First Vatican Council, 4, 49. *See also* Vatican II

FirstWoman, 98

Fisher, James Terrence, 10, 152nn. 29, 35, 166n. 17

Flax, Jane, 23

forgiveness, 62–63, 65–66, 73, 145

fragmentation, 12, 17–18, 21; in Gordon, 60, 69, 72, 75–76, 79; in Haraway, 81, 84–85, 90, 94; in Rodriguez, 129, 134–35

France, David, 76–77, 162n. 90

Freud, Sigmund, 7, 18

gayness, 20–21, 121–24; church teachings on, 131, 132; clergy sex abuse crisis and, 144; crucifix and, 131–32; excommunication of gay celibate priests, 170n. 112. *See also* AIDS crisis

Geertz, Clifford, 35

gene, 90, 94, 102

generations, 105–6

genocide, 90; Holocaust, 7–8, 15, 48–49, 88, 169–70n. 97

Germany, 7–8

Gindhart, Mary, 170n. 1

Girard, René, 43

god-trick, 26, 82

Gordon, David, 52–53, 66–70

Gordon, Mary, 19, 51–52, 143; background, 52–53; church as bedrock in, 53–54, 61, 68, 70–71, 83, 143; on clergy sex abuse crisis, 76–77; disidentifications in, 51, 56, 67–68, 72, 76, 159n. 16; excess figured as Jewish, 68, 70–71; fragmentation in, 60, 69, 72, 75–76, 79; Irish Catholics in works of, 56–57; Italian protagonists, 61–66; Jewish protagonists, 66–70; mourning in works of, 70–72; New Testament stories in, 56, 60, 73–74, 83; non-Catholic works, 53, 55; nonfiction works, 75–77; permeability/impermeability, 19, 53, 55–57, 59–61, 64, 70–72, 144; polarized structure in novels of, 56, 69–70

Grail, the, 118, 140

grammar of suffering, Catholic, 24, 29, 39–40, 46, 106, 152nn. 29, 35

gratitude, 63, 65, 73

Great Depression, 10–11, 12

Greeley, Andrew, 35

Gudorf, Christine, 150n. 11

guilt, 110, 112

Halsey, William, 12

Haraway, Donna J., 143–44; ambivalence in, 83–85; appropriation of

other works, 87–88, 95, 102–3; Catholicism of, 80–81; conversation between actors in, 91–92; diffracted Catholicism of, 101–104; feminist critiques of, 85–87; Hebrew Bible, emendations of, 87–88, 162n. 10; Jewish and Christian figures in, 87–88, 89; move toward mourning in, 88–89; noninnocent diffractions in, 94–97; supplementarity in, 89–91

Harrison, Beverly, 140

Hartmann, Heidi, 42

Hebrew Bible, 87–88

Hecker, Isaac, 30

Hennessey, James, 151n. 15

hero, Christic, 36–39, 142–43

Hoggart, Richard, 110–11

Holocaust, 7–8, 15, 88, 169–70n. 97; Vatican complicity in, 48–49

holy days of obligation, 168n. 50

"Holy Women" (Gordon), 77

homophobia, 18–19; in Carroll's work, 44–45

homosocial bonds, 18–19, 43–44, 48, 143

hooks, bell, 96

Hopkins, Gerard Manley, 33, 155n. 27

host (Eucharist), 67–68

House of War: The Pentagon and the Disastrous Rise of American Power (Carroll), 47

Hughes, Patrick (*An American Requiem*), 36–37, 44

Humanae Vitae, 140

Human Genome Project, 90

Hunger of Memory: The Education of Richard Rodriguez (Rodriguez), 20, 106–10, 121; defense against mourning in, 112, 117–18

ideological hierarchy, 4–5

images, 35

imitation, education as, 111, 113, 166n. 17

"Immaculate Man" (Gordon), 57–61, 63, 66

church, 139; sexualization of, 14–15.
See also women

O'Brien, Justin (*Madonna Red*), 42
oedipal narratives, 96, 102
O'Gara, James, 154n. 4
Oldenhage, Tania, 164n. 67
Oncomouse™, 20, 91, 92–93, 102
O'Neill, Edmund (Brown), 134
optimism, 12, 14, 95, 142; in Carroll's
    work, 27, 32, 37–38, 47; as required,
    137–38; in Rodriguez's works, 117,
    119, 123, 128
Orsi, Robert A., 10, 26, 29, 65, 152n. 30
other: abjection and compulsion to
    expel, 6, 15–16, 19, 132; brown, trope
    of, 132–33; Jews as, 67; legitimiza-
    tion of violence against, 17; sexual,
    Catholics as, 14–17
Other Side, The (Gordon), 55–56, 57
*Our Fathers: The Secret Life of the
    Catholic Church in an Age of Scan-
    dal* (France), 76–77

panopticon, 93, 164n. 48
papal infallibility, doctrine of, 4, 49,
    150n. 9
Paracletists, 58, 59, 59n. 24
parish councils, 139
parish missions, 10
partial perspective, 85–86
patriarchal relations, as traffic in
    women, 42–45
Paulists (Congregation of St. Paul),
    30
Paul VI, 31, 139
Pearl (Gordon), 19, 73
Pelosi, Nancy, 141
perennial philosophy, 53–54
Peters, F. E., 54
"Peter's Avocado" (Rodriguez), 134–36
Pius IX, 13
Pius XII, 25, 48–49
Pohier, Jacques, 170–71n. 3

porousness, 19, 21, 60–61, 65, 72–73,
    75–76
Post, Laura (*The Company of Women*),
    56
postmodern doubleness, 113–14
postmodernity: breaching of boundar-
    ies, 20, 81, 86–87, 89; as crisis of
    figuration, 84–85
preaching, 34–35
Presley, Elvis, 27, 49
presidential inaugurations, 25, 35
pre–Vatican II Catholicism, 20, 38,
    53–54, 68, 71, 127, 167n. 35
priest-poets, 33
Primate Visions (Haraway), 82, 162n. 10
primatology, 82
Prince of Peace (Carroll), 37, 38–39;
    male rivals in, 41–42, 43–44
private/public binary, 109–10, 112,
    117–18, 123–24
Protestant Reformers, 34–35
Puritanism, as metaphor, 116, 124,
    167–68n. 41
purity, 14–17, 19, 30, 67, 93; conse-
    quences of, 7, 15; impurity and, 71,
    106, 134

race, 94
Randolph, Lynn, 93, 94, 103, 104
Ranher, Karl, 141
rationalism, 38
Ratzinger, Joseph, 146
raza national, 114
reconfiguration, 129–30
reform movements, 2, 5, 21, 139
responsibility, 86–87
Rest of Life, The (Gordon), 53; "Im-
    maculate Man," 57–61, 63; "Living
    at Home," 61, 66; "The Rest of Life,"
    19, 61–66; structure, 68
resurrection, imagery of, 11, 73–74
Revival, Thomist (neo-Thomist), 6,
    12–13, 18–21, 30, 38, 53, 66, 69. 72,
    78, 144

supplementarity, 89–91

Tate, Allen, 30, 33–34
Taves, Ann, 36
Taylor, Felicitas (*The Company of Women*), 55
teeth and biting, imagery of, 68, 69
theology of the streets, 26, 64–65
"Third Man, The" (Rodriguez), 133
Thomism, 53; neo-, 6, 12–13, 18–21, 30, 38, 53, 66, 69, 72, 78, 144; Transcendental, 6
Tierney, John (*Madonna Red*), 41, 42
Tracing the Sign of the Cross (Ronan), revision of, 72–73
Tracy, David, 35
tragedy/comedy binary, 119–20, 126
trajectory of the cross, 24; in Carroll, 29, 33; in Haraway, 101, 103–4; in Rodriguez, 106
Transcendentalism, 30
Transcendental Thomism, 6
transubstantiation, 34, 63, 65, 130
Trickster, 85, 86, 90
Treaty of Versailles, 12
Truth, Sojourner, 80
truth and error, boundary between, 53–54
truth telling, 58–59

unconscious, reconfigured, 96
"Unholy Orders" (Gordon), 76–77
Union Theological Seminary, 142
United Farm Workers, 113
United Nations discourse on human rights, 90
universalization, 59, 96

unmarked category, 26, 82
upward mobility, 9–11, 24, 30–31
Uses of Literacy, The (Hoggart), 110–11

Vatican: complicity in Holocaust, 48–49; opposition to liberal state, 14
Vatican territories, 13
Vatican II, 1–2, 138–39; ambiguity and, 4–5; as attempt to regain power, 5–6; loss of Latin, 116, 118. *See also* First Vatican Council
Versailles, Treaty of, 12
vessels, religious, 67
Vietnam War, 30–32
visual metaphors, 85–86, 94, 97

War on Poverty, 113
will, immolation of, 29–30
Wills, Garry, 47
women: in Global South, 146–47; homophobia used to control, 18–19; Irish, 40; ordination of, 3, 65, 140, 146; patriarchal relations as traffic in, 42–45. *See also* nuns
women of color, 90
"Women of God" (Gordon), 75
women's movement, 45
women's movements, religious, 118, 140
Woolf, Virginia, 80
Working Alliances and the Politics of Differences (Jakobsen), 45
working through, 18, 96, 142–47
World War I, 12
World War II, 3, 8–9, 13, 24–25, 136

yearning, 96, 101, 104